Ding Yi

LUND HUMPHRIES | CONTEMPORARY PAINTERS

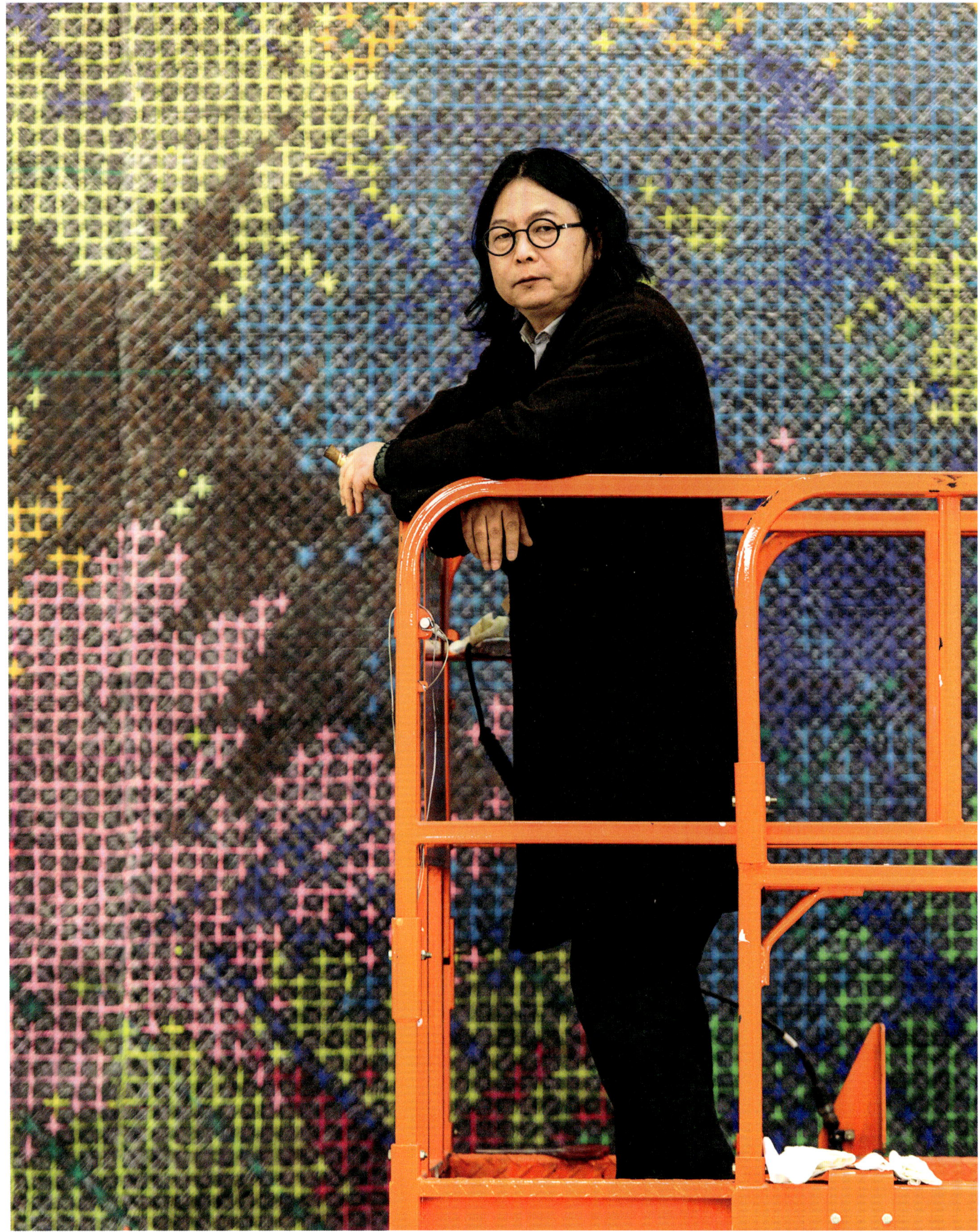

Tony Godfrey and Kaimei Wang

Ding Yi

LUND HUMPHRIES | CONTEMPORARY PAINTERS

Contemporary Painters Series
Series Editor: Barry Schwabsky

The Contemporary Painters Series is a curated series of accessible, authoritative and highly illustrated monographs on the world's leading living painters, which locates painting as a vibrant and vital part of contemporary art.

The series is edited by American art critic Barry Schwabsky, supported by an international advisory board with a specialist interest in contemporary painting. It aims to redefine 'painting' in the contemporary context as work that is done within the conventions and history of painting, but which may incorporate other materials or techniques.

Advisory Board
Paco Barragán, independent curator and arts writer and Contributing Editor of *Artpulse*
Tony Godfrey, freelance writer and curator based in the Philippines
David Pagel, Los Angeles-based art critic, curator and writer
Ida Panicelli, former Editor-in-Chief of *Artforum*
Simon Rees, former Director of the Govett-Brewster Art Gallery/Len Lye Centre, New Zealand
Beatrix Ruf, former Director of the Stedelijk Museum, Amsterdam
Philip Tinari, Director of the Ullens Center for Contemporary Art, Beijing
Gilda Williams, art critic, writer, lecturer and London correspondent for *Artforum*
John Yau, poet, art critic and curator

Also available in the series:
Amy Sillman by Valerie Smith
Bernard Frize by David Rhodes
Etel Adnan by Kaelen Wilson-Goldie
Guillermo Kuitca by Raphael Rubinstein
Jim Shaw by David Pagel
Lois Dodd by Faye Hirsch
Mary Weatherford by Suzanne Hudson
Neo Rauch by Michael Glover
Philip Taaffe by John Yau
Tal R by Martin Herbert
Thomas Nozkowski by John Yau
Verne Dawson by John Hutchinson

Contents

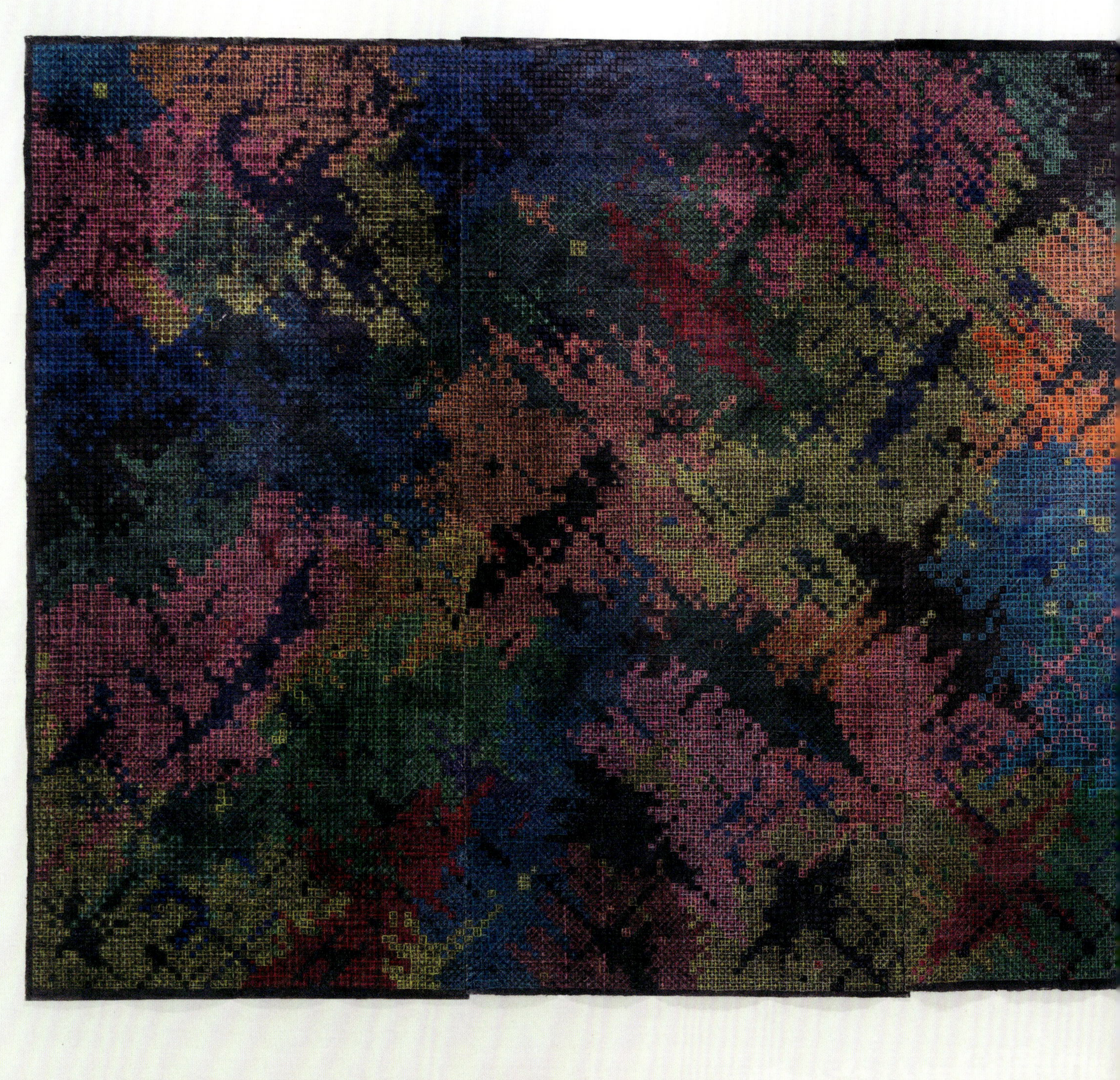

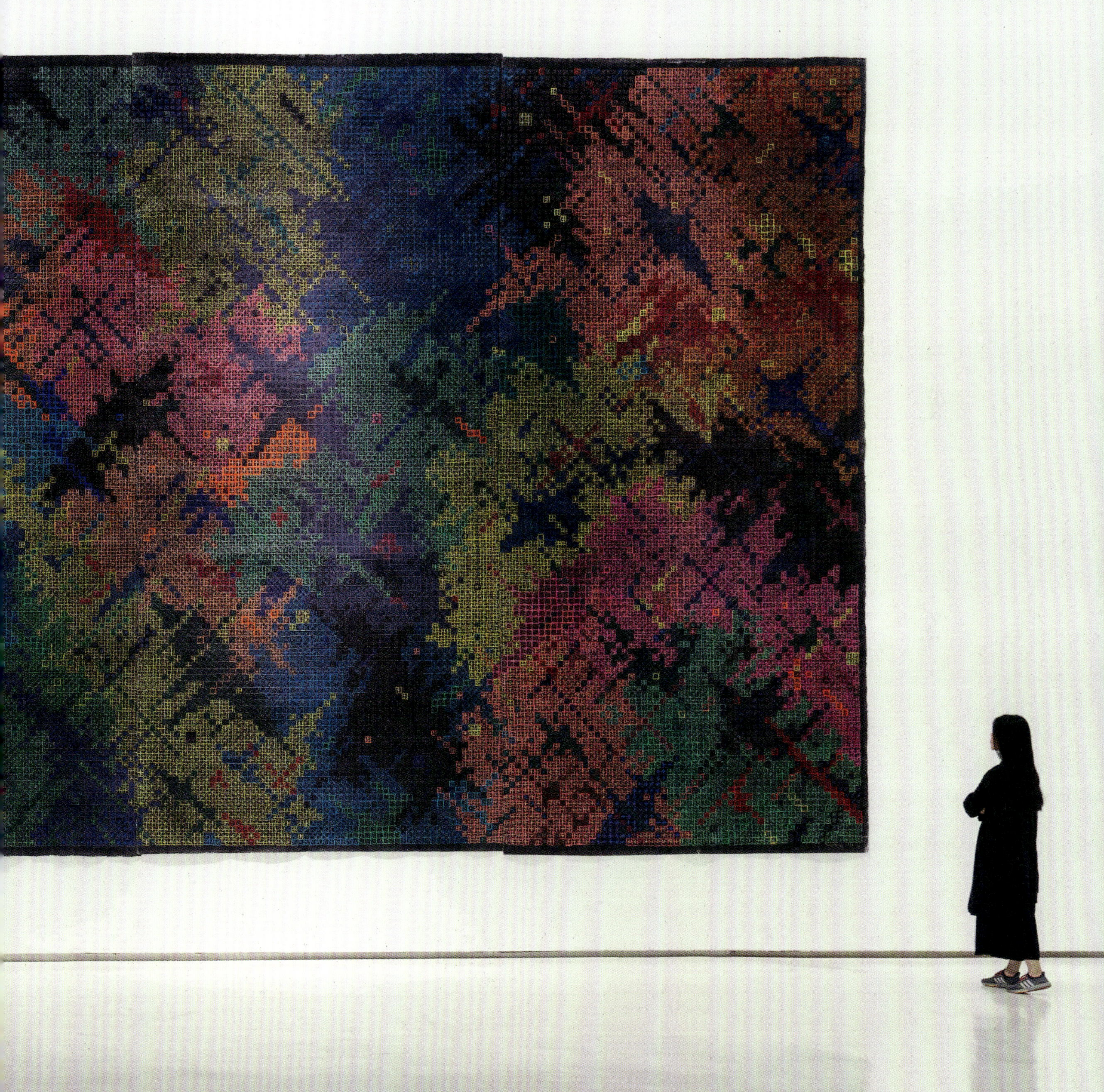

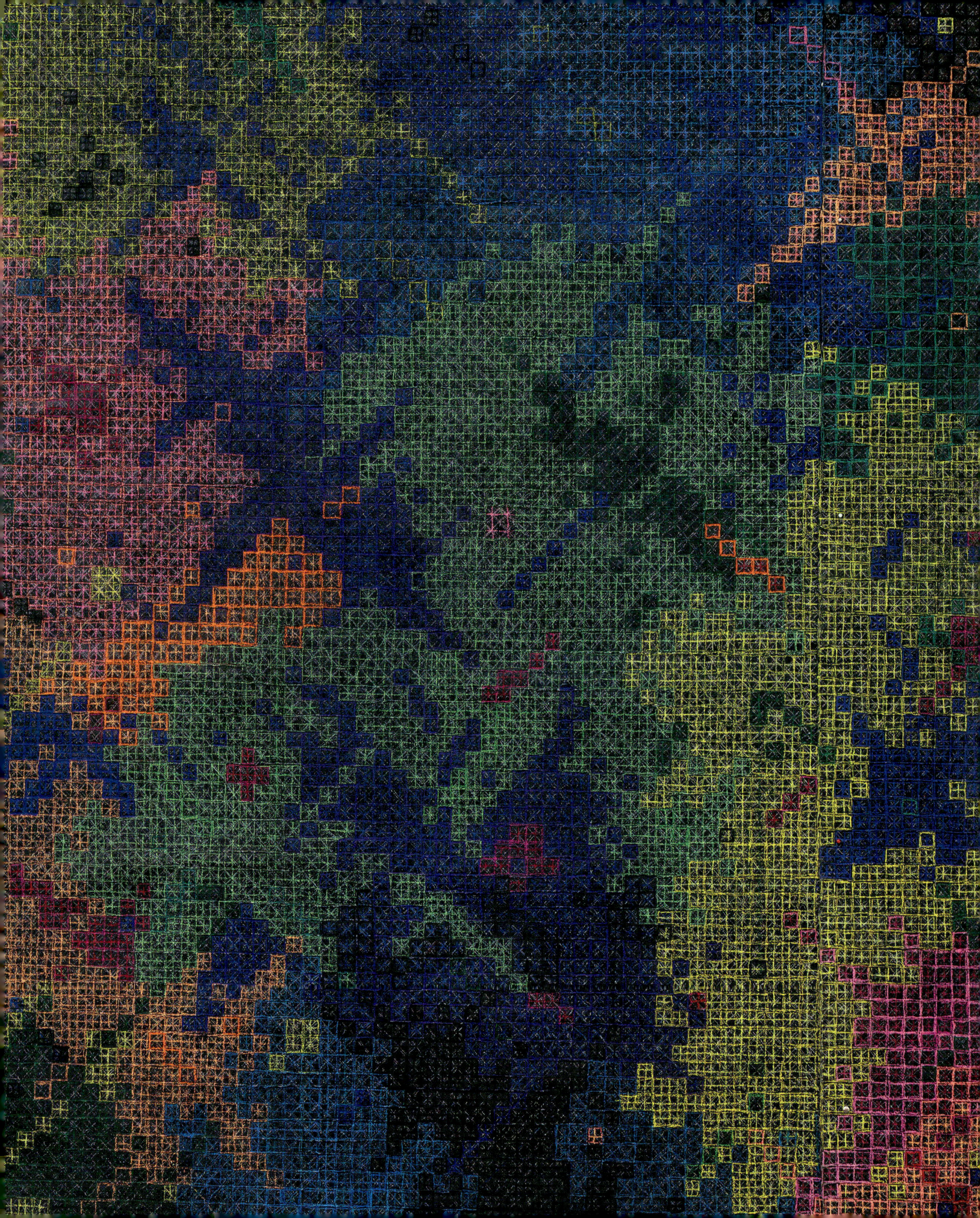

Foreword

Tony Godfrey and Kaimei Wang recount an eye-opening conversation with the painter Ding Yi: he told them that his approach to abstract painting is comparable to the venerable Chinese game of Go – a game, he quickly adds, that he himself does not play. 'I am not painting in order. Sometimes I put one point here; sometimes I start to put another point on the other side of the painting . . . Take the centre! Take the corner! I paint the middle part as the first place . . . After I finish the big frame, I go back to the big square: I would put in something, symbols or cross, not knowing yet what or which colour. Maybe the white here doesn't need to be so white after I finish the work, so I can paint them grey. Sometimes the opposite and I increase the whiteness of the white frame.' It's a kind of improvisation, but one with a goal: to win, aesthetically speaking.

And he usually does win. Ding Yi is one of the most prominent painters of contemporary China, a country that in a very short time has gone from being profoundly isolated from cultural developments abroad to asserting a widespread influence in art, cinema and writing. If Ding Yi is becoming increasingly prominent in the West as well as at home, it's undoubtedly because his originality is easily recognisable in Western terms; to me, for instance, his synthesis of rigour with spontaneity within the constraining yet also liberating structure of the grid makes him a worthy successor of Piet Mondrian.

But perhaps it's a mistake to see Ding Yi's work in such a European framework. It's interesting to learn, as I did from this lively account, just how devoted the artist is to his own cultural identity: he loves listening to podcasts on Chinese history as he paints, and he's undertaken a project to exhibit every year throughout China – not in Shanghai, where he lives, or Beijing, but rather in cities overlooked by the commercial art world: Wuhan, Xi'an, and so on. He studied ink painting, the traditional Chinese medium, not oil painting as it was developed in the West, and cites the influence, early on, of Zao Wou-ki, the Chinese painter who worked in Paris, and whose lyrical works appear very different from Ding Yi's – 'too sweet', Ding Yi now thinks, and more obvious in their attempted fusion of Asian and European modes of art making. Godfrey and Wang help us understand how Ding Yi attempts to reflect the dynamism of contemporary China and thereby 'preserve some kind of cultural ambition for the future'.

Barry Schwabsky

1. Previous pages and opposite (detail)
Appearance of Crosses 2016-B10   2016

Chalk and charcoal on Japanese yuu grid paper
500 × 1185 cm (196⅞ × 466½ in)
Private collection, Singapore

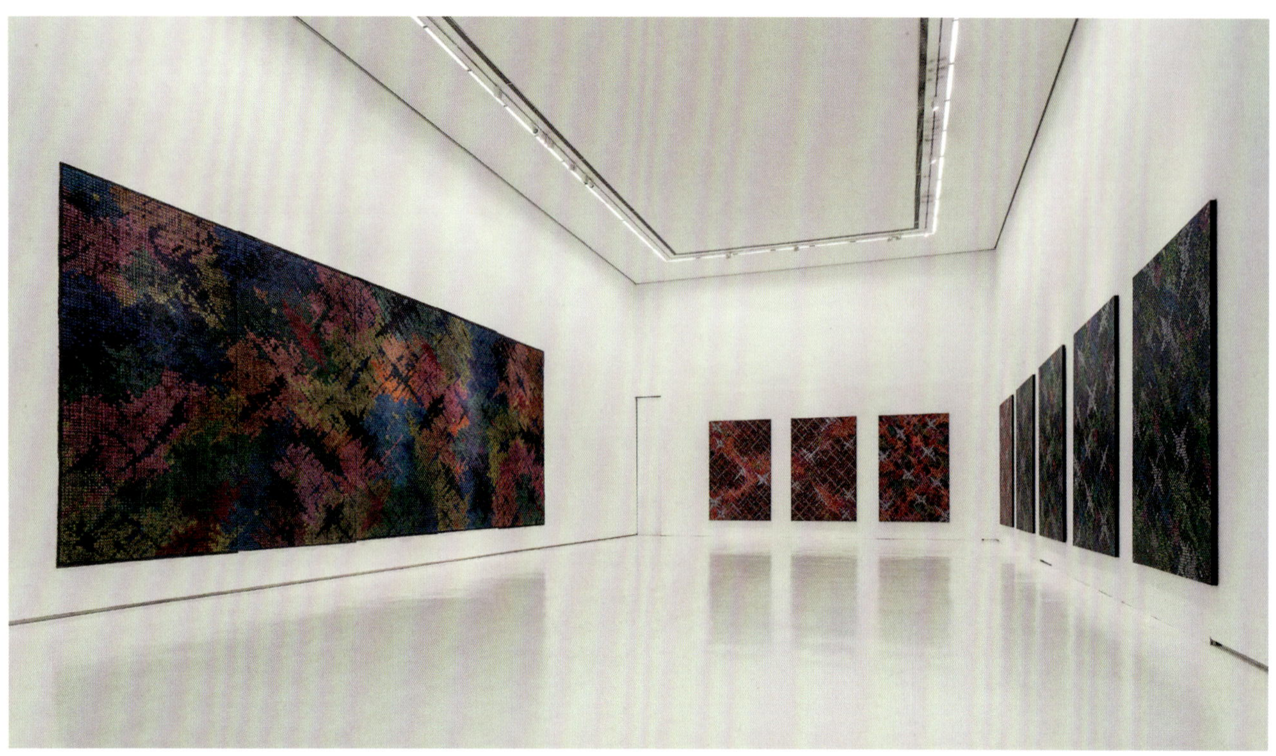

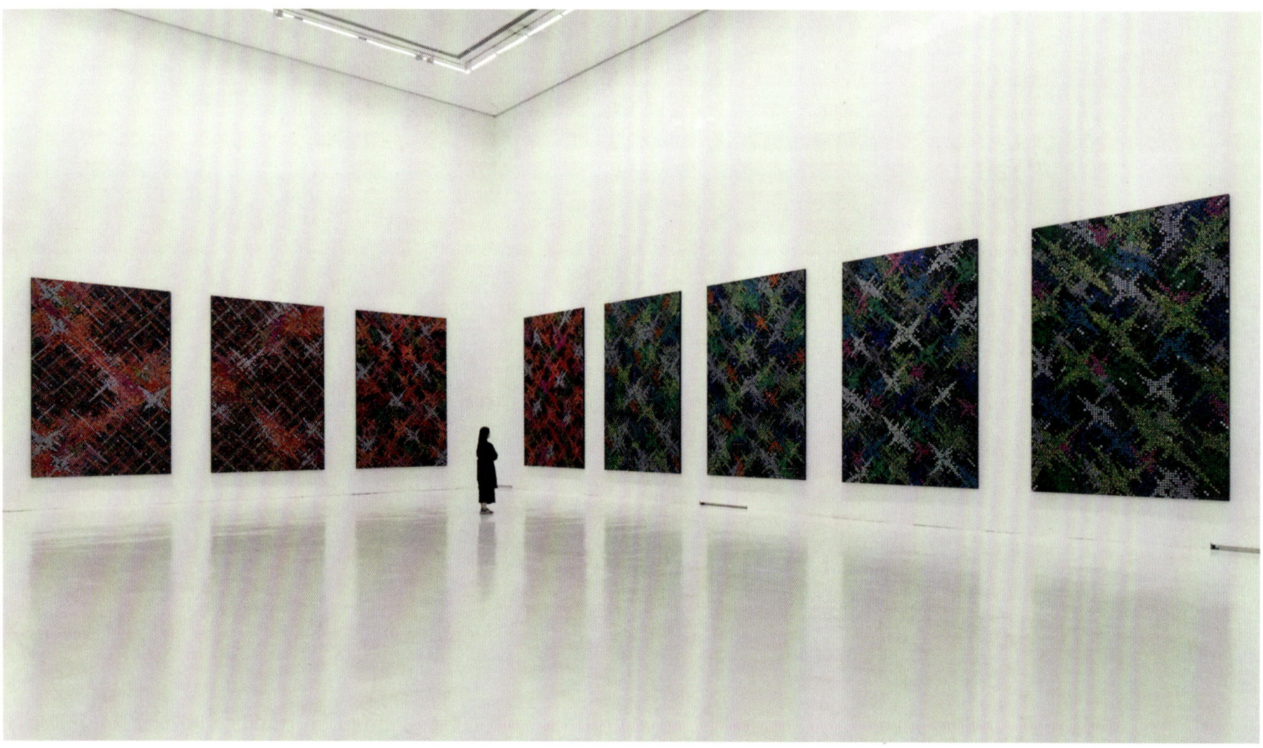

2. Installation view of Ding Yi's solo exhibition in
Xi'an Art Museum, 2017

1   In Xi'an

October 2017. Where are we and what are we looking at?

We are in Xi'an, 1200 kilometres (745 miles) west of Shanghai, in the city's newly built art museum. We are standing in a hall with very high ceilings and we are looking at paintings by the artist Ding Yi (fig.2). What strikes us first is just how very large these works are. To our left is a drawing on paper, five metres high and nearly 12 metres (16 ½ × 39 ⅜ foot) wide. Ahead and to our right are eight paintings, each close on four metres (13 foot) high. People come into the room, look at the paintings from a distance, then go closer, often very close. Sometimes they have their photograph taken standing in front of a painting. They must look as if they are immersed in it, like a swimmer in the sea. Two old women come in, go up to one of the paintings, and one of them knocks on it as if it were a door. The guard, horrified, runs to admonish them. The sound the woman made was like that of knocking at a door: the paintings are on wood.

Looking towards the opposite wall, the large paper work gives one a sense of floating, a little like looking down into a pond. The colours are subtle and harmonious. Perhaps one is reminded a little of Monet's *Water-Lily* paintings. In contrast the eight paintings on wood are very dynamic: the diagonal lines that cover them zip back and forth. As we look at those paintings we see that although the colours seem to settle and form clusters or clouds, one's eyes are always bustled on by the relentless diagonal lines.

Those people were right to go up so close. We realise this when we also get close: the details are everything. Large though the paintings are, they call on one to approach and to become intimate. Technically, there is nothing to see but crosses made with diagonal lines and, less prominently, the traces of a horizontal/vertical grid.

It is as if someone has laboriously filled that massive grid, joining corner to corner. Put like that, it sounds pretty boring. But it isn't. There is a lot to look at. A lot of different things. This is what strikes one as one gets close: the sheer variety of marks, thin and fat, short and long, sharp and wobbly. Our eyes may follow a yellow line that stutters along or a purple line that flashes determinedly from one point to another, or white crosses that coalesce into a cluster. We realise also that some lines are not painted but carved, that Ding Yi has periodically cut away an underlay of black, red and orange paint to reveal the wood itself. We see also that Ding Yi has dug out a small spot at the centre point of each vertical or horizontal line. This makes the painting glow like the star-laden night sky. We are told later that these paintings remind many people of the night sky.

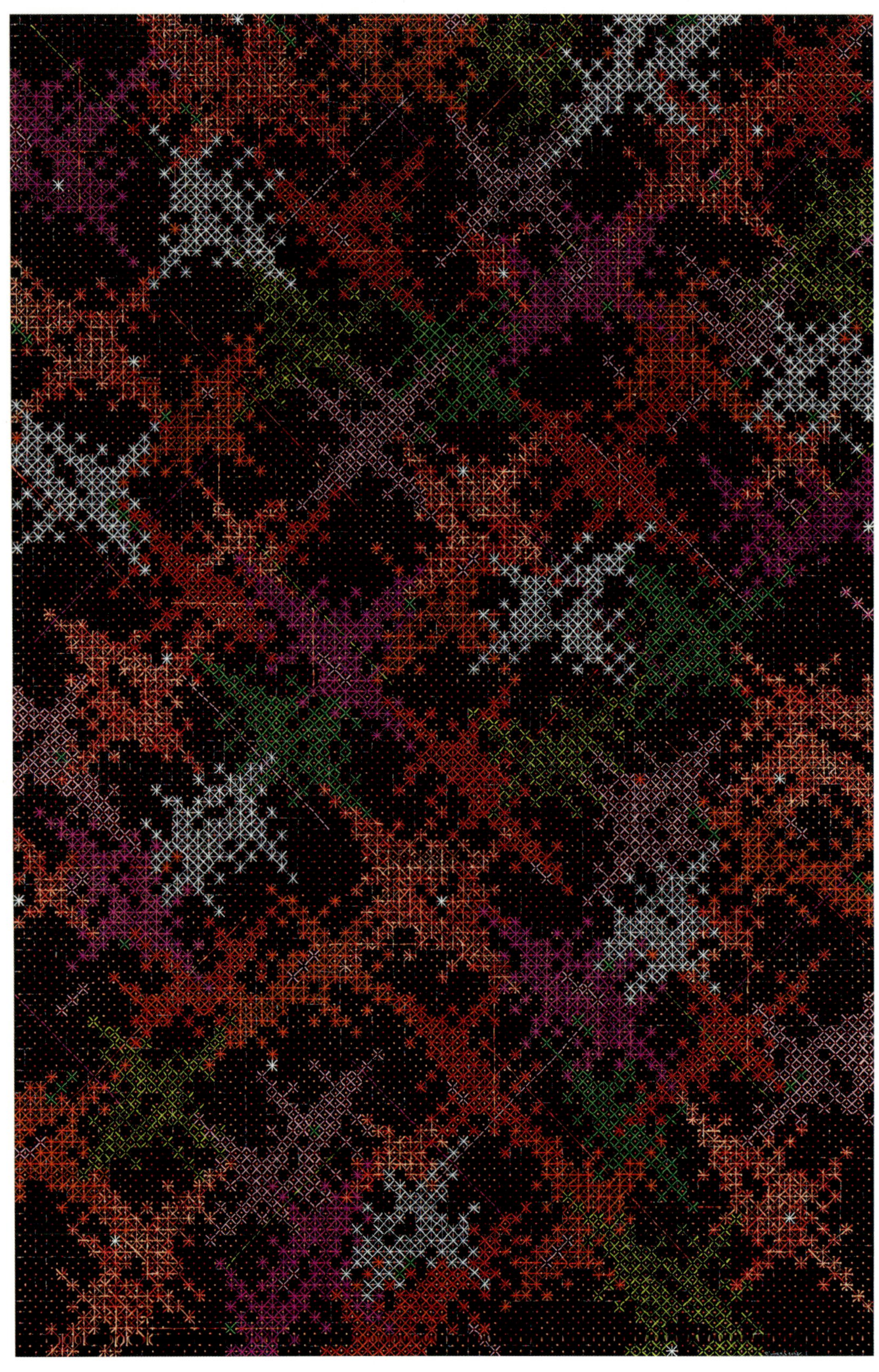

3. Appearance of Crosses 2017·7   2017

Mixed media on basswood
366 × 242 cm (144⅛ × 95¼ in)
ShanghART Gallery, Shanghai

4. Appearance of Crosses 2017·7
2017 (detail)

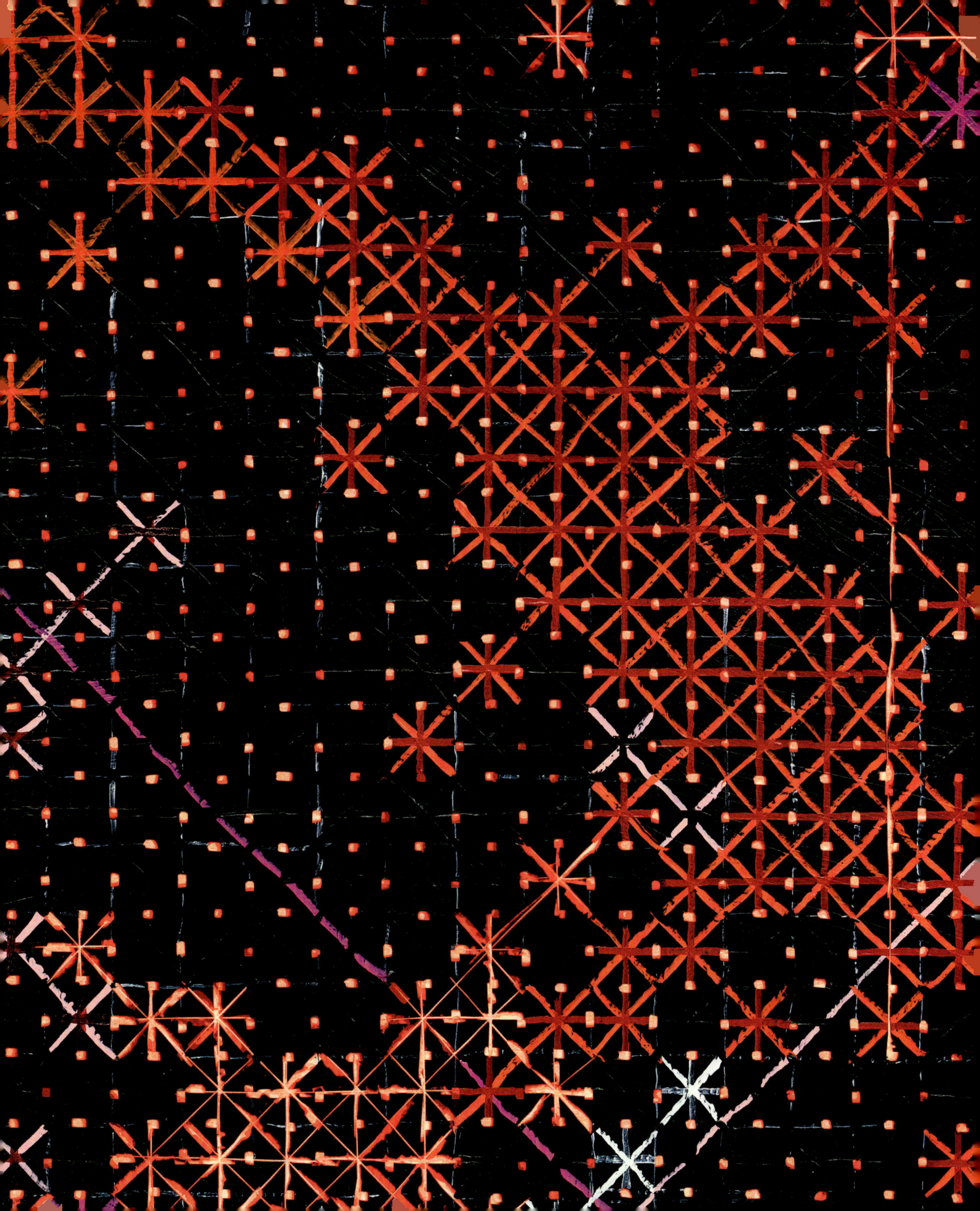

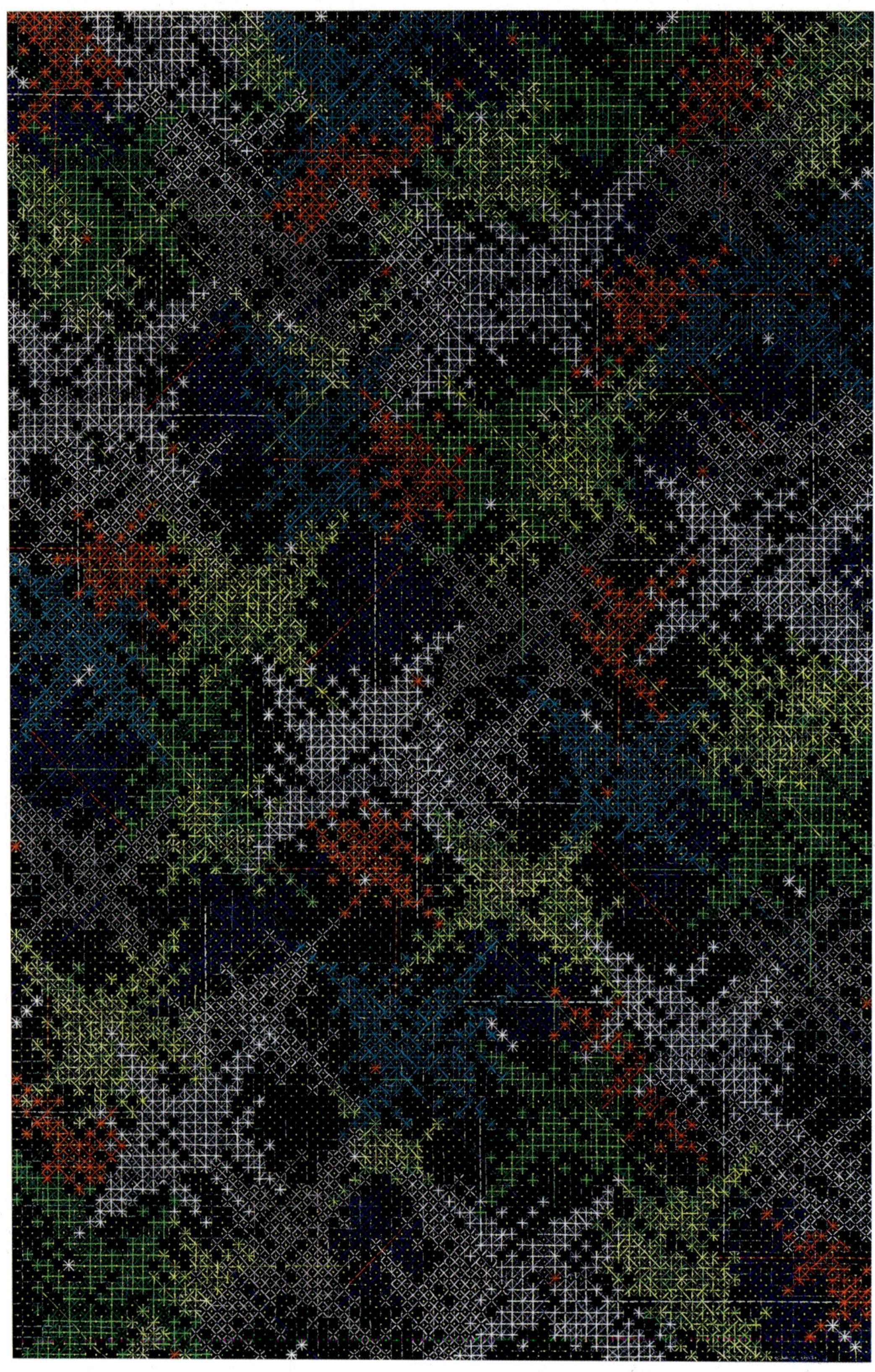

5. Appearance of Crosses 2017-6   2017

Mixed media on basswood
366 × 242 cm (144⅛ × 95¼ in)
ShanghART Gallery, Shanghai

6. Appearance of Crosses 2017-6
2017 (detail)

14

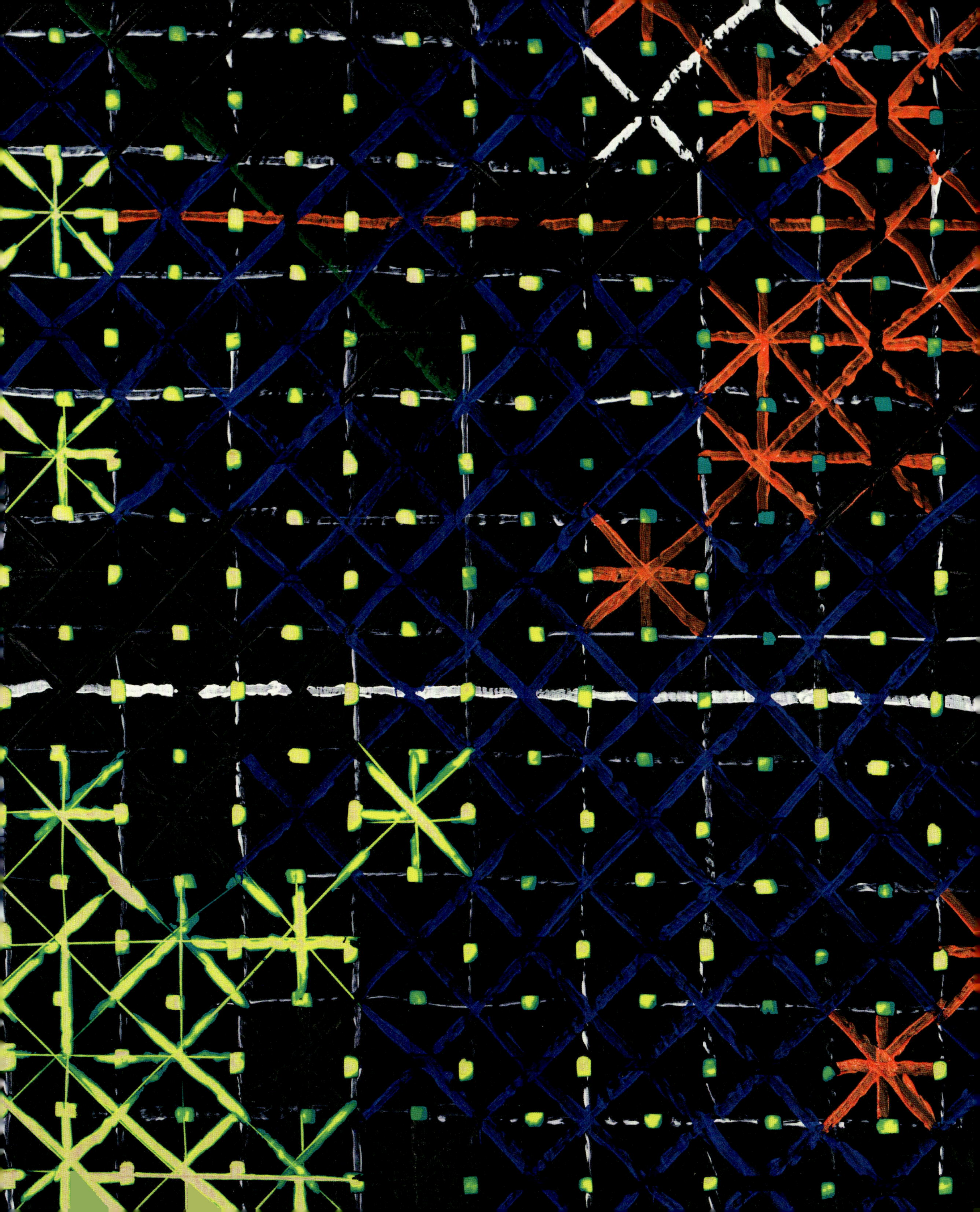

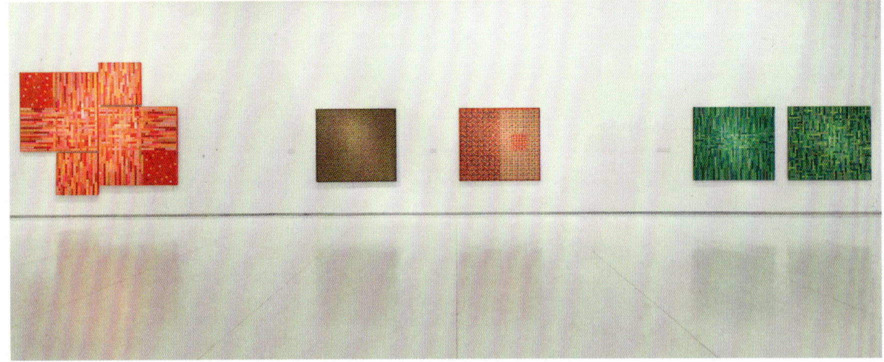

7. Five paintings as shown in Xi'an exhibition
L–R: *Appearance of Crosses* 2008-22, 1998-8, 2000-3, 2003-11 and 2002-12

Acrylic on tartan
L–R: 150 × 150 cm (59 × 59 in) (2 pieces) and 80 × 80 cm (31½ × 31½ in) (2 pieces); 140 × 160 cm (55⅛ × 63 in); 140 × 160 cm (55⅛ × 63 in); 140 × 160 cm (55⅛ × 63 in); 140 × 160 cm (55⅛ × 63 in)

Why is he exhibiting in Xi'an? Ding Yi was born in Shanghai and he still lives there. The Chinese contemporary art market is almost exclusively to be found in Shanghai and Beijing. Xi'an is far away from Shanghai and is better known for that great tourist attraction the 'Terracotta Army' than for its contemporary art scene. But Ding Yi believes that as a Chinese artist he must work for all of China. Starting in 2016, when he showed in Wuhan, his goal is that every year he will make a major exhibition with new work and a selection of old work in a major city other than Beijing or Shanghai. In Xi'an 45 paintings from the preceding 30 years were shown (fig.10), though thematically rather than chronologically.

Two days later when we met with him in Shanghai we asked him whether it was possible to sell such a vast paper work as the one we had seen in Xi'an. He replied that though it would be difficult to sell and impossible to frame and glaze, this was a unique time in China when so many large museums and collections were being created and where there were collectors and curators ambitious enough to consider acquiring and installing such works. We met him in his new studio. We were interested to talk about his working methods, how he planned his day, how he actually made the work, how he brought a painting to a successful conclusion.

His new studio, which he moved into in 2015, is much larger than the old one we had met him in before. It is in the new West Bund cultural zone of Shanghai, close by the Yuz Museum, the Long Museum and many art galleries. At the centre of this new studio is a very large table. On it are laid out his laptop, piles of books and catalogues, jars full of the coloured wood parings from his paintings, cups of tea and some letters to answer.

The table is like an island in the sea, whilst beyond on the walls unknown things grow. It is the place he returns to, where he can reconnect with the world outside. The table is where he answers emails, makes phone calls and drinks tea. It is where he meets with his assistants or visitors. Nearby there is an art deco leather chair for him to relax in and think. Beside that is a smaller table with a selection of paintbrushes and several pots of paint.

What is a typical day for Ding Yi? He has always been a disciplined and hard-working artist. Nowadays his daily routine starts at 10.30 a.m. when he arrives at the studio. Here he meets with his assistants, usually over a delivered lunch box, to go through his agenda and discuss upcoming projects and exhibitions. One assistant, Feng Jingfan, also known as Ariane, deals with administration. Another, Deng Yunfei, who is himself an artist, prepares the surfaces for him to paint on. Originally this meant little more than stretching canvas, but since 2015 when Ding Yi started painting on wood the assistant must cover each panel with, one by one, up to three different colours and then draw a grid over the surface. Only then do aesthetic decisions become needed, and from then on Ding Yi paints everything.

As he remarked in 2005, 'Unlike those artists with teams of assistants I want to keep painting my paintings by myself from the beginning until the end. In this way I make them resemble the world outside.'[1] This was and remains an interesting claim. In what way they may resemble the world outside we shall discover anon.

After lunch, Ding Yi may take a half-hour power nap on the studio sofa before he stands in front of his paintings and starts working. Usually he'll stay until 11 p.m., long after the assistants have left and the studio is empty. Most of the time he stands. Even when he takes a break and smokes a cigar, he will normally stand. He only sits when he starts to work on the lower part of the painting. The physical challenge hasn't increased since he turned to work on wood and carving; after all, either with chisel or brush the hand gestures are quite minimal compared to the huge physical endurance of standing and working continuously for nearly 12 hours a day.

He loses himself in his work. He becomes immersed in it and loses his sense of time. In 2011 when we first met him he told us that sometimes his wife will have to call him late at night and say, 'Ding Yi, it is time to come home.' Back then when we visited him in his studio in the M50 district – a factory-turned-creative zone in downtown Shanghai – he had a small radio. He would often tune in to the local news because his works then were addressing urban life – and the sound from the radio where the Shanghainese discussed their daily lives connected his studio world with the world outside. In 2018 we noticed that there was no radio on his table. Instead he plays podcasts. At the time he was listening to the Israeli historian Yuval Noah Harari's popular trilogy on human history. Normally he listens to podcasts on Chinese history. But Ding Yi, of course, often gets lost in his painting and loses track of the narrative. Frequently, when he goes back to find out what happened he realises that he must have already heard that part of the podcast several times.

It is the accompaniment of a human voice that he needs in this lonely working process. He says he is not really listening whilst working, yet he is still concerned about the contents of his podcasts. The reader's voice shouldn't be over-dramatic, nor should the stories be over-dramatised.

On our next visit in 2018 we saw on one wall of his studio a row of eight medium-size paintings on wood (fig.8). We asked how he began and finished such a set.

'When I compose new paintings', he replied, 'I often work in pairs and in terms of composition they match each other. For example, in paintings 1 and 2 [those on the

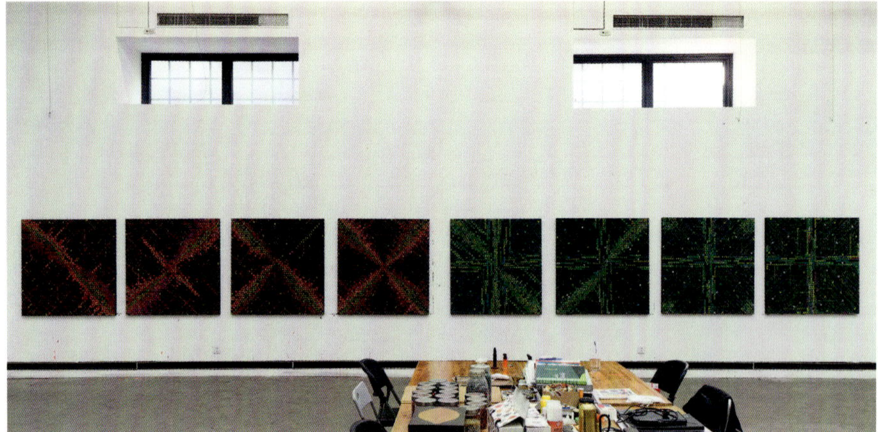

8. Ding Yi's studio with eight paintings, 2017

L–R: Appearance of Crosses 2017-13, 2017-14, 2017-16, 2017-15, 2017-18, 2017-19, 2017-20, 2017-21

Mixed media on basswood
Each 120 × 120 cm (47¼ × 47¼ in)

far left], they have both diagonal crosses whilst the upper left composition in painting 1 matches the lower right in 2. My choice of colour starts from instinct. The choice of red is my starting point but as I work with the other colours I feel that red is not powerful enough. That's when the white appears and then purple. I'd say this process is more an analytic one.'

Asked whether he has failures, he replied, 'It can happen that I'm not 100 percent satisfied. There is always one that I'm most satisfied with. For example, if I had to choose one amongst these eight to represent my works from this exhibition, I know which I would choose. But what would you two choose?'

Tony chose the fifth from the left (fig.9): 'This one that has the most complex corner. Corners are both important and difficult in abstract painting.'

Ding Yi replied, 'Yes, I have put much thought into the corner here, also the space created by the diagonal cross, as if the corner is pushing towards the cross to create an imaginative depth.'

Kaimei chose the second last one from the right (fig.10), saying, 'It feels for me the most harmonious one and fulfilled in all corners and sides.'

Ding Yi smiled and said, 'I would choose the second to the left (fig.11). The diagonal is not completed. There is an unbalanced match between the short line and the longer line around the diagonal. I like the unfinished and unsettled feel of this work. However, now these works are finished I head on to the new project.'

Although painted as a series or sequence of pairs, the paintings are all seen as stand-alone works in their own right and as such were sold separately at his gallery ShanghArt. Smaller paintings such as these also act as seedbeds for what will come next, he explains: 'Working on the smaller sizes is a preparation for larger works. I can finish one such work in a week. It feels like a transitional period for me before working on the larger works and an opportunity to find new expressions in painting. So I have been thinking a lot about my next large painting already as I work on the last painting of these eight. These eight paintings are like a warm-up for my next stage.

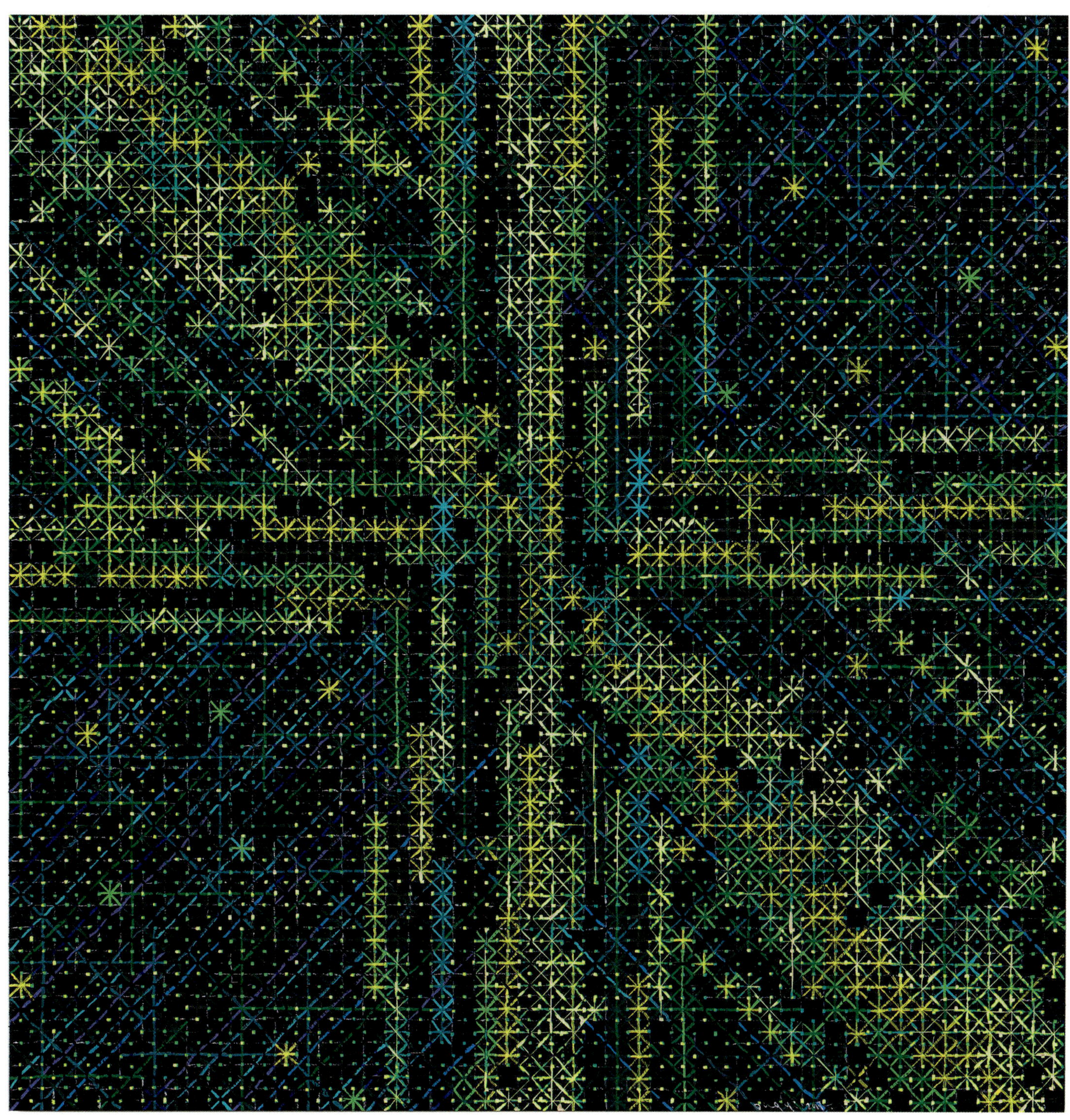

9. Appearance of Crosses 2017-18 *2017*

Mixed media on basswood
120 × 120 cm (47¼ × 47¼ in)
Private collection, Shanghai

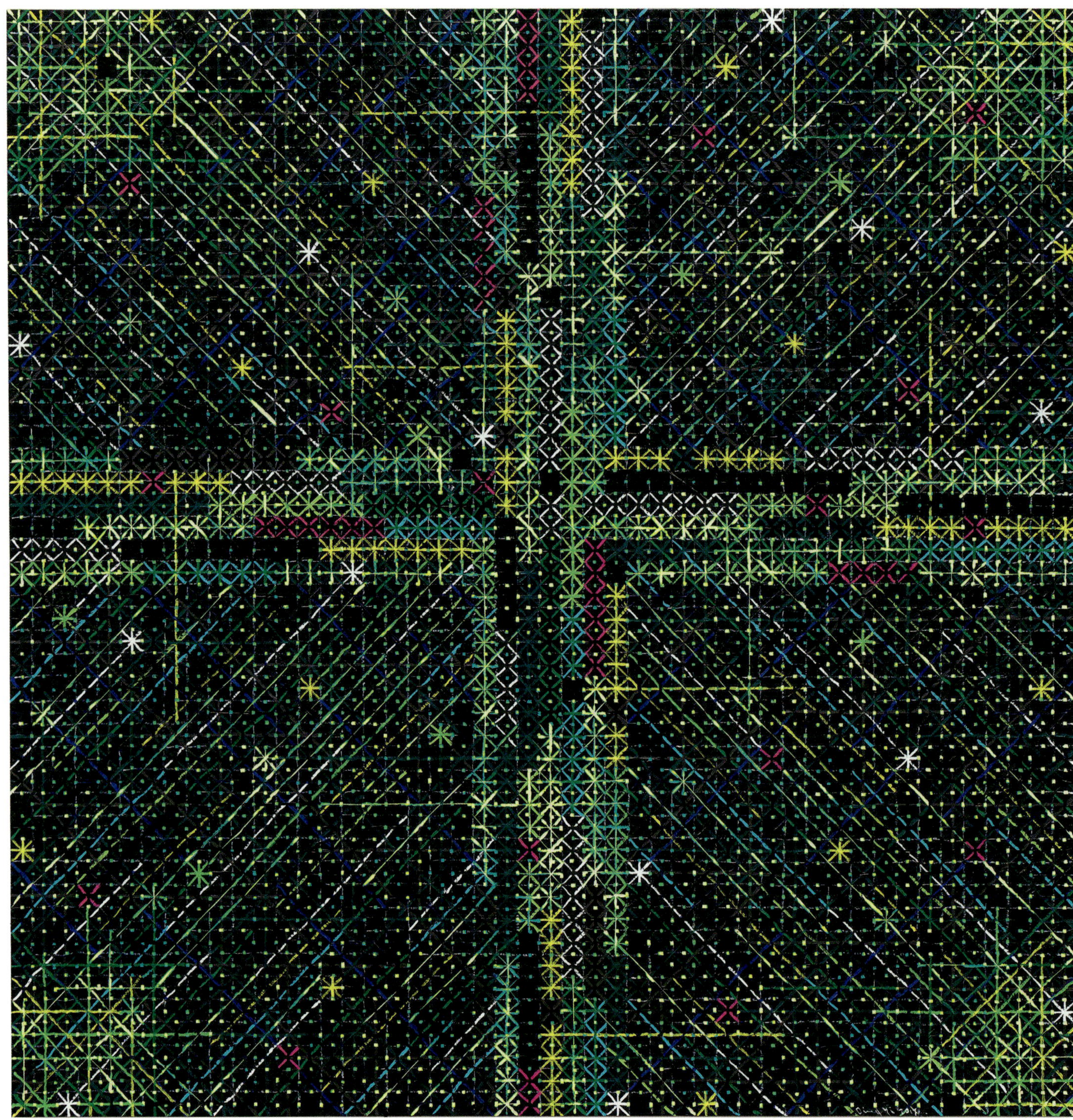

10. **Appearance of Crosses** 2017-20   2017

Mixed media on basswood
120 × 120 cm (47¼ × 47¼ in)
Private collection

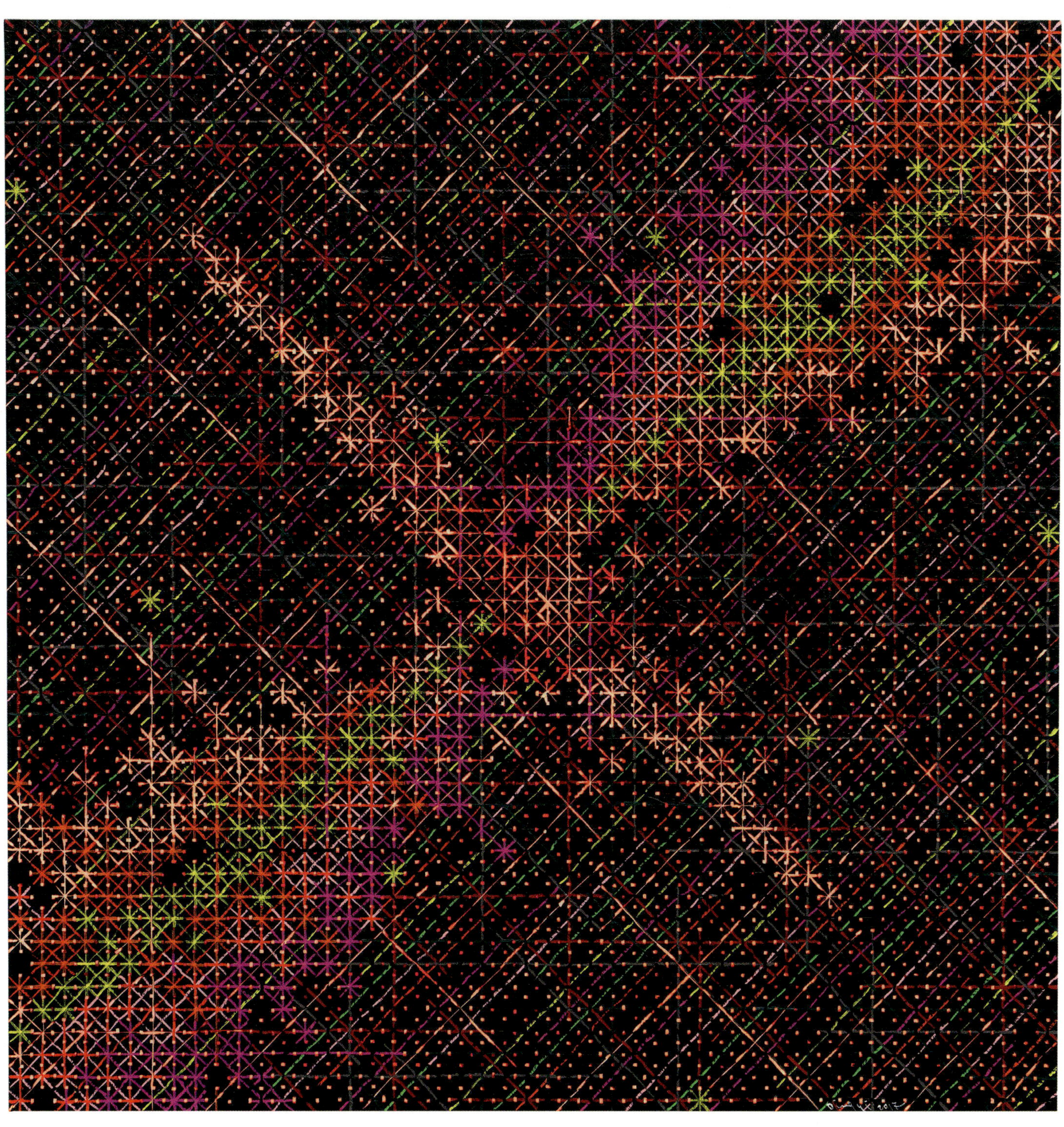

11. Appearance of Crosses 2017-14   2017

Mixed media on basswood
120 × 120 cm (47¼ × 47¼ in)
Private collection, Taiwan

'Then I move to this painting', he said, pointing at a 240 cm square painting on the opposite side of the studio with a similar black ground and red matrix of crosses (fig.12). 'And this painting is an important stepping stone to the next very large painting.' (An as yet unpainted wooden panel measuring 366 × 732 cm hung close by.) 'Already when I work on this one I am starting to plan the very big one. Will it be black or white underneath? How will I compose the painting? I am making a new form now. I have been thinking about how to express power within my painting. The diagonal lines, the parallel lines create power.'

'It looks like *Star Wars* to me', Kaimei remarked. 'The formation of the rebellion's fleet in the galaxy.'

'Do you mind being compared to *Star Wars*?' Tony asked.

'No, not at all', Ding Yi replied. 'Actually, last month after I had made this painting I went to a National Geological Park outside Dunhuang in western China. I was amazed to see how the formation of the land, especially when seen from an aeroplane, looks so similar to my painting. The geological formation was created by wind and sun. The locals call this valley "The West Sea Fleet".' A month and a half later this enormous wood panel was fully painted. (As *Appearance of Crosses 2018-2*; see fig.96.)

Fixed to the wall in one corner of the studio was a small work on paper. Whenever he had to wait for a layer of paint to dry he would work on that.

There was also an earlier work (*Appearance of Crosses 1997-29*) painted on tartan that had returned from his show in Xi'an (fig.13). He felt dissatisfied with it but he couldn't destroy it as it now belonged to his gallery. Therefore he had made several changes to it, including putting white squares round the crosses. In general he had given it a greater complexity. It was the first time he had ever reworked a painting. It made him feel better.

He stands for long hours in the studio and loses himself in his painting. But if making and thinking is a meditative process, he himself is no ascetic monk. As our meeting with him ended he told us of a new restaurant he wanted to take us to for supper later that week. As another Chinese artist remarked to us at a banquet, 'Ding Yi is very good at planning a menu.' In China, where a meal consists of many dishes, choosing a good selection and sequence is seen as a great skill. He appreciates good food and good design. His studio, which, as the photographs show, is notably clean and well organised, contains several elegant objects.

He always gives the appearance of being calm and self-controlled. Yet his way of working is the opposite of mechanistic. In 2011 he told us, 'I am not painting in order. Sometimes I put one point here; sometimes I start to put another point on the other side of the painting. I structure my painting like playing Go. Take the centre! Take the corner! I paint the middle part as the first place. This is like a Go strategy, though I don't play the game myself. After I finish the big frame, I go back to the big square: I would put in something, symbols or cross, not knowing yet what or which colour. Maybe the white here doesn't need to be so white after I finish the work, so I can

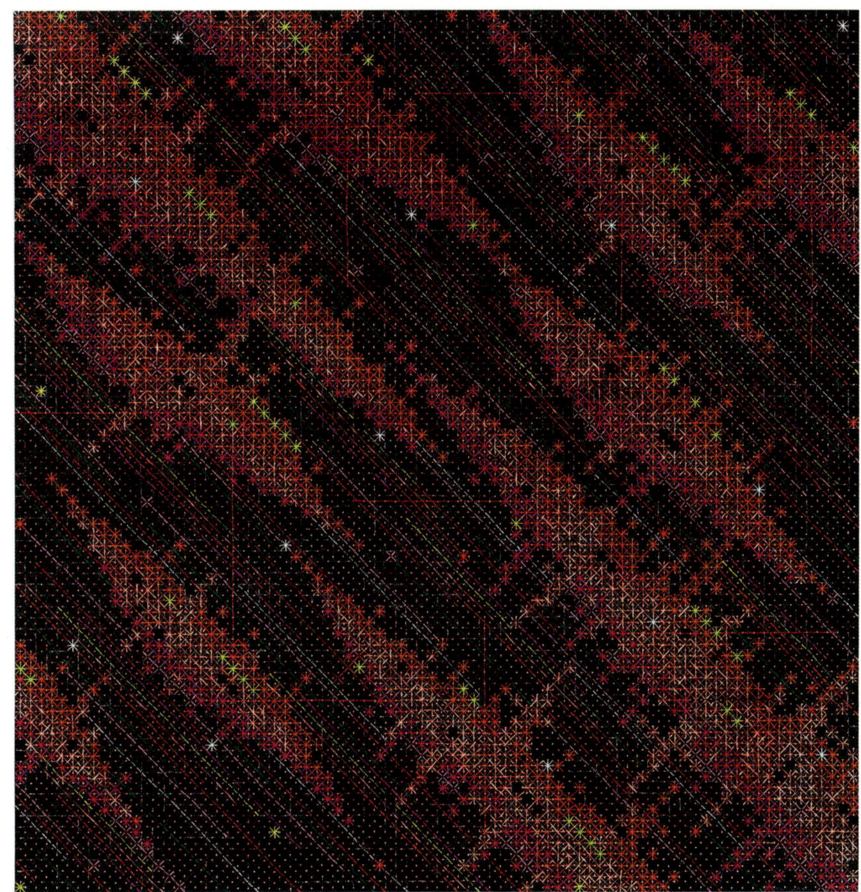

12. Appearance of Crosses 2018-1   2018

Mixed media on basswood
240 × 240 cm (94½ × 94½ in)
ShanghART Gallery, Shanghai

paint them grey. Sometimes the opposite and I increase the whiteness of the white frame.' Then as now, his approach was to deal with the detail but always with a sense of the overall feeling.

We are reminded of a seemingly very different artist, Alberto Giacometti (1901–66). There is a famous film of Giacometti working on a clay portrait bust. His fingers push in the cheeks and then, as if in an essential response, pinch a section of the neck, and then again, as if some invisible balance had been destabilised, adjust a lump on the back of the head. Everything was connected. An action on one part of the sculpture would make another action elsewhere necessary. So it is with Ding Yi. He is always working on details – and there are many details in his work! – but he is also always responding to an organic sense of the whole, of a certain rightness.

He is an intuitive artist who works with nothing but grids and crosses. Can we explain this paradox? How can we persuade the sceptic that it is not 'the same old crosses' but always something new? His work may not seem very 'Chinese' to a Westerner, but to what extent has he been formed by his particular environment, and how does he act within it? How could an abstract artist with such ambition and subtlety emerge from Communist China?

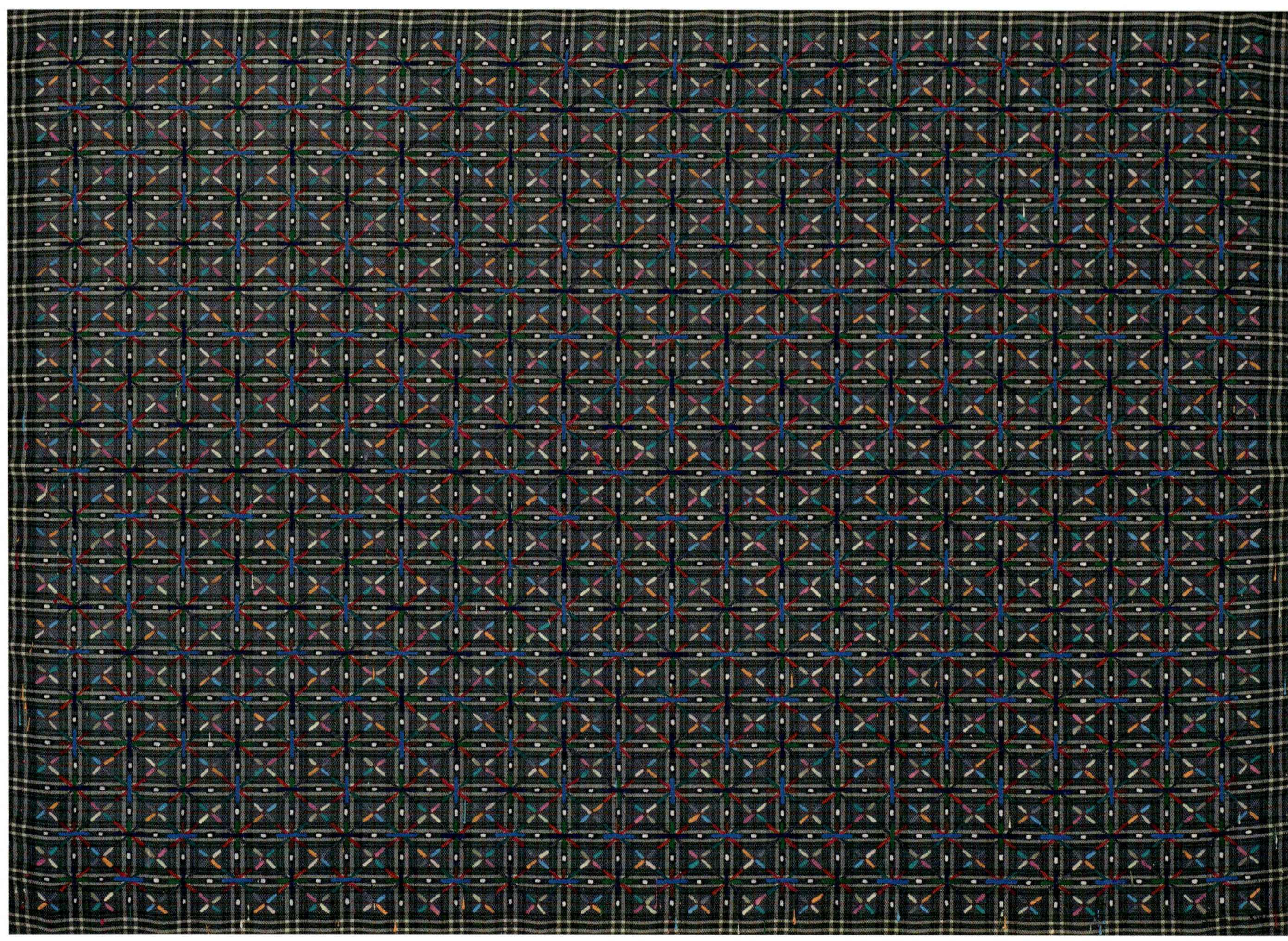

13. Appearance of Crosses 1997-29   1997

Acrylic on tartan
135 × 200 cm (53⅛ × 78¾ in)
Private collection

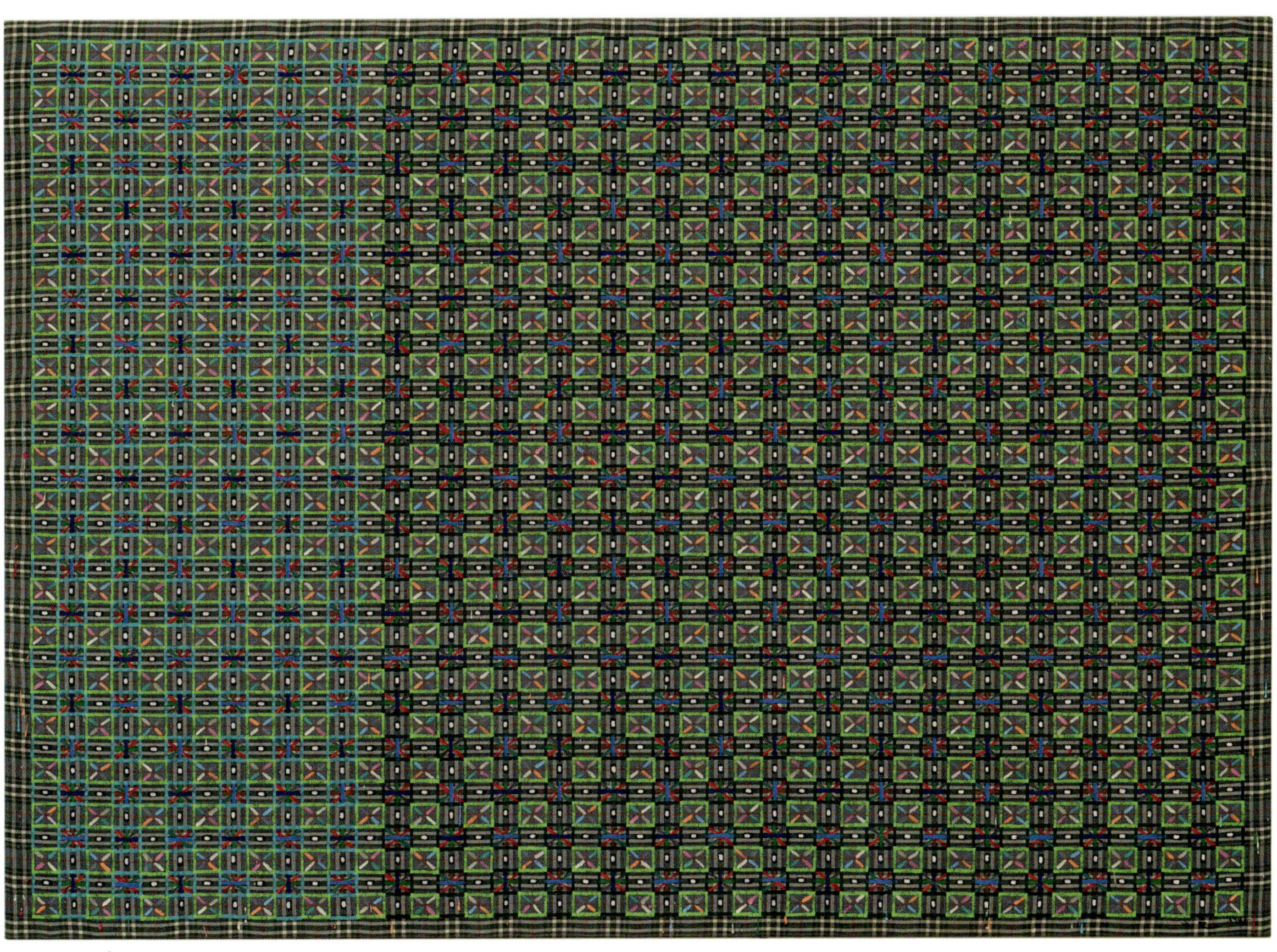

14. Appearance of Crosses 1997·29
(as reworked in 2017)   1997

Acrylic on tartan
135 × 200 cm (53⅛ × 78¾ in)
Private collection, Guangzhou

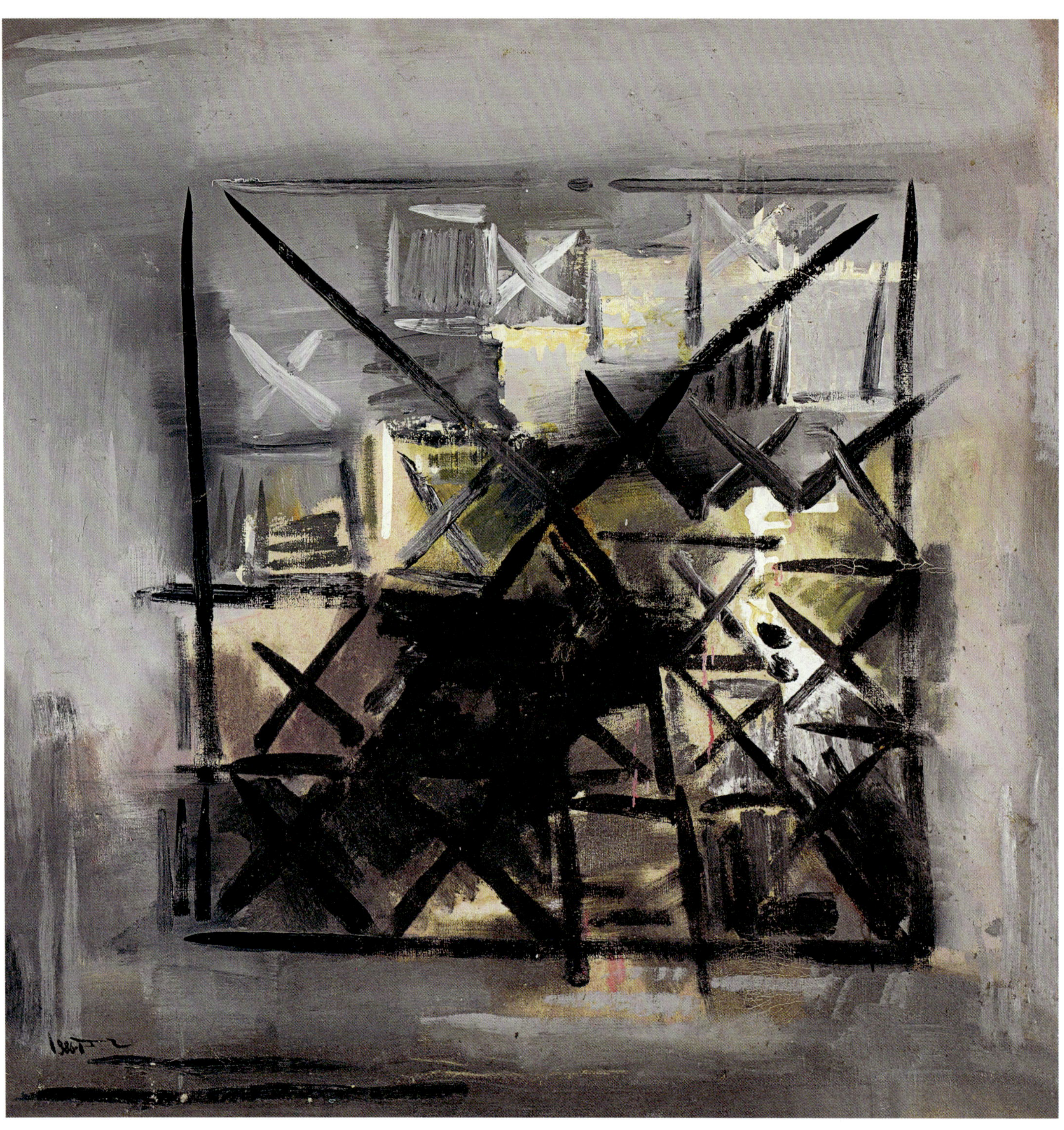

15. Taboo   1986

Oil on canvas
84 × 84 cm (33 × 33 in)
Private collection

2 Early Work

Ding Yi (丁乙), or as he was originally named Ding Rong (丁荣), was born in Shanghai in 1962.

Ever since it was opened to international trade in 1842 Shanghai had been a meeting place of East and West. By the 1920s it was a great city and a vibrant cultural centre. 'Nothing more intensely living can be imagined,' wrote the English author Aldous Huxley then of Shanghai.[1] It was a centre for jazz, dancing, film and whatever the latest Western fashion or fad was. In painting too, it was a place for innovation: it was here that Chinese painters such as Xu Beihong (1895–1953) had tried to find a harmonious blend of Western modernism and Chinese traditions. China's first art institute, its first instance of life drawing, its first modern art society and its first national art exhibition were all born in this Western-influenced rising metropolis. During the 1920s and 30s, a new urban class driven by Westernised education arose, aware of advanced Western literary and artistic thought. In 1925 Liu Haisu (1896–1994), himself a renowned painter and the dean of the Shanghai Fine Art School, was the first to open a life room with nude women posing for the students in his Western Painting department. This caused much controversy: the warlord of the Shanghai region issued an order to ban such an 'obscene' practice.

But by the time Ding Yi was born this international city must have seemed a distant dream. After invasions by the Japanese in 1932 and then again in 1938, the glamour and the gaiety slowly died, though even in 1949 Shanghai may still have had a larger foreign population than any other city in the world, including New York. However, by 1953 the Communist government had cleared any remaining foreigners out along with all vestiges of capitalism and consumerism.

It was in Shanghai in 1966 that the Cultural Revolution started: libraries were sacked and burnt, cultural monuments destroyed. Anyone with links to that earlier international period was likely to be persecuted or even killed, be they businessman or musician. Just as in other towns of China, the streets of Shanghai, including that outside Ding Yi's house, were covered with revolutionary posters, and hundreds of thousands of statues of Chairman Mao were erected in the city. By 1970 over 600,000 Shanghainese had been sent to the countryside for 're-education' following Mao's call that they should learn from the peasants. Torn apart, Shanghai stagnated. By 1972 the hunger for more statues of Mao faded, the giant slogans started to be painted out and the city was cleaned up for US President Nixon's visit. The parks started to be slowly restored.

In 1978 Deng Xiaoping, effectively the new premier of China, pledged to reform the country's economy, but this drive was mainly directed at Beijing. It was only in the

1990s that the government began to focus on Shanghai as the key economic centre, with Pudong on the east side of the River Huangpu set up as a Special Economic Zone and the centre for China's financial market in 1993.

What was life in Shanghai like for Ding Yi as a boy and then as a young man?

Ding Yi was born into an ordinary family: his mother was a kindergarten teacher and his father worked in a state-owned food-distribution bureau. They had secure, uncontroversial jobs. Ding Yi benefited from this stability. He did not go hungry, he was not sent to the country for 're-education'. If his family does not sound particularly artistic, one should note, however, that Ding Yi's father was a very handy person who had made every piece of furniture at home and even all the children's clothing by hand. 'Once my father got hold of some very rare pigments for oil painting', Ding Yi told us. 'For more than half a month, as soon as my father had any spare time, he would lock himself in his room and work on a large fibreboard with his pigments. Finally, one day he came out with a completed oil painting based on a still photograph from the famous film at that time, *The Women's Brigade*. I was so proud of my father that I told all my friends in my class that I had a painter father. No one believed me so I had to prove it. So one day, after we had finished school, I ran home and lifted my father's painting into the window so that as my classmates passed by our house, they would all see it from below.' As a child Ding Yi showed a real interest in painting, so his father took him to neighbours' houses and here he learnt something about traditional ink painting from the uncles and grandfathers. (In China respected older men are often called 'grandfather' and 'uncle' even if they are no blood relation.)

There were no art classes at his junior school, but around the age of eight he began copying comics and revolutionary posters. His classmates were impressed. In every class in those days there was always a second blackboard where chosen students could draw or write news and quotes from Mao's Little Red Book. Even though the anarchy of the Cultural Revolution had ended and the teachers had returned to the classroom, much education was still about ideology. Aged 11 he was chosen by the class propaganda committee to be in charge of this blackboard newspaper. When he moved on to middle school he was once again put in charge of the blackboard newspaper. He received many awards for his work on it.

The house where Ding Yi grew up is located in the older part of the city, the Yang Pu district. Opposite his family's home was the district's Cultural House. The best thing that Ding Yi remembers about this institution was that it showed films. Before each screening a poster of the film would be painted on the billboard outside the Cultural House. The cultural workers in long dark-blue robes covered in flecks of paint, standing on the ladder painting film posters, fascinated him. 'For a long time, whenever I thought of an artist, it was as a man in a blue gown standing in front of a billboard painting film posters.'[2]

He would eventually enter Shanghai Arts and Crafts College in 1980, graduating in 1983. Although the college had no renowned teachers at that time and its main subject

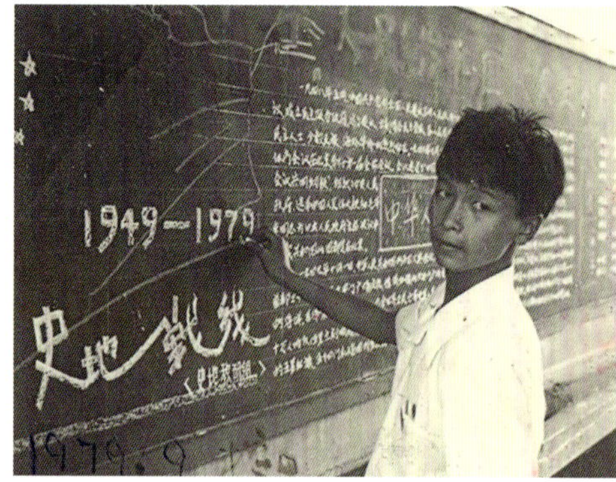

16. Ding Yi working on blackboard newspaper when studying in Kongjiang Middle School, Shanghai, 1979

17. Ding Yi exhibiting his works in the classroom in Shanghai Arts and Crafts College, 1981

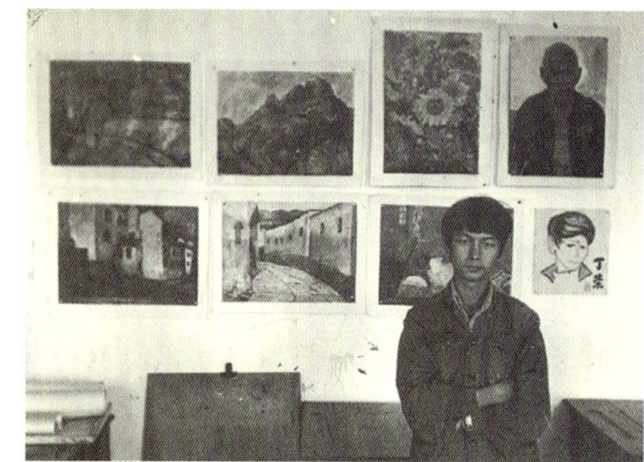

18. Hongkou Park   1983

Oil on canvas
57 × 70 cm (22½ × 27½ in)
Private collection

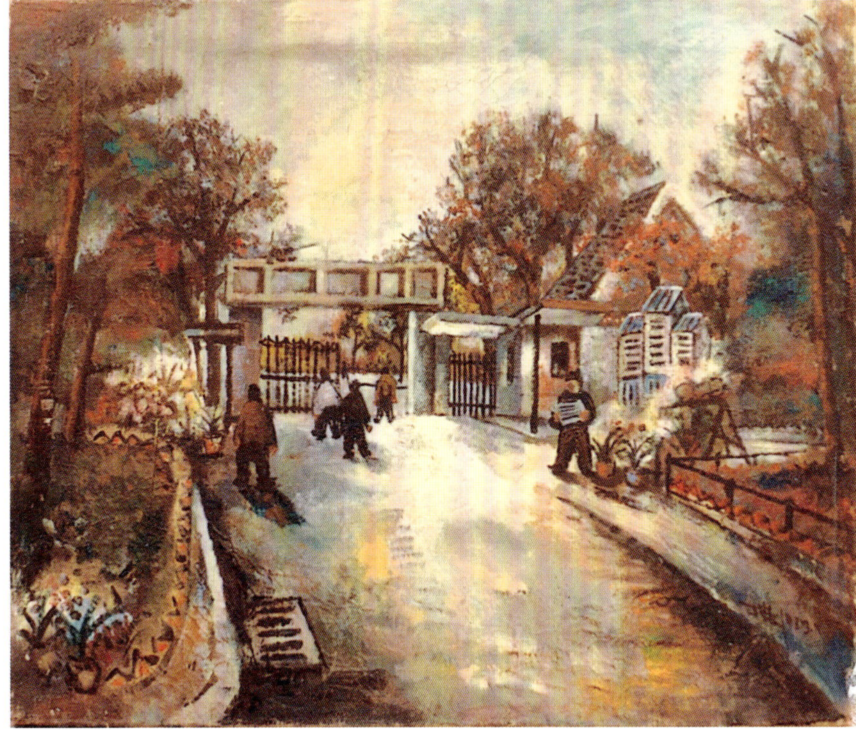

19. Maurice Utrillo *Eglise de village*   1919

Oil on canvas mounted on wood panel
46.8 × 38.5 cm (18½ × 15⅛ in)
Private collection, Shanghai

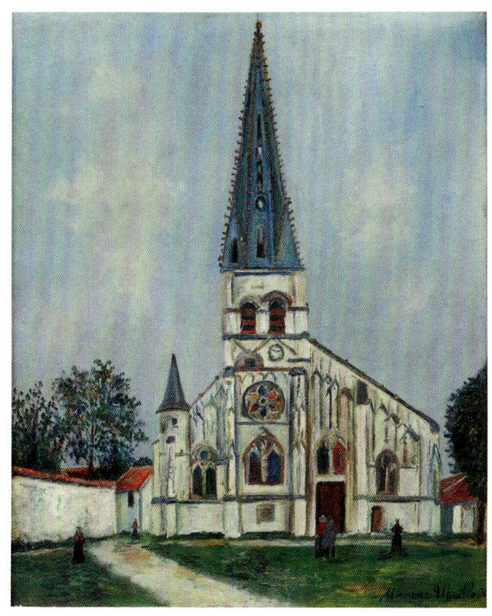

was then product design rather than oil painting, sculpture or calligraphy, it was here that in 1981 Ding Yi met Yu Youhan (b.1943), who was then teaching in the college. Nineteen years older than Ding Yi, Yu was to become the artist who had the greatest effect on him. Ding Yi often took his paintings to Yu Youhan's studio to show him, or sometimes simply went to borrow Yu's camera to photograph his own artworks. They held open and long discussions about art and creativity, and their contact soon developed beyond a student–teacher relationship into a good and genuine friendship.

Yu introduced Ding Yi amongst other things to the work of Maurice Utrillo (1883–1955), a once fashionable but now rather forgotten Parisian artist. Ding Yi has often cited him as a key influence. Why? 'Because what he showed us of Paris looked very much like the Shanghai of my formative years',[3] or at least the Hongkou district which was part of the International Settlement once occupied by the British and later by the Japanese. 'By imitating him and painting Shanghai so that it resembled his Paris, my technique improved . . . Utrillo with a Chinese twist.'[4] Yu also 'taught us to figure out what Cézanne was. At that time to be able to understand Cézanne was a watershed. It was extremely important.'[5]

It should be emphasised that there was little access to Western art in China at this time. The exhibition of French landscape paintings from the Musée d'Orsay shown in Beijing and then Shanghai in 1978 was the first, rare chance he and others had to see real works of Impressionism or Fauvism. After 20 years when only socialist realism had been exhibited, the formal freedom and inventiveness of these Impressionist and Post-Impressionist works was a revelation to artists. In October 1981 an exhibition of works from the Boston Museum of Fine Arts was an even rarer opportunity for Ding Yi to see abstract paintings by Jackson Pollock, Hans Hofmann and others. But generally knowledge of Western art was limited to reproductions, and of those only a limited and haphazard selection was available.

In a way this was to prove for many Chinese artists an advantage; they were not weighed down by all the theoretical and ideological baggage of late modernism. This relative lack of historicist preoccupations meant they could approach old problems in a new way. It has been noted that the emerging generation of Chinese avant-garde artists leapfrogged modernism, jumping from socialist realism straight to post-modernism. However, in Shanghai, because of the memory of modernism during the 1930s, artists had a stronger yearning to re-embrace modernism per se.

Though he only became well known for his pop paintings of Mao from 1989 onwards, since 1979 Yu Youhan had been exploring abstraction and abstracted landscapes. Although he was just as interested in political or ideological art as Beijing artists were, he was more focused on exploring the language and materials of art. Li Shan with his *Beginnings* and *Expand, Extend* series and Zhang Jianjun with his *To Have* and *Have Not* series were other artists in Shanghai who were also exploring abstraction at this point.

Was abstraction merely, as some have suggested, 'an alternative to seemingly unavoidable political or sociological subjects'?[6] Scarcely! Abstraction was neither a convenient and comfortable hiding place for the timid in China nor a practice devoid of ideological thinking. In the reform years of the early 1980s abstraction was as likely as pornography to be denounced as 'bourgeois spiritual pollution'. In 1983 Deng Xiaoping had initiated his anti-spiritual-pollution campaign which strove against Western hair-dos, high heels, short skirts, moustaches and the 'worship of individualism'. In line with this, an editorial published in the Shanghai-based party newspaper *Liberation Daily* the same year described artists who painted abstract paintings as 'self-indulging and self-admiring' and urged such artists to 'wake up' because 'people cannot understand it [abstract painting] and therefore do not welcome such works'. The editorial ended by saying: 'abstract painting has no future in our country'.[7]

After college Ding Yi got a job in a toy factory as a package designer. He worked there for three years but spent most of the time in his own studio, painting. For his first studio he rented a room in a farmer's house. It was basic: if he wanted to use a toilet he had to go to a nearby hotel.

While working as a designer he became familiar with the + marks used in mock-up pages to indicate where the different colours should be aligned and printed. This was to be the germ that grew into his *Appearance of Crosses* paintings. Importantly, this is a + with no meaning, linguistic or symbolic. All it does is mark a spot with cross hairs.

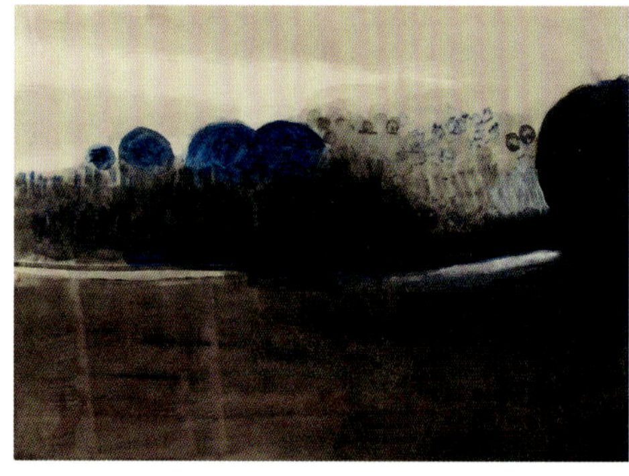

20. Yu Youhan *Abstract*   1983–10

Acrylic on paper
81.5 × 112 cm (32 × 44⅛ in)
Private collection

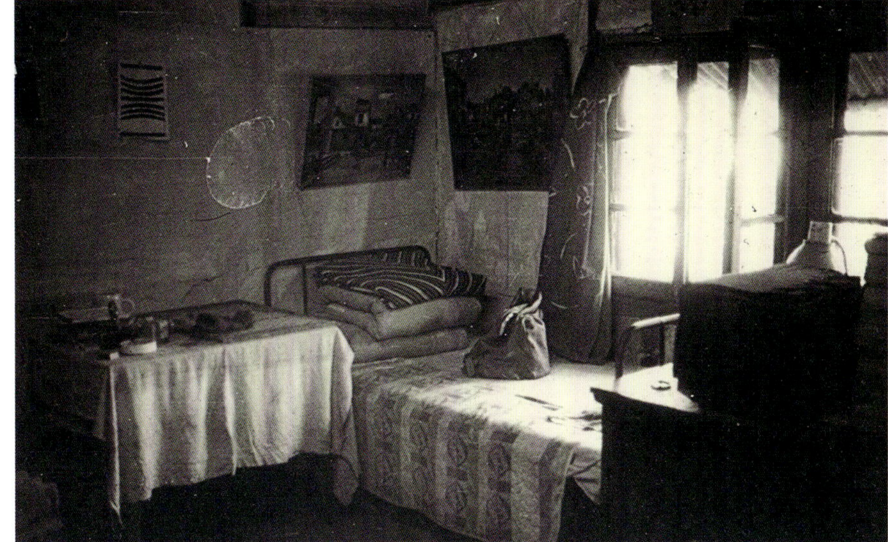

21. Ding Yi's first studio
in Wang Jia Lou, Shanghai   1986

22. Zao Wou-ki *Vent*   1954

Oil on canvas
195 × 96.5 cm (76¾ × 38 in)
Centre Georges Pompidou

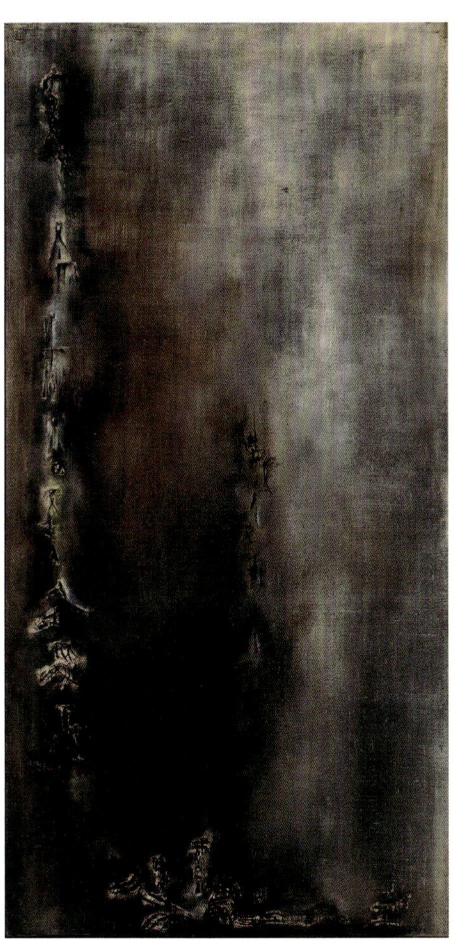

During this time he travelled to cities nearby to visit exhibitions. Only a week after his registration at the factory in 1983, he went to Hangzhou to see an exhibition by Zao Wou-ki (Zhao Wuji, 1921–2013) without asking for leave. He was reprimanded for this, but for Ding Yi this encounter with Zao Wou-ki's abstract work was crucial. It was the first time Zao Wou-ki had shown his large abstract paintings in China. Having left his homeland in 1948 he had become established and famous in Paris, hence an obvious role model for young artists fretting at the conservatism of their education.

In 1982 Guan Liang (1900–86), another artist known for his ingenious integration of Chinese and Western cultures, had a retrospective in Shanghai.[8] This was part of the process of rehabilitation and opening up known as *Ping Fan* ('Correct the wrongdoings') during the 1980s, when Chinese artists and writers who like Guan Liang had suffered badly during the Cultural Revolution were given back their status. The early 1980s is marked as the most liberal period in China's politics, and the party apologised for the brutal treatment they had received and tried to make up for the loss. There were several international exhibitions in China at this time, and many foreign books on philosophy, psychology, social science, art and political science were translated and published.

Guan Liang's and Zao Wou-ki's fusion of Western and Chinese styles into abstraction was important to Ding Yi as he began to make his own first forays into abstraction in 1983. He was aware by now of Frank Stella and Piet Mondrian (1872–1944) but, of course, only knew their work through reproduction. His first encounter with Mondrian had been in 1981 through the small black-and-white reproductions in the book *A Short History of Western Modern Art* by Herbert Read, recently translated into Chinese. A little later, he saw for the first time works by Frank Stella and Barnett Newman – albeit only as reproductions in a catalogue about Ad Reinhardt that belonged to a friend. It was to be much later that he got to really know, understand

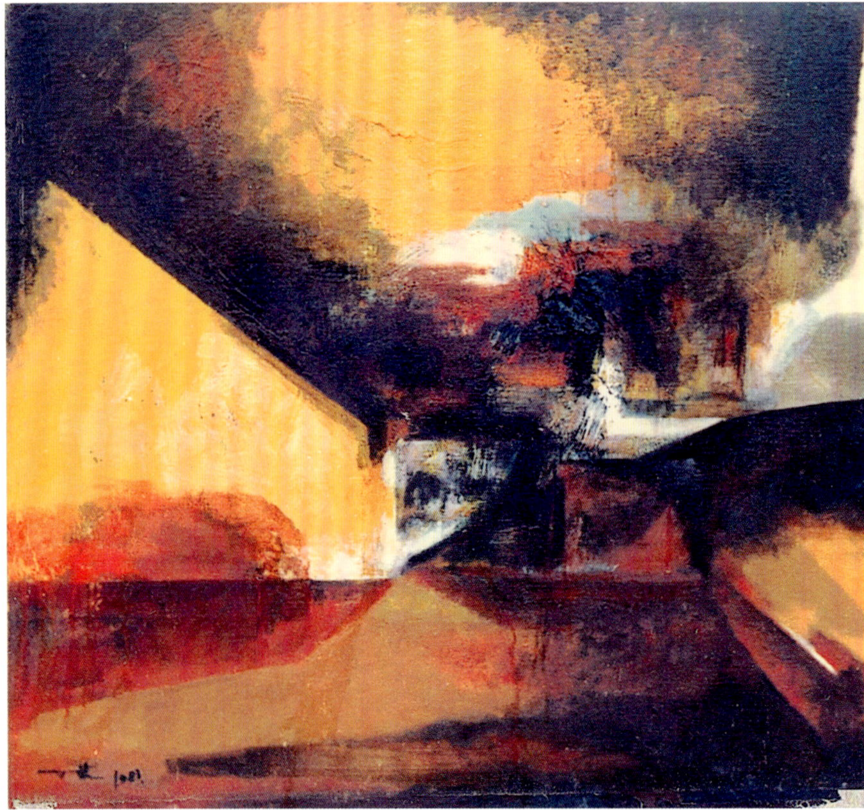

23. Heroism   1983

Oil on canvas
78.5 × 95 cm (30⅞ × 37⅜ in)
Collection unknown

and think about Mondrian's work. An early abstract by Ding Yi from that year, *Heroism*, has some hard edges but is still mainly characterised by Zao Wou-ki's sort of space and chiaroscuro (fig.23).

Yet for some time he was more obviously influenced by the views Maurice Utrillo painted of Paris in the late 19th century. 'I was painting cityscapes, the colonial architecture on Dalian Road. I went to see every exhibition in Shanghai at that time, and I came to the conclusion that there was nothing new amongst Shanghai artists. At that time, I was learning instead from Utrillo and Cézanne, the French Post-Impressionism styles. I was developing a more skilful technique. I knew that I was doing something different, but I couldn't have predicted that I would be making something historically new. By 1985 I had made my last street painting, then I moved on.'

As a painter of 20th-century Parisian streets, Utrillo inevitably painted, however indirectly, many grids, albeit with an all-too-often wobbly brush. Importantly Ding Yi learned by painting streets and houses – not trees and hills and rivers, nor the human figure. He was and remains an urban artist. As Xiao Kaiyu pointed out in an early essay on Ding Yi in 1997, his townscapes were notable for some 'abnormal perspective relations'.[9] Space could be twisted. Xiao also remarked that Ding Yi had a habit of adding iron fences to the houses he painted – perhaps an early sign of his propensity for grids.

After decades of isolation from the outside world, the liberal social atmosphere in 1980s China led to an embrace of Western thoughts and ideas but at the same time witnessed the revival of traditional Chinese culture and values. The debate about cultural identity and fusion of the East and the West influenced young artists like Ding Yi.

Ding Yi realised at this point that his understanding of Chinese traditional art was not profound enough. He also wanted to be a student again rather than work at the toy factory. In 1986 he applied to the Chinese painting department of Shanghai University. Without a solid Chinese painting foundation, Ding Yi had to seek help from his friends and fellow students in Shanghai University to prepare for the exam. With ten days to go, Han Feng, a student in the department, taught him the basic patterns and rules of Chinese ink painting and advised him on some shortcuts that would help him score highly. Eventually Ding Yi entered the Chinese painting department with the highest marks. He was equally amazed that his final essay there as a student was well received by the department although its thesis was 'Anti-Chinese Painting'. As he remarked,

> You can imagine therefore that the Chinese painting department of Shanghai University was quite open-minded and tolerant towards different voices. I was a student at the ink painting department in Shanghai University from 1986 to 1990. A period when we tried to invent experimental ink painting. I think the most important thing I learned from this period is that I started to think abstractly. It was an open and chaotic period for me as I was experimenting with various art expressions – I even did performance art. Experiments in ink painting initiated my abstract thinking. I was working on some pieces for the experimental ink painting exhibition. I made sketches for my paintings. This was in fact the only period when I made sketches before actually making a painting.[10]

In 1986 an exhibition entitled *Modern Painting: Six Men Group Exhibition* took place at the student club at Fudan University. The exhibition was led by Ding Yi's former teacher at the Arts and Crafts College, Yu Youhan, and Ding Yi was included as one of the six participating artists. All six artists presented purely abstract works, which was a very radical approach at the time. Ding Yi presented paintings in the style of Zao Wou-ki. For his artist's statement, he wrote:

> I used a large painting brush to draw big blocks of colours, eager to search for a serene space to reflect and meditate. The horizontally parallel traces restored the harmony and mystery of the world. The shaky and colourful thickness gave out a sense of movement, highlighting the oriental in my mind. Within such a universe I created. The paint I used was like numerous tiny black, brown and white dots, studding all over my mind. It reminded me that I was a Chinese. Only by injecting national dynamism and emotions into works could one truly understand one's own strength.[11]

24. D84-8 Poetry   1984

Acrylic on paper
109.5 × 79 cm (43⅛ × 31⅛ in)
Private collection

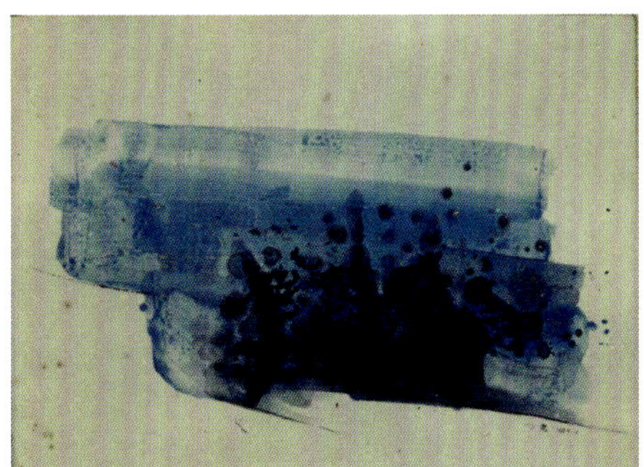

Looking at these paintings today, there are not many similarities with Ding Yi's present cross paintings, save the fact that already at this early stage Ding Yi has developed his own way of identifying his artworks. The titles of two works from 1984 *D84-8* or *D84-9*, were both also subtitled *Fu (Poetry)*. Such evocative subtitles soon disappeared and from then on we have been told nothing but the year of the creation and the sequence within that year. The surface of *D84-8* contains an intense cluster of blue in the centre applied with a large painting brush. What Ding Yi describes as horizontal parallel traces were made with the same brush with less paint on it. The entire work demonstrates fast gestural painting and leaves large areas of emptiness around the central motif, a device that is often found within traditional Chinese ink painting. The void around the main subject invites the viewer to meditate on the universal nature of existence; it also challenges them to find something to fill it in with.

The intellectual ferment that since the end of the Cultural Revolution had manifested itself in independent art exhibitions, avant-garde groups of artists and actions was coming to a climax – often called the '85 Art New Wave. By that year throughout China there were at least 100 art groups working collectively and making art, especially performances and installations, that was very different from the art approved of by the government and exhibited in state museums. Although the art scene in Shanghai may have remained less politicised than elsewhere, the desire to experiment and to try and break the barriers between art and life also affected Ding Yi. Like other artists he tried making performance art: on 12 and 13 October 1986 he collaborated with Zhang Guoliang and Qin Yifeng to stage performances in which they wrapped themselves in yellow fabric. 'The first was held at Wusongkou

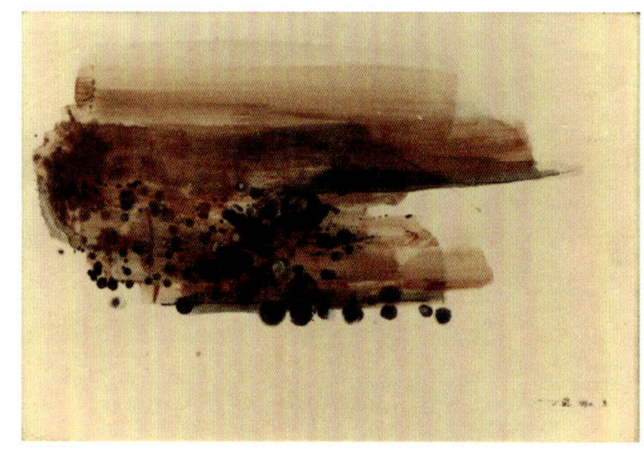

25. D84-9 Poetry 1984

Acrylic on paper
109.5 × 79 cm (43⅛ × 31⅛ in)
Private collection

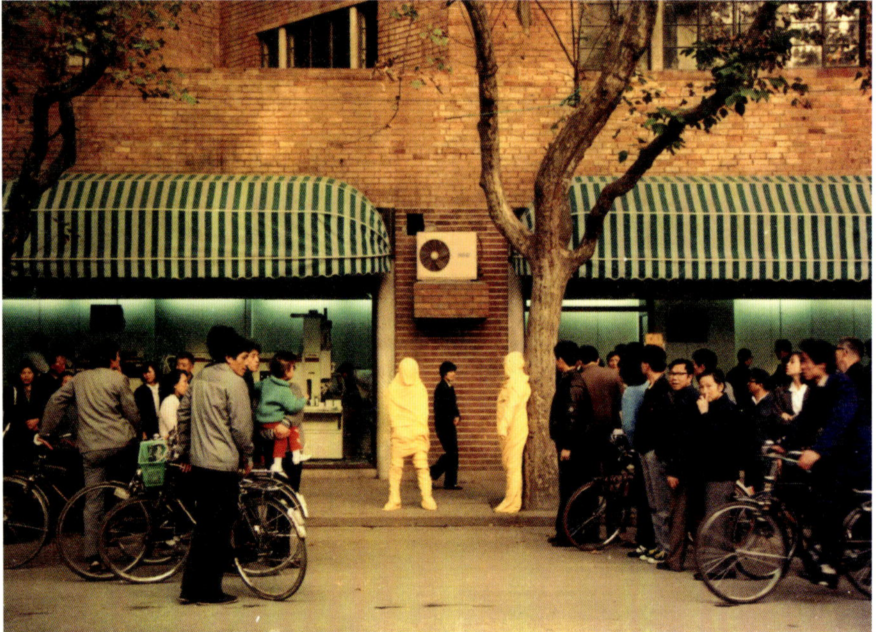

26. Ding Yi, Qin Yifeng, Zhang Guoliang,
Cloth Sculptures 1986

Performance

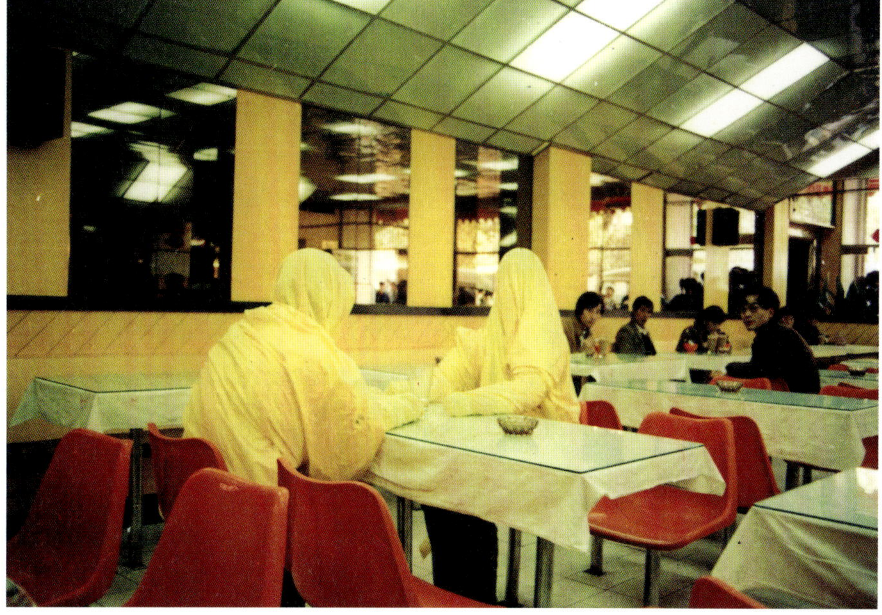

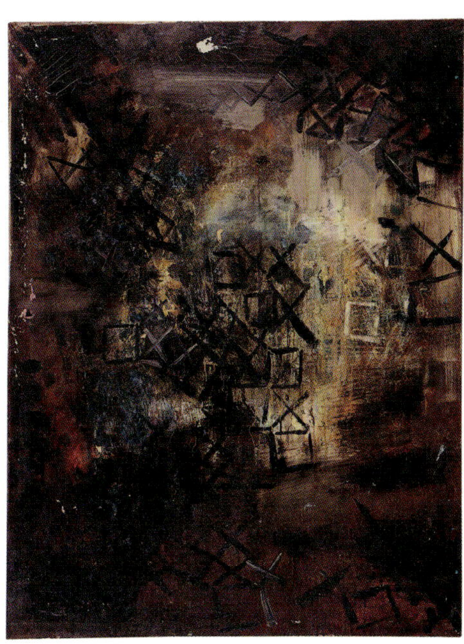

Wharf in Shanghai and a series of abstract sculptures were made by creating shapes through body poses inside the pieces of cloth. A day later the artists moved to a coffee shop across the road from the Shanghai Fine Art Department of Shanghai Normal University in the city centre, where they sat down behind one of the tables, again dressed in yellow fabric, Thereafter, the three artists moved from the front gate of the East China University of Political Science and Law to the streets surrounding the newly opened People's Hotel and the Bright River Hotel in Honqiao District, where they continued performances in which the artists posed as human sculptures.'[12]

On 22 November 1986 Ding Yi, Yu Youhan and others participated in the *Concave-Convex Exhibition* (also translated as *Exhibition Full of Bumps and Holes*). For this exhibition, Ding Yi created another performance outside the newly opened Shanghai Art Museum, wrapping a long stretch of yellow cotton around two people sitting on a bench. The museum, he noted, 'was new but represented tradition. It was I who represented modernity.'[13] As he admitted, the work was influenced by the famous wrapped sculptures of Christo. Back in 1986 Ding Yi had no knowledge of these other than a small picture he had seen in an art magazine – but he got the basic idea. (This very patchy, limited knowledge of Western art was typical of this period in China.)

By then the cross-shaped symbols and the form and style of his paintings had started to emerge. In 1986 he had painted what he has come to see as his first cross painting, *Taboo* (fig.15). Asked why he called it *Taboo*, he replied that that was what it was: it was just not done in China then to paint this way. Even earlier, his 1985 painting *Breaking the Shrine* (fig.28) contained many crosses, though they float in a rather murky space, whereas in *Taboo*, aligned on a grid, they give at least the centre of the painting a compositional structure. As he said, 'At the time I did not realise these would lead to something truly new, but, yes, these two works gave birth to my cross paintings. At that time, I was influenced by Zao Wou-ki with his mixture of figuration, landscape and abstraction in the same painting. As you know, I went to see the exhibition and admired his achievement. Today when I look at his paintings again, I feel his works are too sweet, too much in the Chinese manner.'

With the arrival of his first cross paintings something else, apparently small, but highly significant happened: before then he had signed all his paintings as Ding Rong (丁荣), the name given to him by his parents, but now he used Ding Yi (丁乙), the name he gave to himself, as his signature. Why? The radicals in the characters 'ding yi' couldn't be simpler and the given name Yi is just an anonymous ordinal number. It was a gesture of departure from the calligraphic tradition and certainly the first sign of a minimalistic pursuit. (It should be noted, at this point, that the assumption by some Western writers that his work is about calligraphy is wholly incorrect: he has no interest in it.) In 1995, as more and more invitations for overseas exhibitions were sent to Shanghai addressed to 'Ding Yi', to simplify applications for travel documents he officially changed his name to that.

Entering Shanghai University was mainly a way to get a studentship and time to continue with his own work. But he had hoped to learn something from studying Chinese painting (fig.29). However, eventually, as he put it, 'I realized that this artistic style did not correspond to the modernity of contemporary Chinese society. I was unsettled by this. I didn't know what to do or how to find my way out of the maze. I decided to forget everything I had learned on both the European and Chinese sides and to explore a completely different route.'[14] So he turned away from Chinese painting as he also had from the influence of Utrillo and Cézanne. He has talked of how he felt not only excited by the influx of Western art and ideas but highly perplexed on how to harmonise them with Chinese thinking. This was the crunch point. He felt the need to go back beyond both ways of art making to the most basic forms.

In 1988 he began his *Appearance of Crosses* series proper. This title (sometimes also translated as *Manifestation of Crosses*) comes from 十示 – the term used in China for the markers that show how to align the four different colours (CMYK) that make up a colour reproduction. In English we would probably say 'cross hairs' or 'registration crosses' – a term that is perhaps more correct as it does not have the human or religious associations of 'appearance' or 'manifestation'. 十示 is pithier and simpler than any English translation.

Though these new paintings used the cross shape and grid that appeared in *Taboo* they were remarkably different: the cross and grid were no longer motifs floating in space but a structure that covered the whole of the canvas. There was no longer any freehand gesture, no depth, no expressionist or humanistic mood, no message. *Appearance of Crosses I* of 1988 (fig.30) was no doubt produced as a manifesto for what he would now seek to do. It must have seemed outrageous to viewers in China:

29. Xujie 87-10   1987

Ink on paper scroll
210 × 60 cm (23⅝ × 82⅝ in)
Private collection

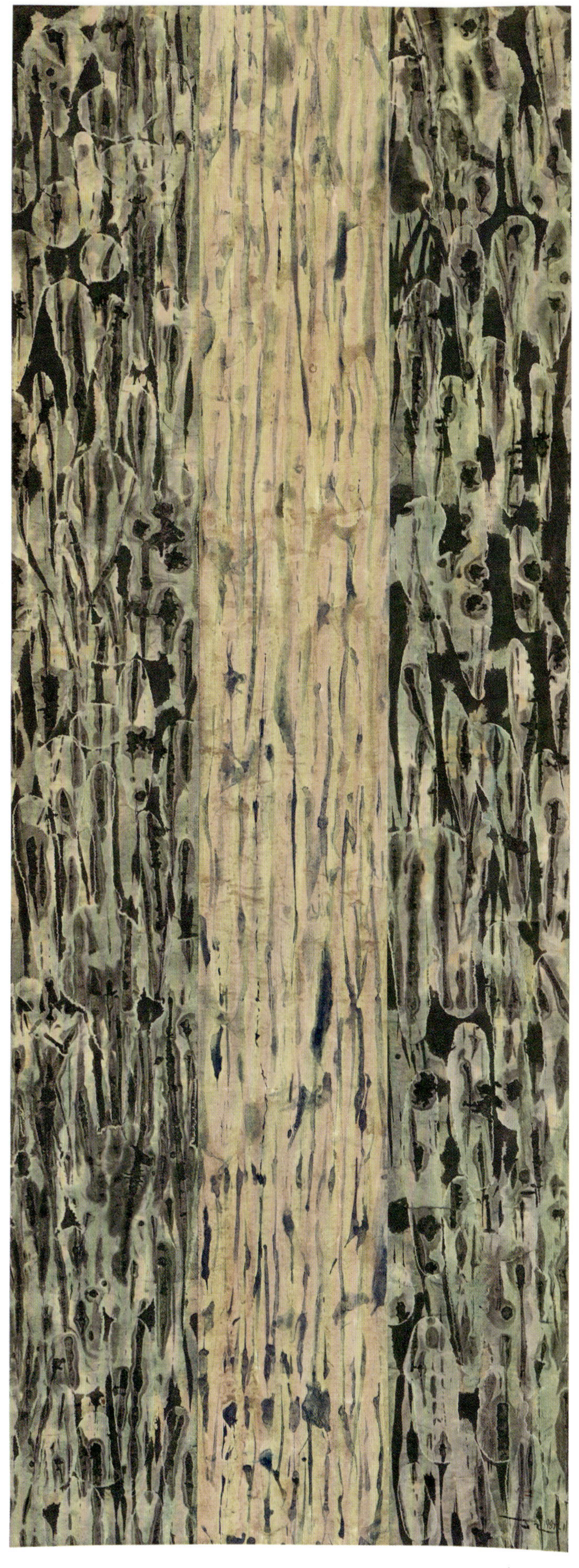

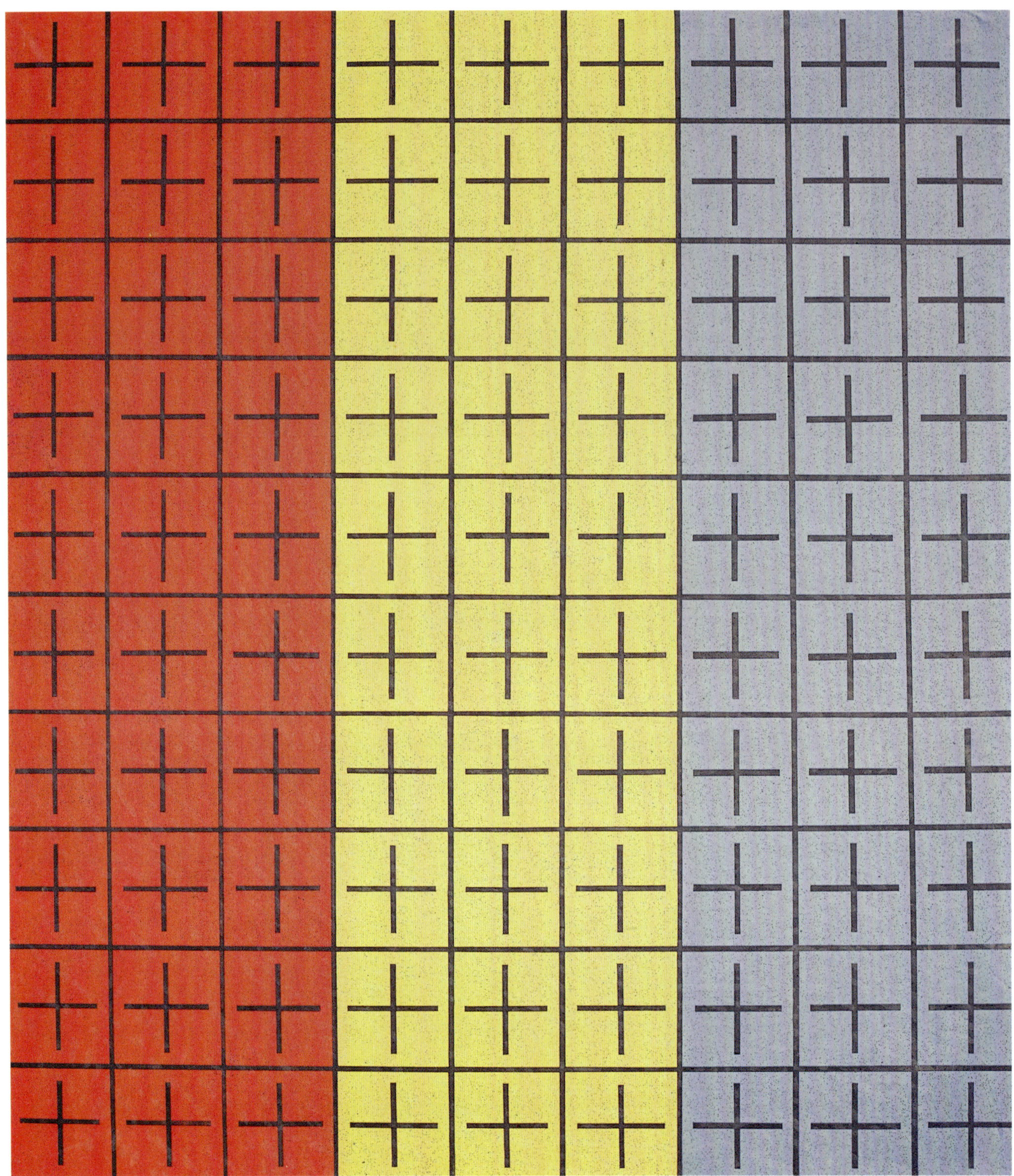

30. Appearance of Crosses I   1988

Acrylic on canvas
200 × 180 cm (78¾ × 70⅞ in)
Private collection

nothing but the three primary colours, and no image save a simple grid of repetitive crosses that had obviously been drawn with the aid of rulers and masking tape. This was not what people who were used to either traditional ink painting or socialist realism understood as art.

For just over three years he was to make such works, using rulers and masking tape. They were as exact and machine-perfect as he could make them, though, as he now remarks ruefully, 'the masking tapes available then were not good quality so they left marks'.

It is difficult now to appreciate how radical these paintings were: in his annual exhibitions, which are always partly retrospective, one rarely sees more than one or two of them, and they are always overshadowed by the larger, brighter, more dynamic paintings that followed. But within Chinese art history they have an equivalent status and effect to Frank Stella's Black Paintings of 1958–9. Of those Carl Andre noted that 'art excludes the unnecessary. Frank Stella has found it necessary to paint stripes. There is nothing else in his paintings.'[15] One could equally say, 'Ding Yi has found it necessary to paint crosses. There is nothing else in his paintings.'

'When I started making cross paintings in 1988', Ding Yi later said, 'no one in my surroundings could accept my art. My art looked strange to the public.'[16] However, he persisted because he believed his 'non-mainstream works would bring new life to art'.

It is ironic that the crosses began when he was studying traditional Chinese art because, as he said in 2004, 'when I started working with crosses, I was making a break with traditional Chinese painting'.[17] It was also a rejection of the sort of in-between art of Zao Wou-ki which, as Ding Yi pointed out, mixed European painterly abstraction with a style of painting from the Song Dynasty. The atmospherics and space of Zao Wou-ki or *Taboo* had been wholly edited out.

During this time of experimentation throughout China there was a great hunger for ideas and images from the West, but there was little interest in minimalism or other reductive art forms. As the famed scholar of Chinese art Michael Sullivan pointed out, 'these forms of expression were too remote from the gesture with the brush that is at the heart of Chinese painting, or too unsettling . . .'[18] The austere machine-style drawing of Ding Yi's first *Appearance of Crosses* paintings was perhaps a more decisive rejection of that 'gesture' than any performance or installation. It must be emphasised again that at this time he knew very little about Western minimalist art. He had other reasons to follow his route than imitating Western artists, as he told us: 'Perhaps in the 80s when China was still quite backward, artists were more interested in industrialisation. That was the time when I was using rulers and painting very exactly. I wanted to avoid personal expression in my painting.' As he said combatively in 2001, 'Only art that isn't art-like is art. I am convinced that a breakthrough requires that I make use of other elements.'[19]

'When I began', he said in 2009, 'to paint *Appearance of Crosses*, I chuckled to myself, for no one understood my paintings. They thought it was mere fabric design. But that was exactly what I wanted.'[20]

In earlier paintings such as *Taboo* he had used oil. In these new works he turned to acrylic. He needed something that dried quicker; its more synthetic nature was also appropriate.

How isolated was he at this time? How eccentric was his position? As he was so often the only abstract artist included in exhibitions of Chinese art abroad, his work has often seemed anomalous – and hence not been discussed. Although there were more abstract painters in Shanghai than elsewhere in China and people do sometimes talk of 'Shanghainese abstraction', this was discounted in the text for his first catalogue (1994), presumably with his approval: 'Shanghai does not have schools of painters but has more individuals with their own character. The avant-garde artists try to avoid any resemblance to each other, and try to develop their own style. In this Ding Yi is typical.'[21] Others have observed the same characteristic. The artist Yang Fudong, born in the countryside outside Beijing in 1971 and trained in Hangzhou, decided, after initially moving back to the capital, to go and live in Shanghai: 'I like the way I think in Shanghai . . . People in Beijing live gregariously, but in Shanghai they don't even keep in regular touch by phone. Artists don't hang out unless there's a reason to do so.'[22]

The climax of this intense period of experimental art throughout China was the February 1989 *China/Avant-Garde* exhibition at the National Museum of Art in Beijing. The organisers had asked Ding Yi to bring photographs of his performance art and two paintings, including his first works in the *Appearance of Crosses* series. He packed his artworks in two rolls – the paintings in the larger, the photographs in the smaller – and got on a train heading to Beijing. Unfortunately, as a student he could only afford to purchase an economy ticket. After over 20 hours travelling, sitting on a very hard seat, he finally arrived in Beijing, not feeling at his best. As he stepped out from the train, he took only the bigger roll from the luggage rack and forgot to take the smaller roll. Therefore, at the exhibition, Ding Yi was represented by his paintings only. No one was to know that he had also made performances.

This was the most famous (and notorious) exhibition of the new Chinese art movement. After Xiao Lu came in with a gun and fired twice at the work she had made jointly with Tang Song, police were called and the exhibition was closed for three days. Following anonymous bomb threats, it was closed for three more days. In all, it was only open for eight of its scheduled 15 days. Against such a scandal and compared with such works as Geng Jianji's gigantic paintings of laughing heads or Xu Bing's now famous installation *A Book from the Sky*, Ding Yi's work must have seemed strange, modest and unassuming. It was, however, one of only 30 works reproduced in the rather humble catalogue of the exhibition, which gathered over 300 artworks by 180 artists.

In May that year the students in Beijing gathered in Tiananmen Square to demonstrate against corruption and call for freedom of expression. Such a call for a more democratic society was, of course, to culminate in bloodshed when

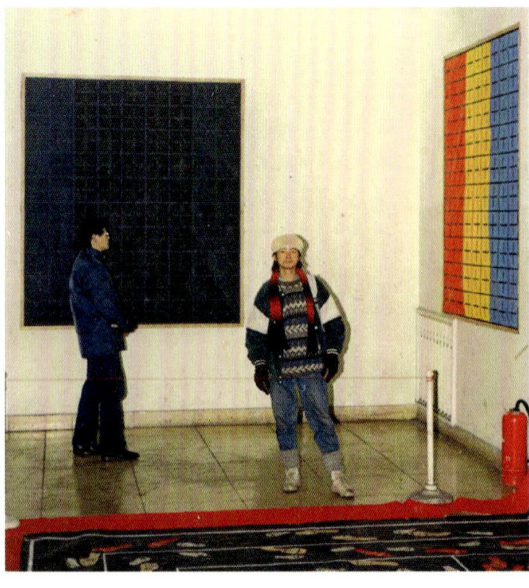

31. Ding Yi at *China/Avant-Garde Art Exhibition*, National Art Museum of China, Beijing, 1989

the government, fearful of anarchy, sent in the military to clear the square. The
4 June massacre was followed by a brutal crackdown on the student movement.
Contemporary art, together with everything else that sought freedom of expression
in the country, entered into an ice age. Independent art exhibitions and publications
were banned for a while. It was a time to keep one's head down. Like other avant-
garde Chinese artists, Ding Yi did not exhibit much over the next three years.

There had been four other students in his class on the ink-painting degree. All of
them got jobs at a state-owned publishing enterprise – safe jobs with a secured future
– when the course ended in 1990, but Ding Yi wanted to be an artist. To survive he
took a teaching job in 1990 in his old college, teaching design students and, after
1992, the foundation course. He had to teach three days a week during two months
of each semester. This left him with long holidays to work in and he was also given
accommodation.

In late 1992 a delegation from Germany arrived in China, led by Hans van Dijk,
a Dutch curator who based himself in Beijing in subsequent years and who played
an important role in introducing Chinese contemporary art to the West. They made
several studio visits to Ding Yi and others as part of their plan for a grand exhibition
of Chinese avant-garde art in Berlin. At the end of 1992, a delegation from the Venice
Biennale also came to visit Chinese artists. Ding Yi's works were chosen for four
major international exhibitions in 1993, including *Chinese Avant-Garde Art* at Haus der
Kulturen der Welt, Berlin (this travelled to the Netherlands, Denmark and the UK);
Post 89 Chinese Modern Art at Hong Kong Arts Centre; the First Asia-Pacific Triennial
of Contemporary Art at Queensland Art Gallery; and the XXXXV Venice Biennale.

Ding Yi made his first overseas trip, to Italy to participate in the Biennale. He stayed
for two months. Since his visa was for Italy only, he travelled to more than 20 cities in
the north and south of the country and visited every museum in every city he got to.

He has two strong memories from this Italian trip. One is that when he was
invited to the homes or parties of Italian friends, people looked up to him when they
found out that he was participating in the Venice Biennale. Before that he didn't know
that an artist could have such a high status in the West. Another memory is from
Rome. Before the Venice Biennale, Mr Chang Tsong-zung of Hanart TZ Gallery
in Hong Kong was preparing the famous exhibition *Post-89 New Art from China*.
Chang had ordered many works from several artists and paid some deposits to the
artists in advance. Ding Yi received a pre-paid US$2000 deposit for the nine works
that Chang intended to buy, which enabled him to make his first overseas trip to
Italy. Ekeing out his few dollars on food or hotels was painful for Ding Yi: the prices
were so high for someone coming from China in the early 1990s. However, an artist
from Taiwan whom he had got to know in Venice let him stay in his studio in Rome
free of charge. One day there Ding Yi passed by a gallery with elegant windows,
situated on a fashionable street. He looked through the window and saw how well the
artworks were hung on the wall. He remembers telling himself, 'Such a nice gallery.

I'll never make it into such a nice gallery in my whole life.' Thirty years later, Ding Yi is represented by famous galleries in the West and in China. His works are shown in large-scale exhibitions all over the world. What enormous changes have taken place in the Chinese contemporary art scene in the short space of 30 years!

It was perhaps, if not unfortunate, certainly problematic that in these 1993 exhibitions he was showing not in a context of painting, especially abstract painting, but one generally dominated by large installation art or the new Chinese pop paintings with their attention-grabbing big faces and parodic representations of Mao.[23] His work was not noticed as much as it should have been, and being so consistently shown in a specifically Chinese context it was not considered beyond that Chinese context.

How Chinese is his art? As we have seen, contrary to what many people in the West assume, he has no interest in calligraphy; indeed, his signature work began as a rejection of traditional Chinese painting. But he is very aware of working in China and reflecting the culture of contemporary China; talking in 2004 of the by then extended period in which he had carried on painting crosses, he remarked that 'in these last seventeen years or so the whole situation in China has changed enormously. The development in my painting might look like something simply happening just on the surface, but instead it reflects the profound changes that are happening in Chinese society.'[24]

The first cross painting had been a simple expression, pared down to a basic grid and the three primary colours. Although he was to stick to rulers and masking tape for over three years, there was much development.

A year later in his painting *Appearance of Crosses 1989-4* (fig.32) we see many more in-between colours: lilacs and pinky greys, thicker and thinner lines. It's more complicated. The colours and the difference in line widths make the painting wobble before our eyes. We cannot see it any longer as flat. The structure is geometric but creates an optical shimmer.

Most of these paintings were relatively small. *Appearance of Crosses 1989-7* (fig.33) at a metre high was an unusually large one. It is a work he has always refused to sell despite his collectors' clamour for such early work: it is one he is still satisfied with. 'This work is well balanced and has a complete feeling,' he notes. It is also one of the first in which the + is overlaid with the x. The diagonals make for a less minimal, more dynamic experience. It is even more complex than *1989-4*: there are, we find ultimately, 11 separate colours. Also, deliberately or not, the thick purple lines never cross the orange-yellow diamonds at exactly the same spot. There is a wiggle in the system that gives the painting that necessary bit of vitality. It also gives our eyes a narrative as they slide from diamond to diamond, detecting differences. As our eyes close in on those orange-yellow diamonds, we realise they are not yellow at all but a mixture of strips of yellow, red and orange in two tones. Obviously, an earlier painting lies underneath this one. Close up too we can see that the marks are far from machine-perfect: the whites in particular vary considerably in density.

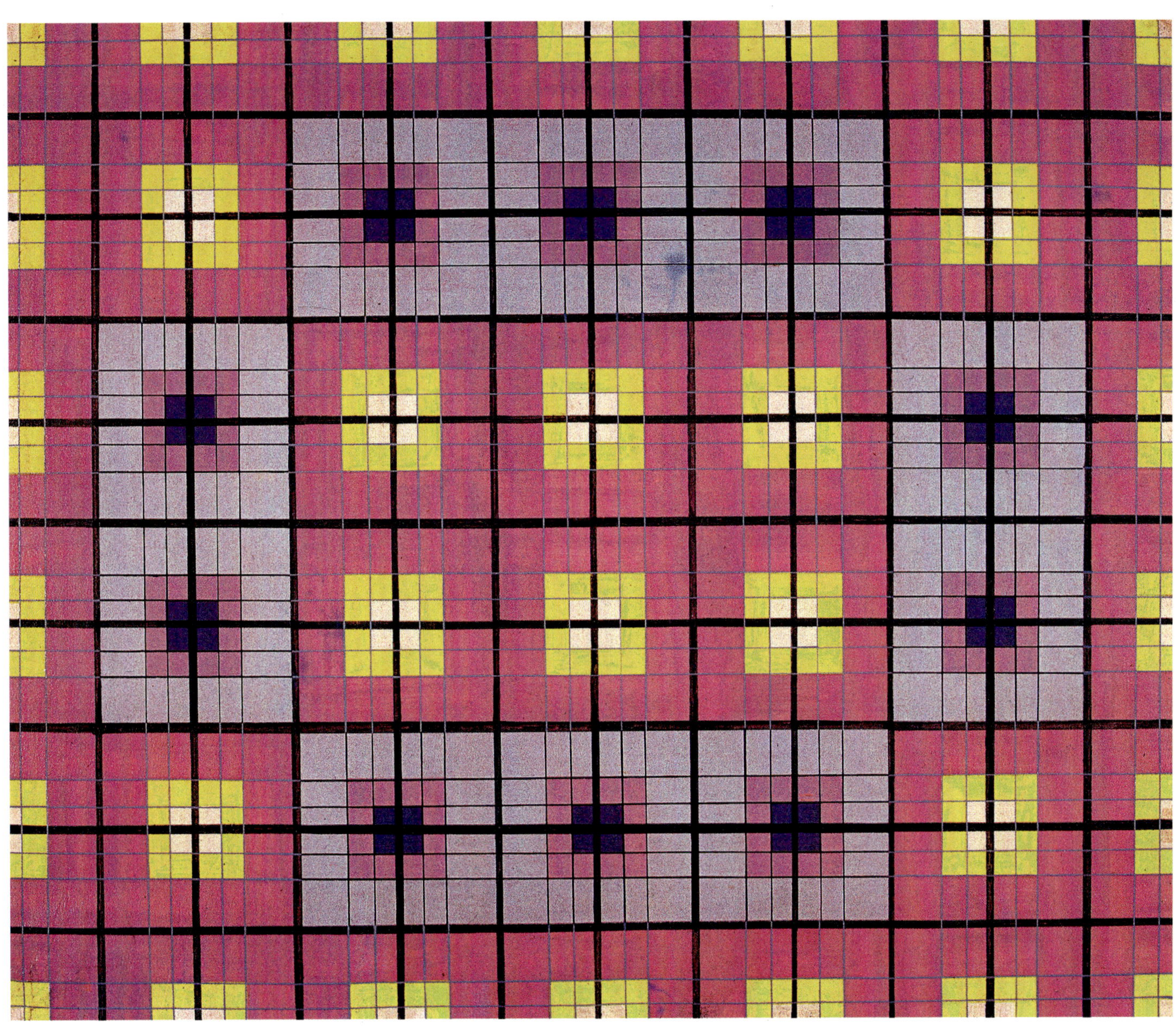

32. Appearance of Crosses 1989-4   1989

Acrylic on canvas
50 × 60 cm (19⅝ × 23⅝ in)
M+ Collection, Hong Kong

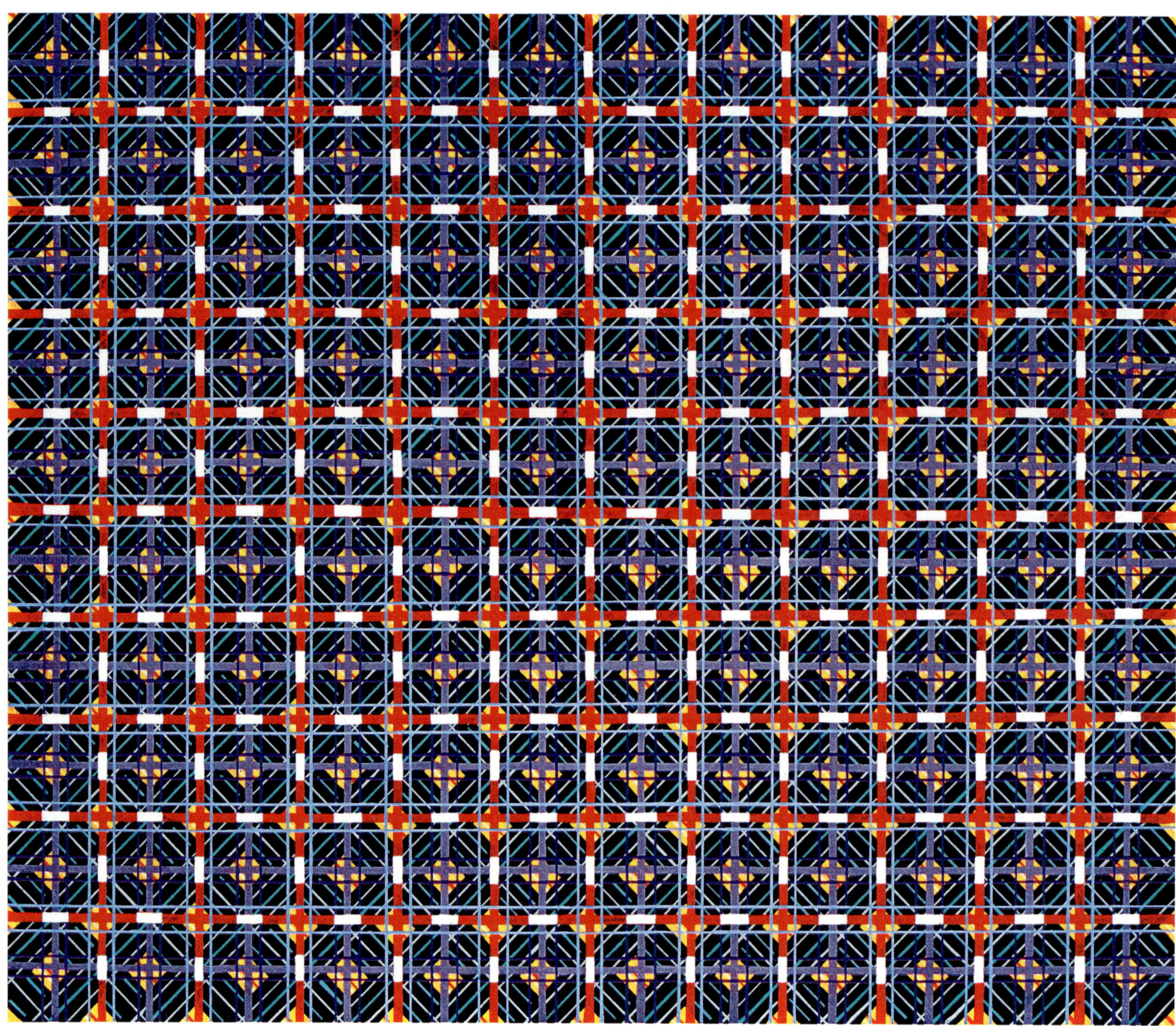

33. Appearance of Crosses 1989-7   1989

Acrylic on canvas
100 × 120 cm (39⅜ × 47¼ in)
Private collection

44

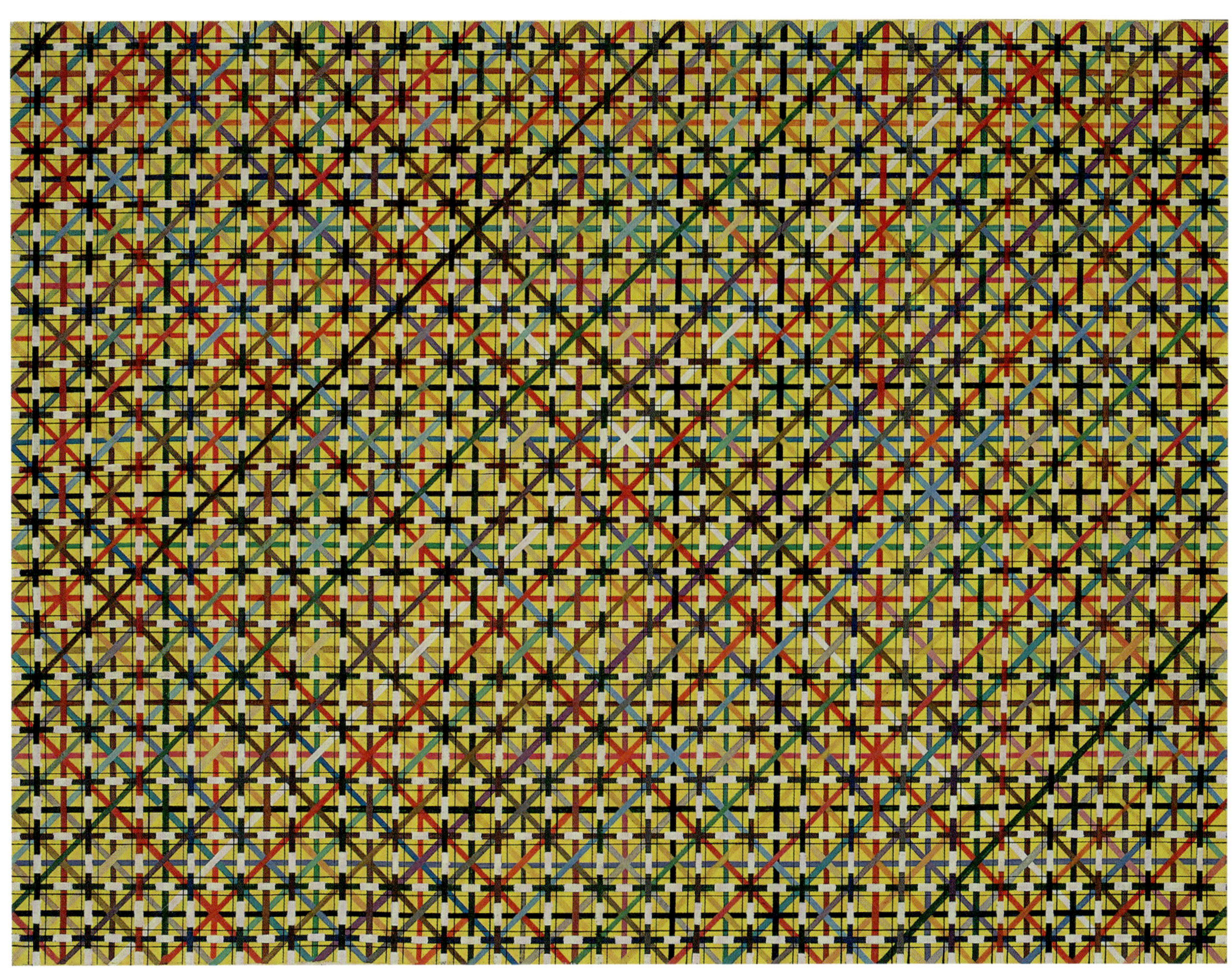

34. Appearance of Crosses 1990-7   1990

Acrylic on canvas
90 × 120 cm (35⅜ × 47¼ in)
Private collection, Hong Kong

This is not an Op art painting. Our eyes don't get confused, we don't get funny after-images when we look away, but it is complex – no longer reductive.

Even the system itself is getting more complex in *Appearance of Crosses 1990-7* (fig.34). As with *Appearance of Crosses 1989-7* the top layer of lines is composed of dashes in white and black, though now this last colour can oscillate to brown, grey, blue or even red on occasion. Is this random or part of a system too intricate for us to easily deduce? Or is it a need to loosen the painting up and vary it in a way no commercial fabric designer would do? Perhaps, though it does not have such an overall feel as *Appearance of Crosses 1989-7*: the reds and darker colours are dominant.

By *Appearance of Crosses 1991-3* (fig.35) we have even more complexity, even more intricacy. Also, something new has happened: the pattern, the system, has grown wilful. The symmetry of the painting is broken by two diagonals, one orange and one yellow, that move down from the upper right to the lower left, crossing near the centre. And then we start to notice more and more of such – to use the geological term for rocks that are in the wrong place – 'erratics'. It seems more an evocation of chaos theory than minimalist rigour.

We are pulled in, absorbed by all this intricacy and variability, but if we step back we are likely to wonder, 'How long did this take to paint? How much masking tape did he use? Does making this not hurt his eyes?'

With that in mind perhaps we are not surprised when we see the next painting, *Appearance of Crosses 1991-4* (fig.36) and observe that only the bottom-most lines seem to have been drawn with masking tape. Indeed, the painting consists primarily not of lines but of short dashes or dabs. From now on his paintings are constituted at the atomic level by such dabs and dashes rather than crosses. They form crosses, of course, but close up our experience is of these often stitch-like marks. (It is not out of place to remember that 'point' in the French-derived word 'pointillism' also means 'stitch'.)

In the summer of 1991 Ding Yi put aside the ruler and masking tape. Had he come to see this expressionless, austere way of working as a trap? A shift in painting procedure hastened the change: 'From 1988 to '91 I worked with the canvas installed between two stools horizontally. As I used ruler and masking tape I needed to work that way on the canvas. It was very demanding for my back, so after some years, I couldn't do this any more because of my sore back. From 1991 I started to work with canvas stretched against the wall. I made long and continuous lines that often go across the entire surface of the canvas. But as I grew skilful in making lines, I started to feel uncertain. Perhaps because it was too easy to make straight lines, I began chopping the complete lines into smaller pieces and using more complicated constellations. In this way I'd stay a longer time with each painting and this allowed me to think more.'

Things had also been happening in his paper works, which were and have remained important to him, forming a parallel but often diverging narrative to his full-scale paintings. In many of his publications Ding Yi reproduces what he calls

Thirteen Pieces of Draft (fig.37). (The architectural term 'draft' is the word he then used in the English titles, rather than 'sketch' or 'drawing'.)[25] These works, made on paper between 1987 and 1989, start with the most basic of configurations and increasingly allow more complexity and variation. He begins to leave a margin around the composition and leave all his mistakes, drips and colour samples there. There is a tendency to state things less emphatically, but to exhibit process more. This fuzz or shimmer of apparent accidents becomes an important aspect of his work.

Years later, as we looked with him at his *Appearance of Crosses 1992-15* (fig.38), we suggested that it looked as if he had been much more relaxed in the way he had painted the crosses. 'Actually,' he replied, 'there are only eight colours in this painting. I repeated patterns and different angles of the crosses, but always kept within eight colours.' How many marks did he paint before reloading the brush? 'From then on I would dip the brush into the jar and apply colour to the canvas directly from the jar. I don't mix colours any more. Each time I dip the brush in the jar, it will allow me to work on three to five brushstrokes, then I will dip it again. I always work on one colour until I finish it for the whole painting.'

He was interested in different surfaces and different objects to paint on: in his exhibition at Shanghai Art Museum in 1994 he included a fan he had painted on and a six-part screen. Perhaps it shows his continuing interest in design objects, though of course fans and screens have both historically been frequent forms in Chinese art. However, it was not something he pursued further. (Hans van Dijk, who helped organise the exhibition, noted that the works sold to Belgians, Swiss, Germans, Brazilians and Swedes. The Chinese were not yet buying their own contemporary art.)[26]

However, experimentation with different types of surface was much more long-lasting: by 1994 he was sometimes using chalks and charcoal on canvas or linen. In 1995 he had his first overseas one-person show, in Sicily. Staying beforehand with Monica Dematté, an Italian art historian who worked closely with Chinese artists in the 1990s, he found he lacked sufficient money to buy good art paper to draw on, so he started using the cardboard he found on the street. It is a material he has continued to use. As an artist he is extremely sensitive to surface and the feel of differing surfaces. Despite the anonymity of the earliest cross paintings, touch – the act of touching a surface on which one leaves a mark – is central to his work.

At this time there was a plan for a collaborative exhibition with German painter Katharina Grosse (b.1961), then making more subdued paintings than she later became famous for. He met with her but the exhibition did not happen. Nevertheless, he got something important from their meeting. Grosse would construct a model of any space she was going to exhibit in, so as to make the right size and shape of painting. It is a practice he too adopted.

How did he present himself to this new, wider world? In 1995 this was his statement for an exhibition in Brussels organised by the Hong Kong gallery Schoeni:

35. Appearance of Crosses 1991-3   1991

Acrylic on canvas
140 × 180 cm (55⅛ × 70⅞ in)
Private collection

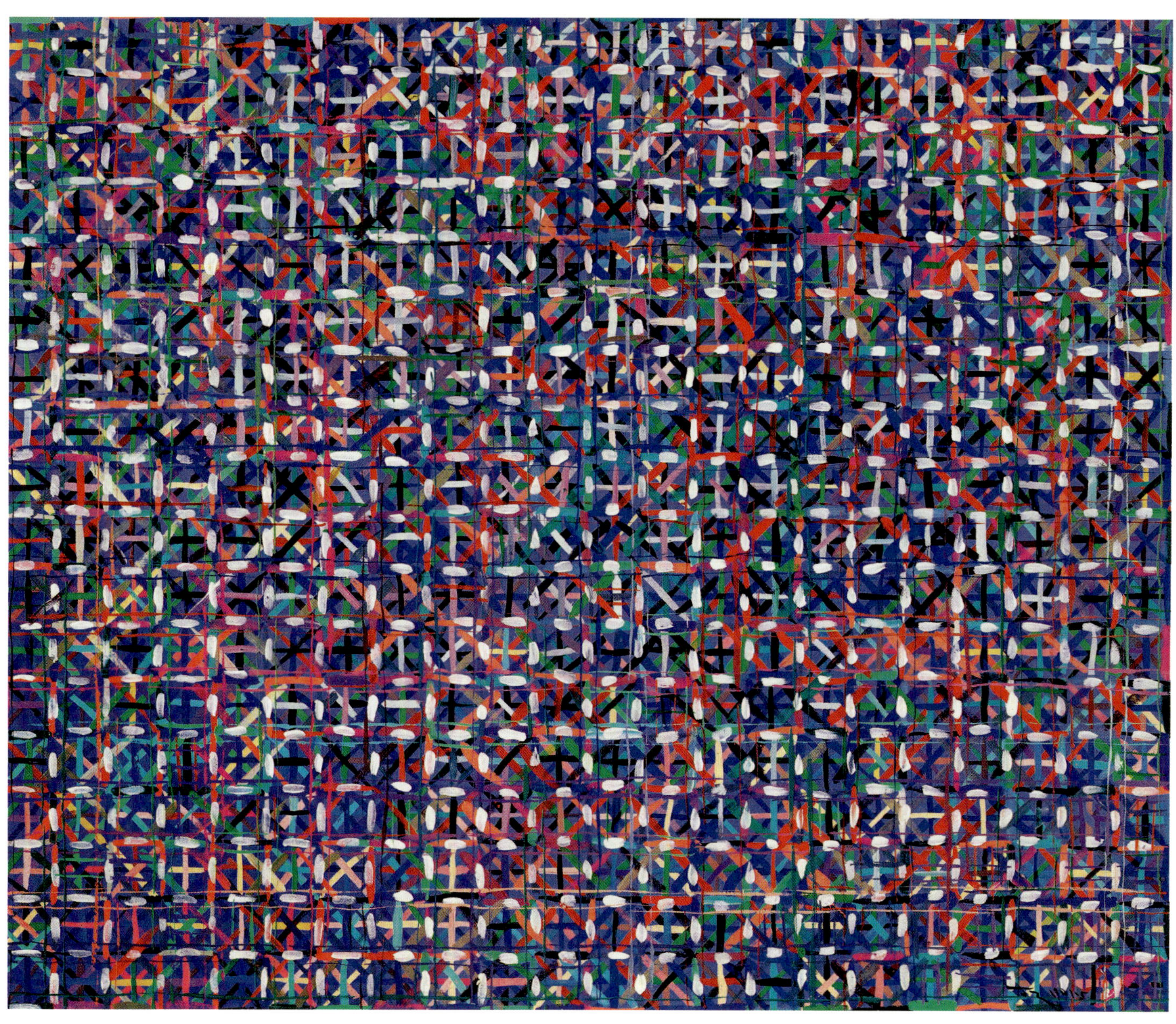

36. Appearance of Crosses 1991·4   1991

Acrylic on canvas
90 × 110 cm (35⅜ × 43¼ in)
Private collection

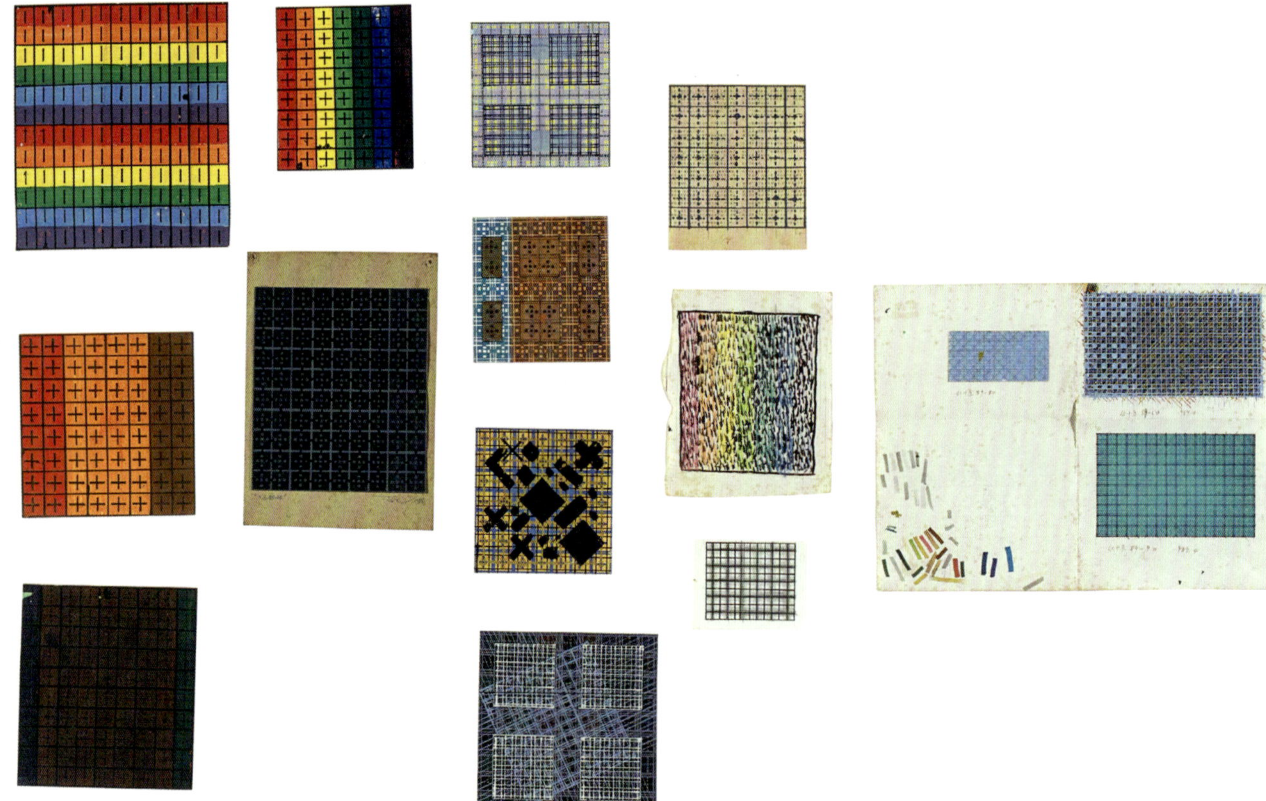

37. Thirteen Pieces of Draft 1987-9   1987

Acrylic and pencil on paper
94 × 144 cm (37 × 56¾ in) (frame size)
Private collection

38. Appearance of Crosses 1992-15   1992

Acrylic on canvas
140 × 160 cm (55⅛ × 63 in)
Private collection

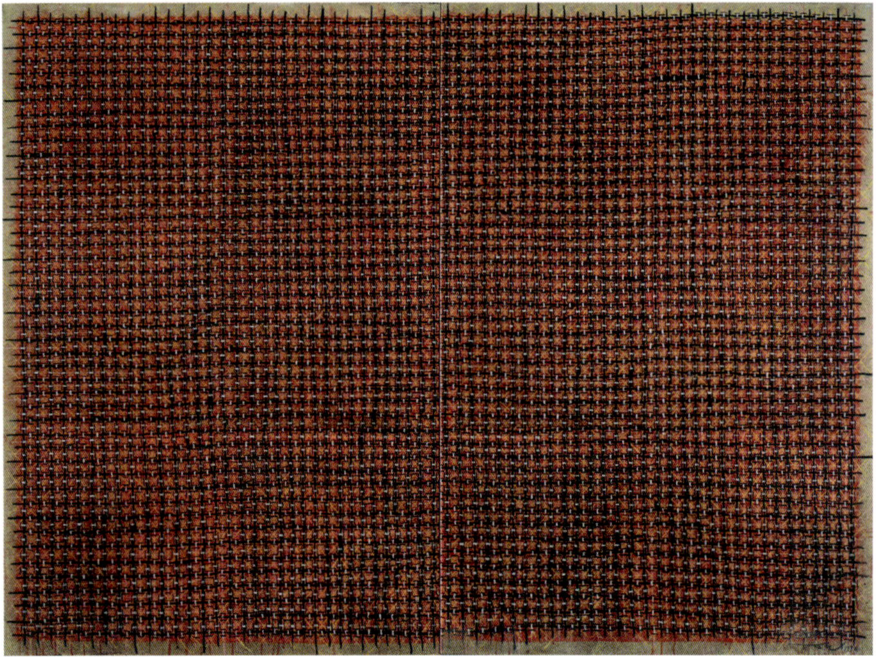

39. Appearance of Crosses 1994-18   1994

Chalk and charcoal on linen
140 × 160 cm (55⅛ × 63 in)
Private collection

40. Appearance of Crosses 1995-29   1995

Chalk and charcoal on linen
200 × 280 cm (78¾ × 110¼ in) (in 2 pieces)
Private collection

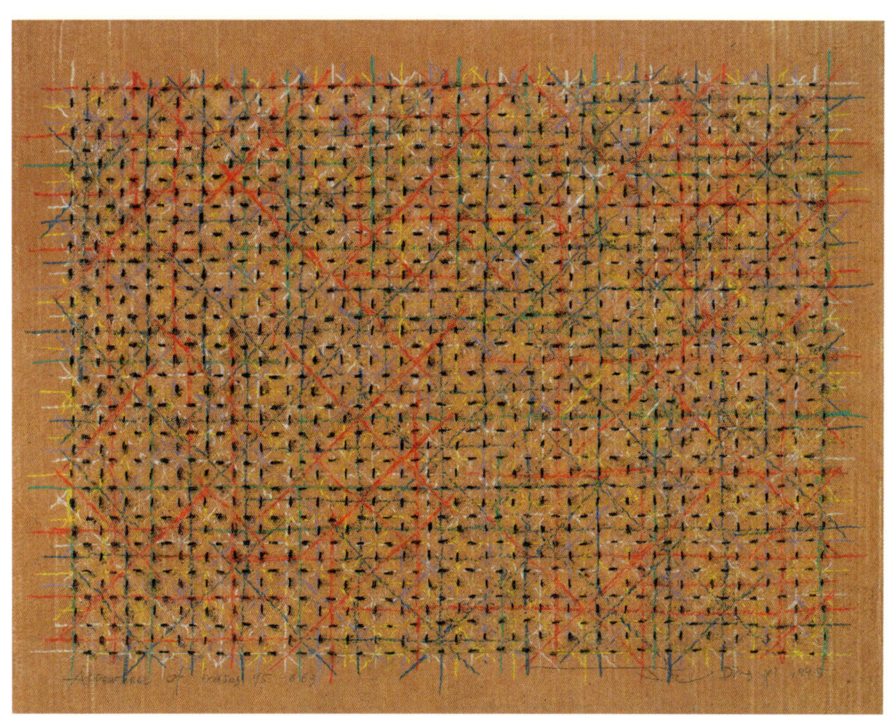

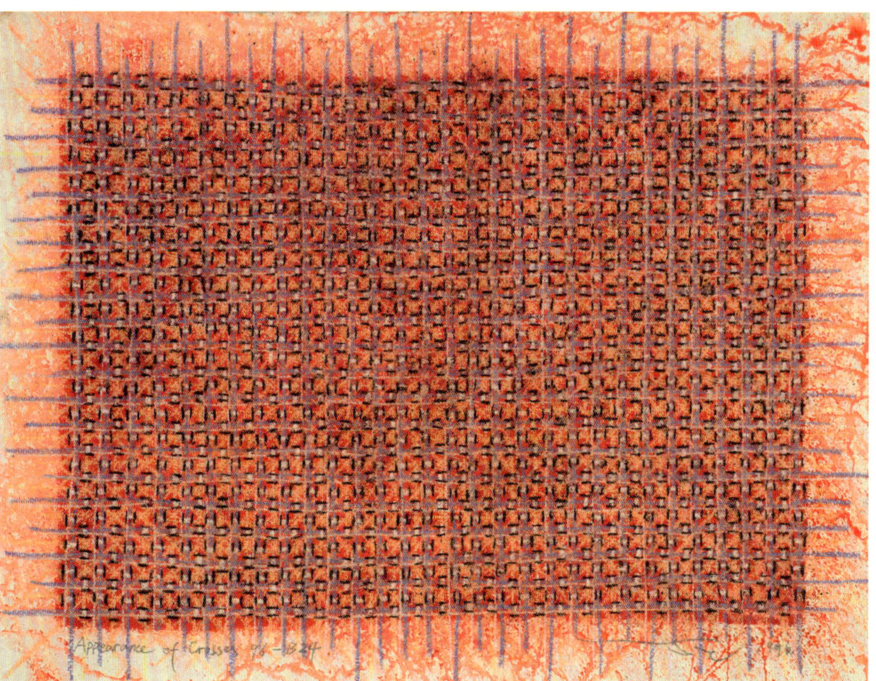

41. Appearance of Crosses 1995-B63   1995

Acrylic, chalk and charcoal on corrugated paper
60.5 × 79.5 cm (23⅞ × 31⅛ in)
Private collection

42. Appearance of Crosses 1996-B24   1996

Mixed media on paper
52 × 69 cm (20½ × 27⅛ in)
Private collection

I have always wished to be more free-handed than technical. The techniques and materials embodied in the traditional painting as it is taught in the art schools hinders artistic advancement and freedom. Painting is initially both a spiritual methodology and a visual perception. It is the collaboration of the various physical characters of painting such as the weave and weft of the canvas, the charcoal and the chalk. It is through the collaboration of these physical characters that painting produces its constant changing force and its independence.[27]

Ding Yi has never been a mere formalist, never seen painting as just a 'sophisticated entertainment'. He has always been prepared to use such loaded words as 'freedom', 'spiritual', 'force' and 'independence'.

In 1996 Ding Yi had his first exhibition with Lorenz Helbling at his ShanghArt gallery. The gallery was then located in the corridor of the Portman Hotel, where Helbling was able to present works on the walls for guests to view. There was effectively no commercial gallery at that time in Shanghai. There was no space for non-official art exhibitions except at foreigners' homes or hotels catering for overseas visitors. The patronage of non-Chinese collectors was of great importance in these early years of Chinese avant-garde art. 'I showed 15 works on paper. All were red colour. They all sold.' In the same year he began to use what would come to be seen as his trademark material – tartan.

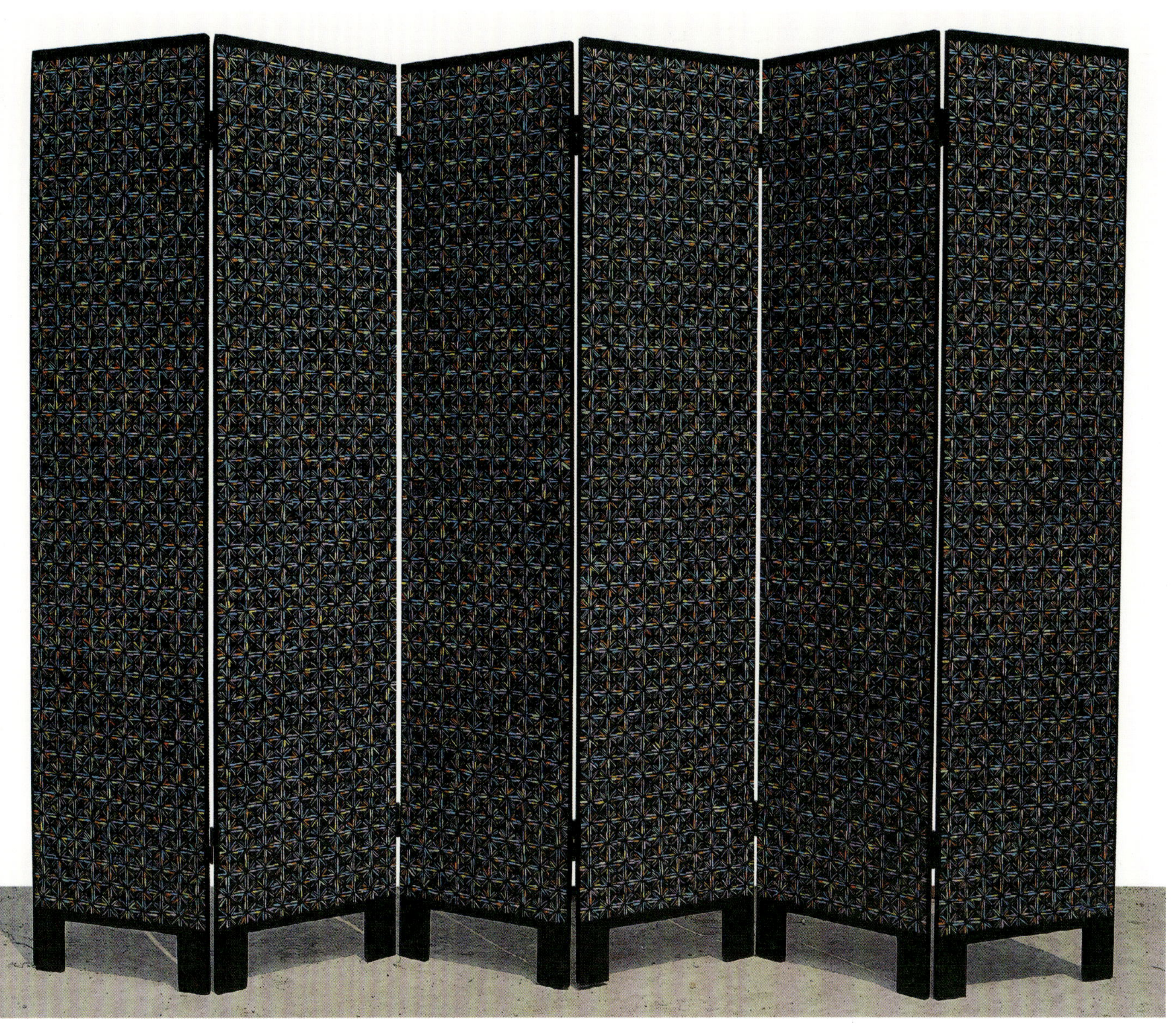

43. Appearance of Crosses 1994-3   1994

Acrylic on wooden folding screen
174 × 240 cm (68½ × 94½ in) (in 6 pieces)
Private collection

55

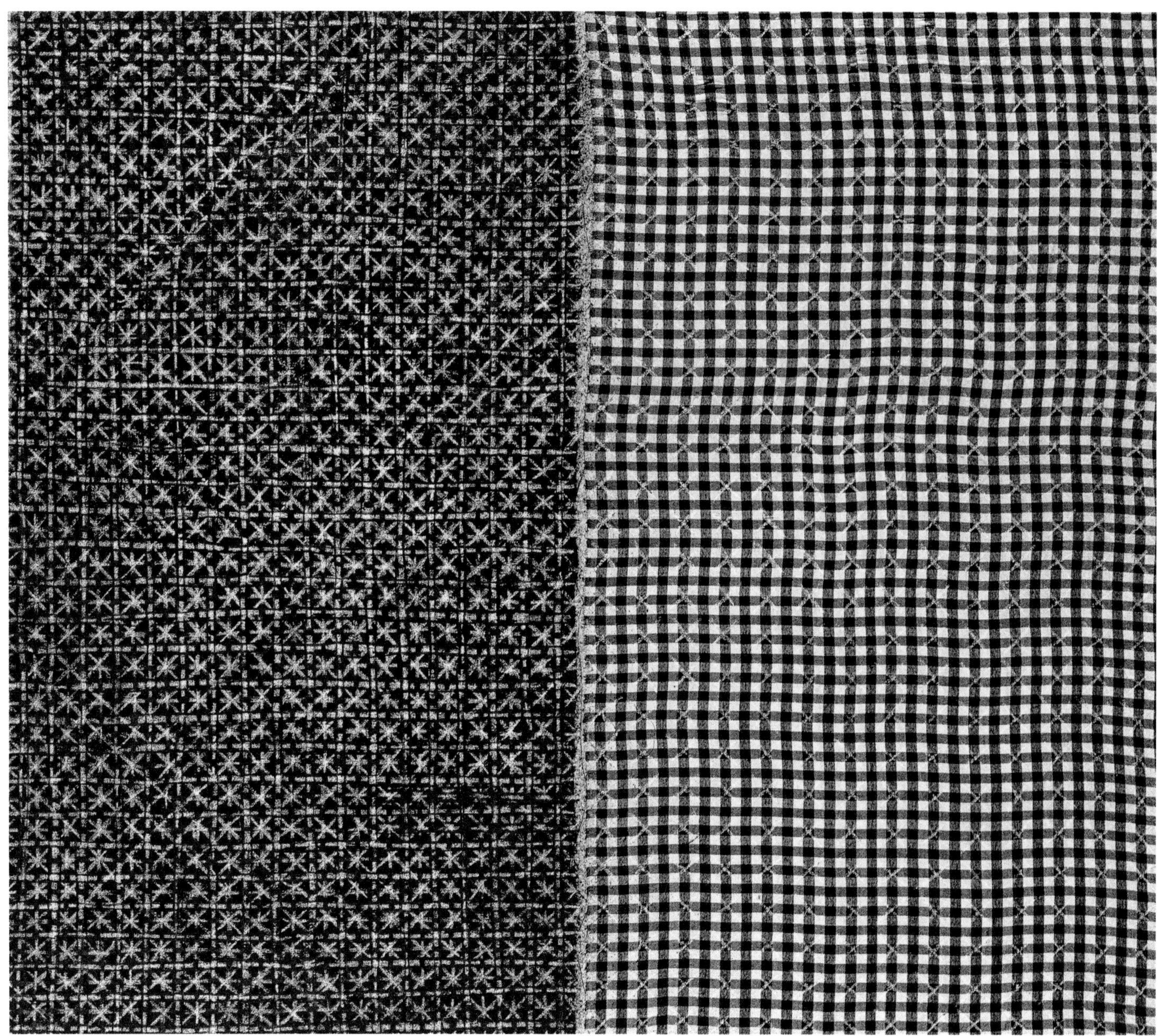

44. Appearance of Crosses 1996-37   1996

Chalk and charcoal on tartan and linen
120 × 140 cm (47¼ × 55⅛ in)
Private collection

Why did Ding Yi start painting on tartan fabrics in 1997?

Possibly, the cost of good canvas was one issue. One of his friends had a girlfriend who worked in a Western-style restaurant; he gave Ding Yi a linen tablecloth from there. More importantly, Ding Yi found he liked the feel or resistance of it. As with his use of waste cardboard he had an impulse to work with whatever material was to hand. As so often he responded to a particular surface or texture, especially one that gave a certain inconsistency or wobble to the composition. Moreover, it was easy to get other commercial fabrics with a 'tartan' pattern. 'These fabrics', Ding Yi told us, 'were often seen in Chinese homes, especially in the seventies and eighties. Many families used and still use them for making tablecloths, curtains or children's clothes. The Chinese people were very fond of this kind of fabric. Back in 1997 and '98 when I went to fabric shops to buy cloth, the shopkeepers often thought that I was a children's clothes designer.'

It was certainly not because of any interest in Scotland or the Scottish clan system, which supposedly identifies each clan by a different tartan.[1] Rather, he was interested in any commercial fabrics 'with stripes of various colours crossing at right angles', as the *Oxford English Dictionary* defines tartan. The definition also covers plaids, ginghams, checks and madras designs. They are all the same to Ding Yi: they are all designs based on a grid. He was fascinated by the ubiquity of such patterns: 'today,' as he remarked, 'you can find them everywhere: on clothes, sofas, sheets, blankets, design objects'.[2] Moreover, such readily available commercial fabrics were seen in China, as elsewhere, as the very opposite of high art – and that intrigued him.

His first use of tartan was at the very end of 1996 in *Appearance of Crosses 1996-37* (fig.44), in which the left half is worked on linen and the right half gently drawn on a black-and-white check pattern. He was playing the relatively loose left-handed side against the more mechanically woven right-hand side. Subsequent tartan paintings such as *Appearance of Crosses 1997-8* (fig.45) were more unitary, painted more consistently all over.

Was this an anti-art gesture? The tartan a sort of readymade? A sort of readymade grid? In 2004 he noted that 'in 1997 I started working with tartan and by this time, of course, I knew about Western conceptual art and minimal abstract art'.[3] Both minimalist and conceptual artist had often used grids, readymade or not.

Perhaps we should stop and consider what the grid meant to Ding Yi.

Ding Yi may not have read the famous essay on grids in modernism by Rosalind Krauss,[4] but he understood her premise, or, perhaps more accurately, her problematic. The grid is 'what art looks like when it turns its back on nature', she wrote. It cuts visuality away from language and narrative. It is an emblem of the autonomy

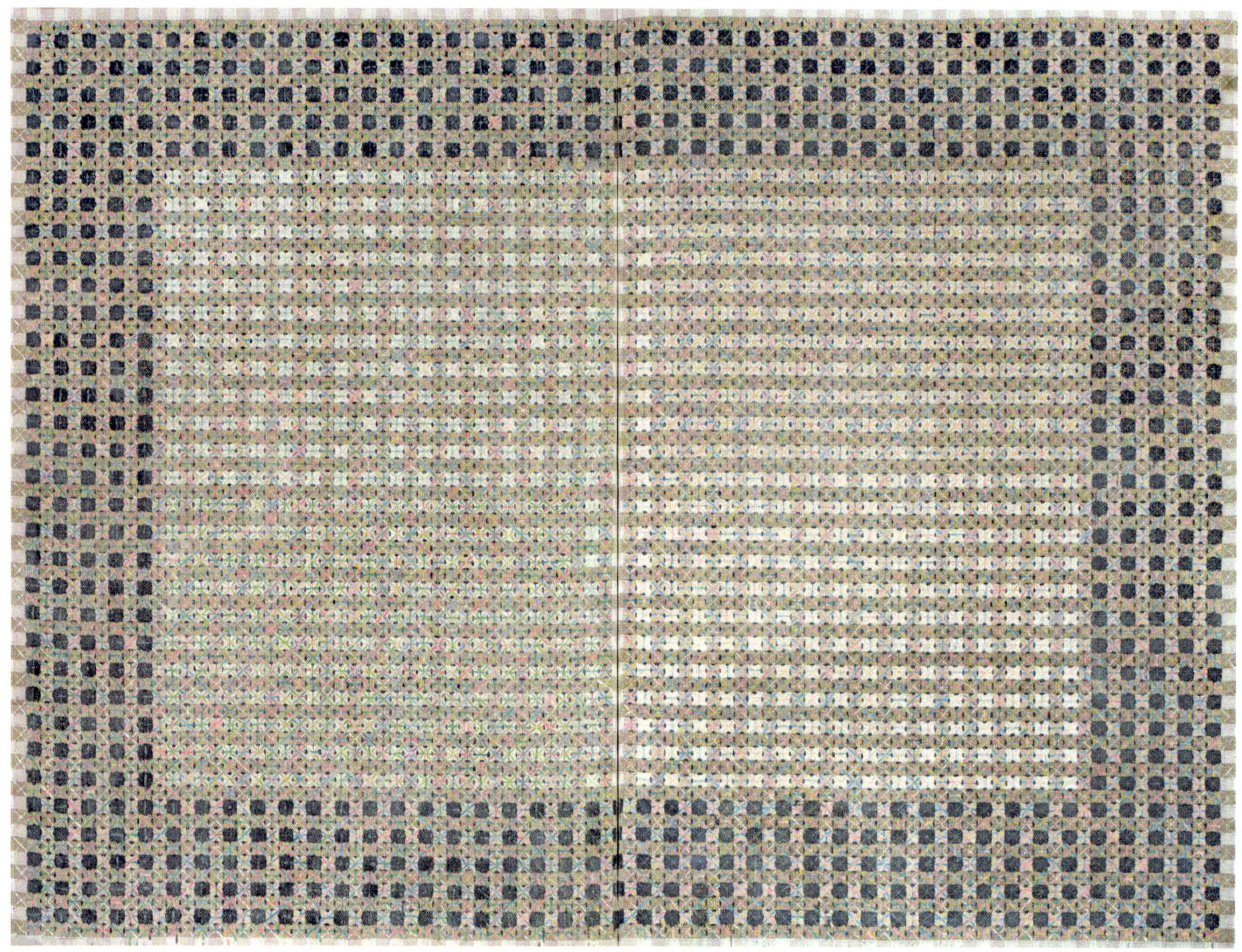

45. Appearance of Crosses 1997·8   1997

Acrylic on tartan
200 × 270 cm (78¾ × 106¼ in) (in 2 pieces)
M+ Collection, Hong Kong

of art and of modernity. 'The bottom line of the grid', she noted, 'is a naked and determined materialism . . . there seems no other logical way to discuss it', but, as she acknowledged, that is not how artists had discussed it: Mondrian and Kazimir Malevich (1879–1935) talked instead about 'being', 'mind' or 'spirit'. But the grid, she suggested, was a myth, a smokescreen that allowed us to be materialists but still hold on to antiquated notions of spirituality. It was a place where the apparent contradictions between science and art were not resolved but, paradoxically, kept in balance. Krauss proposed that underlying all 20th-century Western uses of the grid there is the Christian motif of the cross. This, of course, does not apply to Ding Yi. She also suggests that behind every modernist grid there is the window painted by so many 19th-century artists (Caspar David Friedrich and Odilon Redon are the two she cites) – a window that can look out on both the real world and a different state of being.

Although the cross paintings began as a sort of materialist manifesto, they have changed: both they and Ding Yi's thinking about them have developed. Indeed, his career refutes Krauss' claim that development is not possible for the grid-based artist – as we are seeing, there is a complex development in how Ding Yi both makes and thinks about his work. Unlike Krauss, Ding Yi does not see the grid in modernist practice as shameful. The ambivalence of the grid, its paradoxical status – material but ineffable, dumb but numinous – which we may experience as mechanical repetition or a mantra-like chant, was for him, as it was for Agnes Martin and many others, not an aesthetic cul-de-sac but a surprisingly rich ground for exploration.

Even Louise Bourgeois had remarked in 1977 that 'the grid is a very peaceful thing because nothing can go wrong . . . everything is complete. There is no room for anxiety . . . everything has a place . . . everything is welcome.'[5]

Although Ding Yi has written periodically (a recent bibliography lists 40 items), has given many interviews and also taught for 25 years it is important to remember that he is primarily practice-led, not theory-led. He was, however, being a pragmatic person, becoming unusually concerned with how people experienced his art. What he takes from minimalism is more the way it can be experienced than any predetermining theory.

It is possible to argue that the minimalist he is most akin to is the composer Philip Glass. Perhaps the best way to elucidate this is to draw a comparison with another artist, Sol LeWitt, specifically his wall drawings and two early critical essays on his works. Firstly, Lawrence Alloway writing in 1975:

Sol LeWitt's wall drawings are a brilliant reconciliation of the two senses of drawing that have co-existed, fluctuating in dominance, since the sixteenth century. There is the notion of drawing as graphological disclosure, the most direct marks that an artist can make and hence, because of their intimacy, authentic evidence of the artist's presence. Personal touch is based on this basis. There is another notion, which is that drawing represents not genetic freedom but the artist at his most rigorously intellectual. In this sense drawing is the projection of the artist's intelligence in its least discursive form: line is the gist, the core of art. The term *disegno* has moved, often ambiguously, between the two senses. LeWitt's drawings propose a new relation between drawing as touch and drawing as intellectual content.[6]

Of course, a substantial difference between LeWitt's practice and Ding Yi's is that LeWitt produced written instructions and let other people execute them, but it is important to note that LeWitt saw such other draughtsmen much as a composer of music regards the performers: it was up to them to experience making the work and potentially imbue it with their presence or character. When we think of what happens in Ding Yi's work, when, around 1992, he abandoned the use of rulers and masking tape, we can see this as re-imbuing the canvas with such presence or character.

Secondly, Robert Rosenblum writing of LeWitt in 1978:

A musical analogy may be apt here. LeWitt's wall drawings, in their detail, have the calculated look of a computer world but soon dissolve into diaphanous veils of a strange, engulfing sensuality. It is a quality found as well in the music of Philip Glass . . . Glass's music is constructed from what at first may seem monotonous and endlessly repetitive units of rudimentary melodic and rhythmic fragments . . . But if the intellectual order of Glass's work is as rigorous and systemic as that of LeWitt's, yet again the effect is not of a dry reason. The experience becomes rather a kind of a slow immersion in a sonic seam where the structural anchors of the score, discernible by the intellect's intervention, tend to be washed away by the mounting sensuous force of the cumulative sound. The musical precedents for such a gradual overwhelming of the senses lie in late impressionism, in the engulfing swells of Debussy and Ravel at their most shimmering just as the twinkling expansiveness of LeWitt's wall drawings evokes echoes in late impressionist paintings, especially in the panoramic extensions and vibrant fragility of Monet's waterlilies.[7]

If we think of what happens when we go up close to a work by Ding Yi, especially the larger ones, this seems a comparable experience. We are immersed, floating in a sea of 'sounds' or marks.

In a sense, though, Ding Yi is *not* a grid painter: rather, to use the musical term, he riffs on the grid. Since 1988 all his wall-based works have been variations on the grid, much as a composer might make endless variations on a tune. This became explicit with the tartan paintings.

With his use of tartan fabrics Ding Yi no longer painted grids. Instead he took pre-existing grids and painted on them. He adapted them. He transformed them. Likewise, in the more recent paintings on wood he first gets his assistants to make a grid, a mechanical one using carpenter's string, and then starts painting on that. The starting point may be the grid, but the end point is somewhere else.

Indeed, it was only in the earliest years of his cross paintings that he used rulers and masking tape to create exact grids. (Or tried to, as he admits: because the masking tape he had was so poor, they were far from perfect. Being rougher than he wanted, he has kept those paintings himself.) Since 1992 everything has been hand-drawn. The lines that he paints or draws over and across the grid wobble, stutter, pulsate, jump, stop and sprint.

Using the tartans was not, as it was with Marcel Duchamp and his readymades, an anti-art gesture; it was about taking something that was everyday, banal and ubiquitous, and transforming it.[8]

In 1997 Ding Yi told Monica Dematté that even though a tartan is most unlike nature, when he is in front of a new tartan and is deciding how to 'intervene' his feeling is not unlike that of 'a landscape painter who has to translate a natural scene onto canvas. The artist becomes a medium between what he sees and what he wants to convey.'[9]

One limitation of the commercial fabrics he was using was that they were never more than two metres wide. As at this point he wanted to make larger paintings, he could only do so by joining fabrics together. In *Appearance of Crosses 1997-34-37* (fig.46) he put together four. Scale mattered: in this and other joined-up paintings he could make colour fields as large as a Pollock drip painting or a Morris Louis floral, or for that matter a large water-lily painting by Monet. One could go in close to such a painting and feel absorbed in it. When Mark Rothko was asked the ideal distance from which to view one of his larger paintings he reputedly responded, 'Eighteen inches.' Barnett Newman likewise wanted viewers to immerse themselves in his paintings: in a statement for his second exhibition in 1951 he wrote, 'There is a tendency to look at large pictures from a distance. The large pictures in this exhibition are intended to be seen from a short distance.'[10]

If we look at *Appearance of Crosses 1998-8* (fig.48) we see Ding Yi (as he did in *Appearance of Crosses 1997-29* before it was repainted) leaving the edges unpainted to demonstrate what he had transformed. In a sense it is similar to the way he left the margins in drawings such as *Appearance of Crosses 1996-B24* (fig.42) empty. However, he did not allow the 'noise' of excess chalk and ink to spread onto the fabric as he did on paper. Drawing could be a less formal, dirtier, more impromptu medium for him.

Drawing always runs parallel to his canvas work. He never makes studies for specific paintings. Sometimes the drawings are small. Sometimes, even in the 1990s, they could be very large, for example the eight panels of *Appearance of Crosses 1999-B1-B8* (fig.50) which are always shown together like a monumental stela. Such drawings have much to do with the texture of the paper or cardboard and how it interacts with chalk or pen. Periodically he has also made concertina books – a traditional Chinese format – in which each page has a separate drawing, each drawing different from but developing from the previous one, and all, exhibited normally in a vitrine, visible at once.

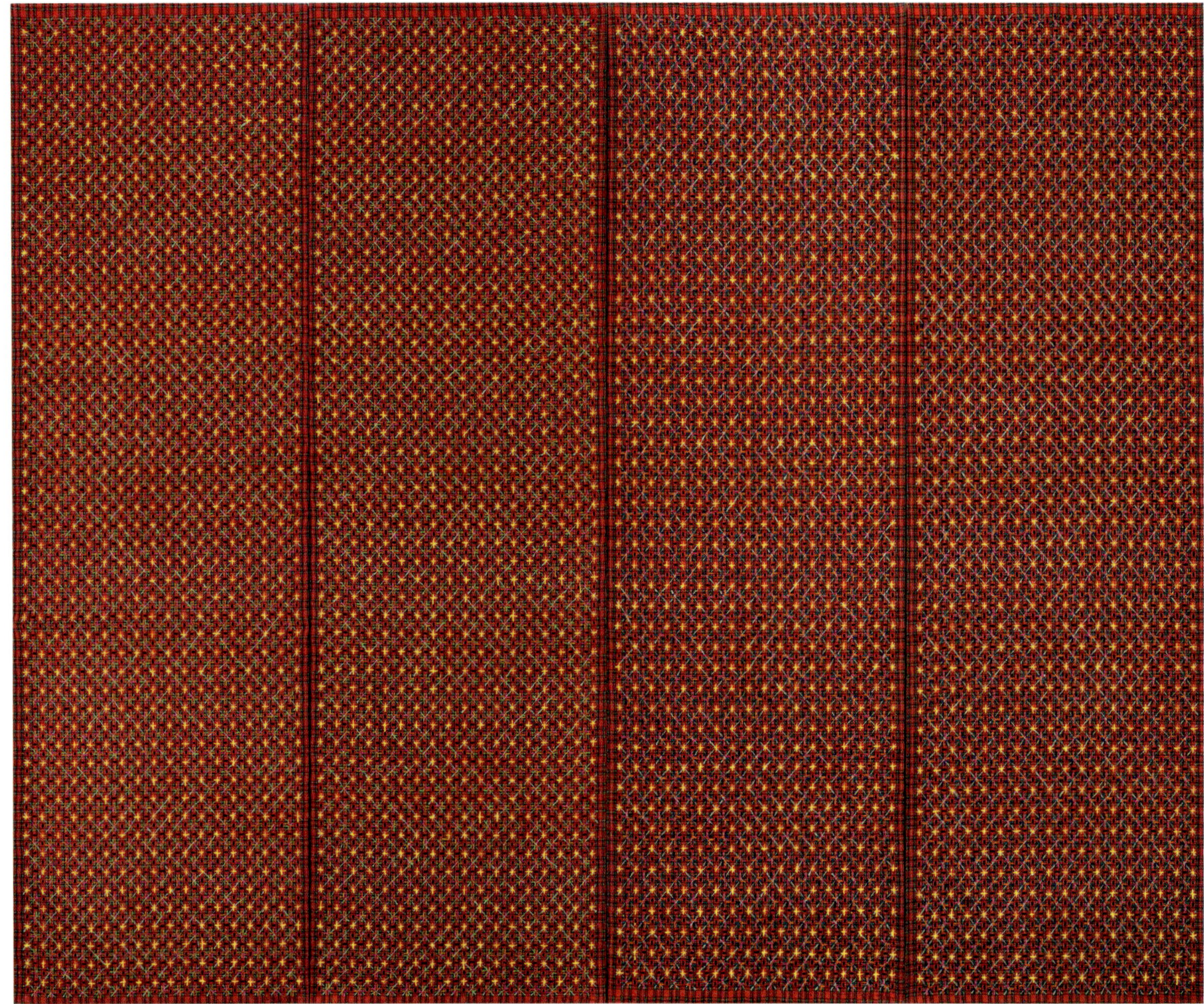

46. Appearance of Crosses 1997-34-37   1997

Acrylic on tartan
260 × 320 cm (102⅜ × 126 in) (in 4 pieces)
ShanghART Gallery, Singapore

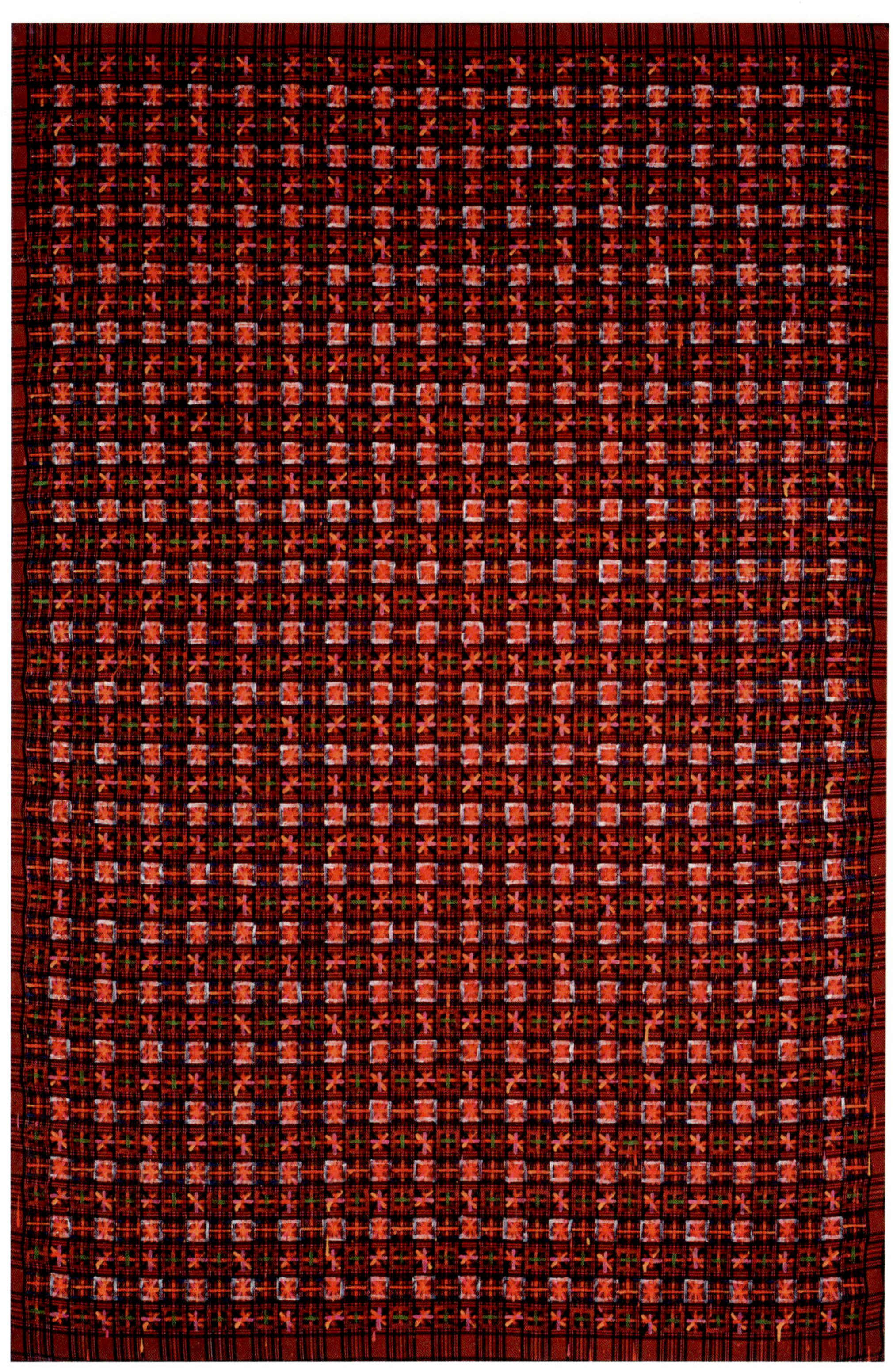

47. Appearance of Crosses 1999-2   1999

Acrylic on tartan
200 × 135 cm (78¾ × 53⅛ in)
Private collection

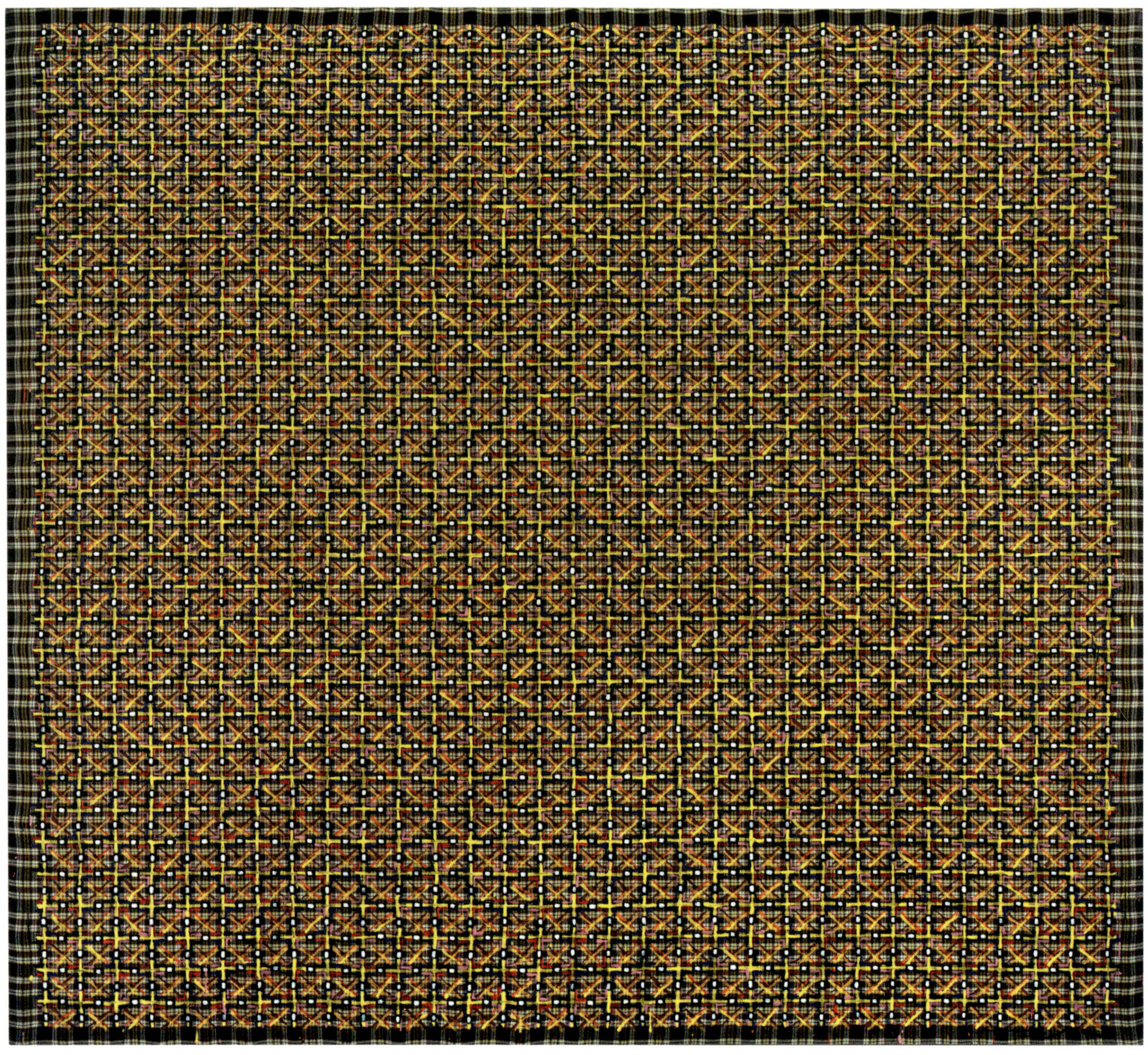

48. Appearance of Crosses 1998-8   1998

Acrylic on tartan
140 × 160 cm (55⅛ × 63 in)
Private collection

49. Appearance of Crosses 1998-8
1998 (detail)

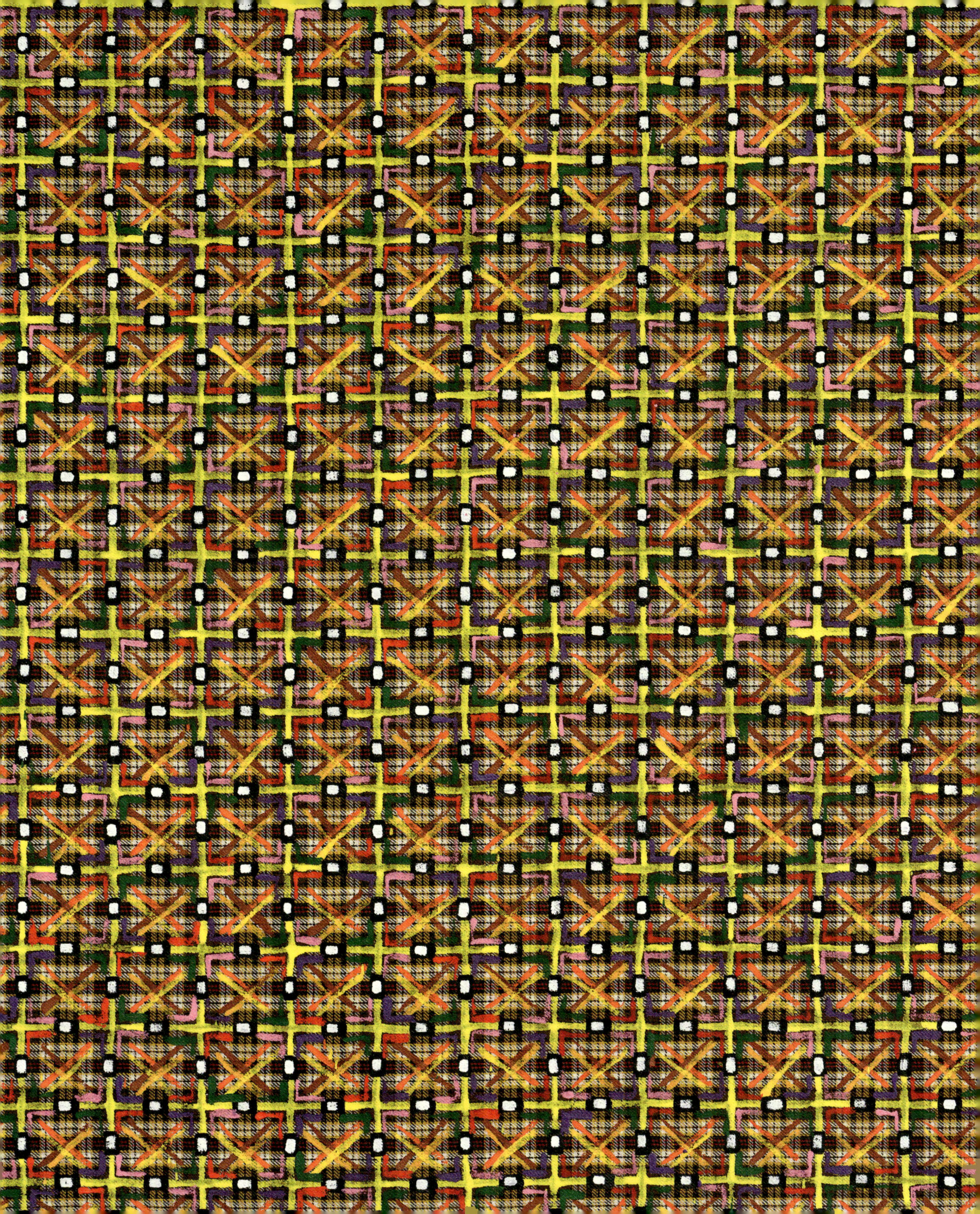

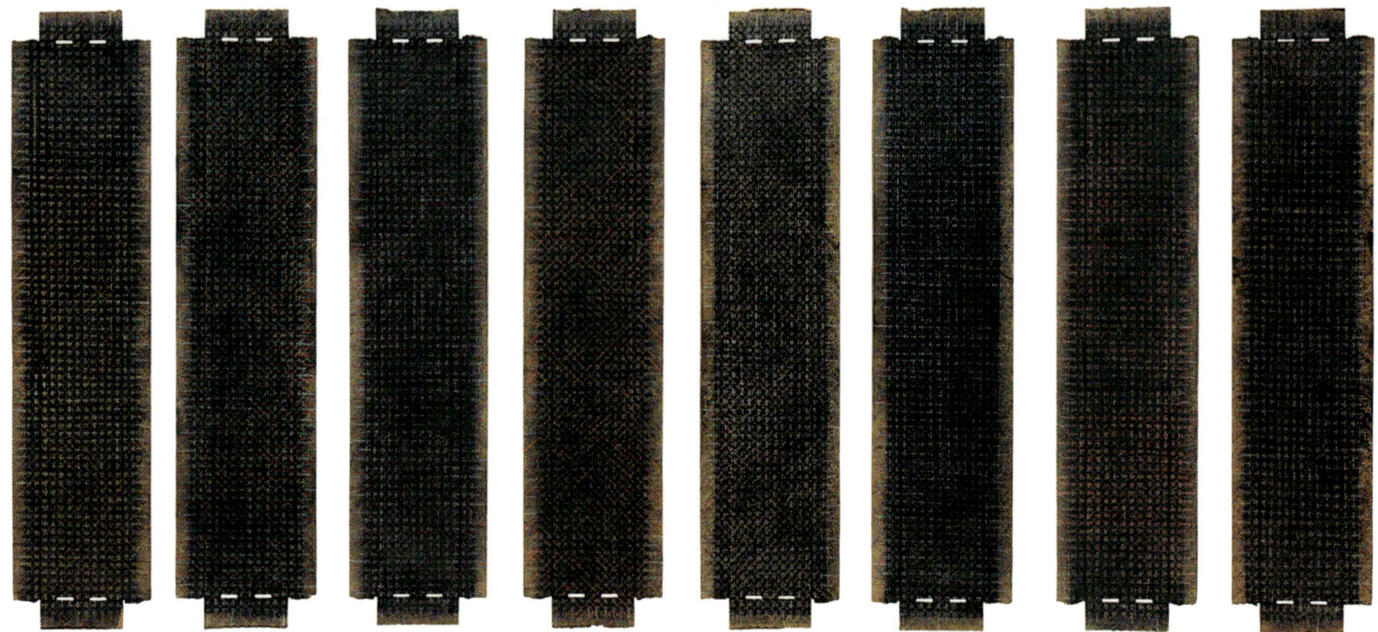

50. Appearance of Crosses 1999-B1-B8   1999

Charcoal, colour pencil and chalk on corrugated paper
In 8 pieces, each 144 × 34 cm (56⅝ × 13⅜ in)
Private collection

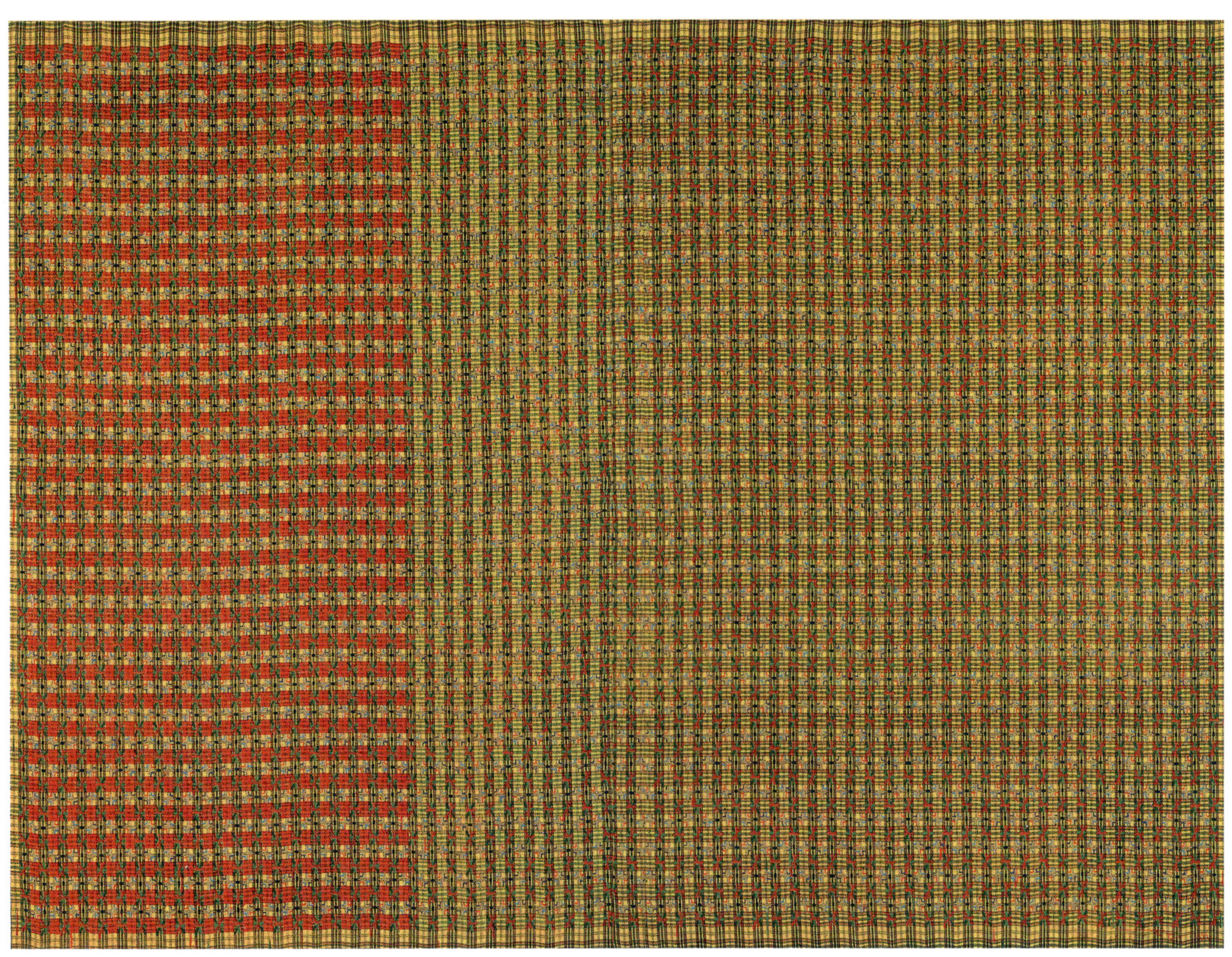

51. Appearance of Crosses 1999-5   1999

Acrylic on tartan
200 × 270 cm (78¾ × 106¼ in) (in 2 pieces)
Private collection

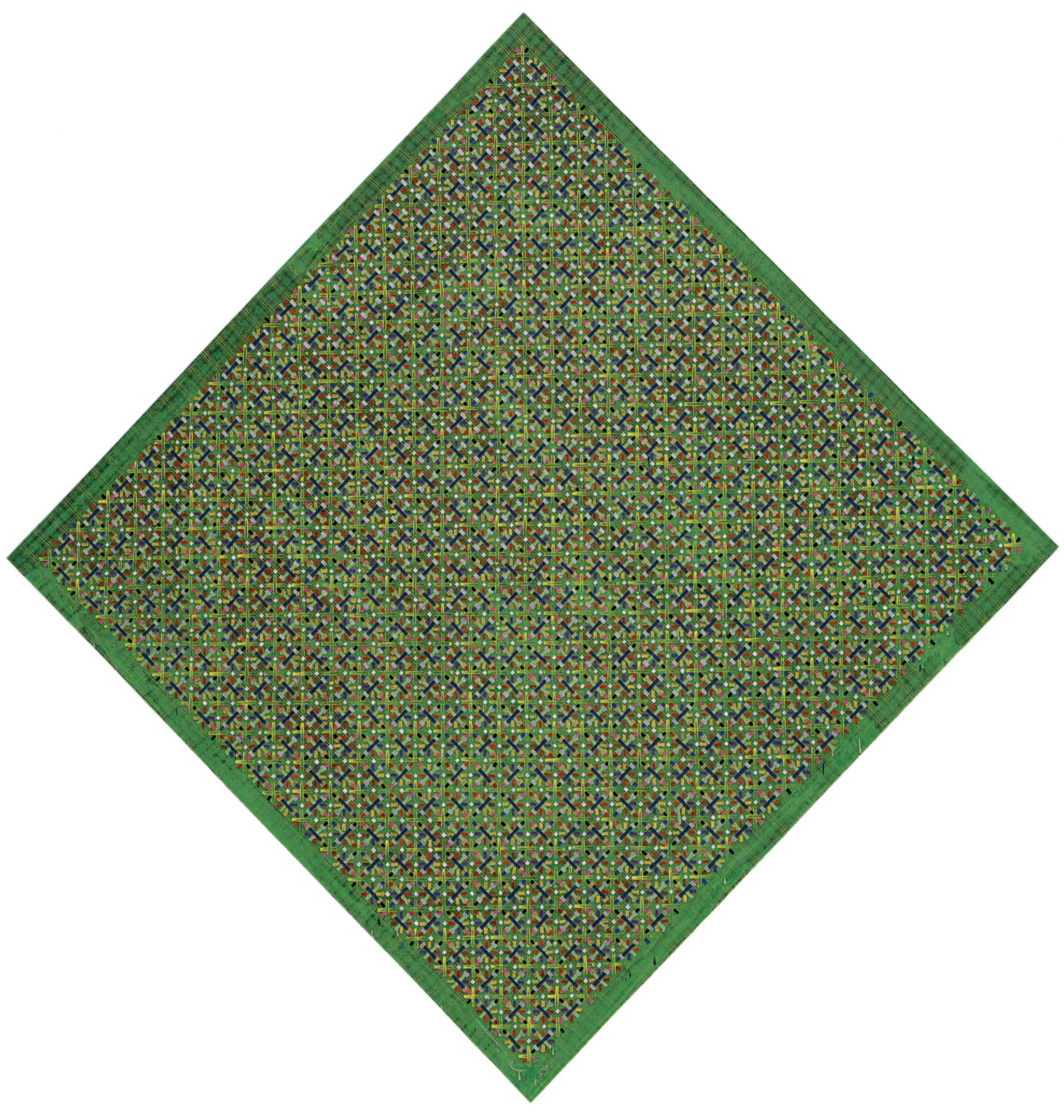

52. Appearance of Crosses 1999·15   1999

Acrylic on tartan
197 × 197 cm (77½ × 77½ in)
Private collection

One element of 'informality' was the way that when these commercial fabrics were stretched the grid came out slightly uneven or warped, as for example in *Appearance of Crosses 1999-2* and *Appearance of Crosses 1999-5* (figs 47, 51). By this point he was starting to use brighter colours – for reasons we shall discuss later. There was a growing emphasis on dynamic diagonals. Given this growing interest it was logical to also make some paintings, such as *Appearance of Crosses 1999-15* (fig.52), in a diamond shape. But generally, diagonal lines, especially ones as zippy as those in *Appearance of Crosses 1999-2* or *Appearance of Crosses 1999-15*, animated the horizontal grid, sending syncopated rhythms weaving back and forth.[11]

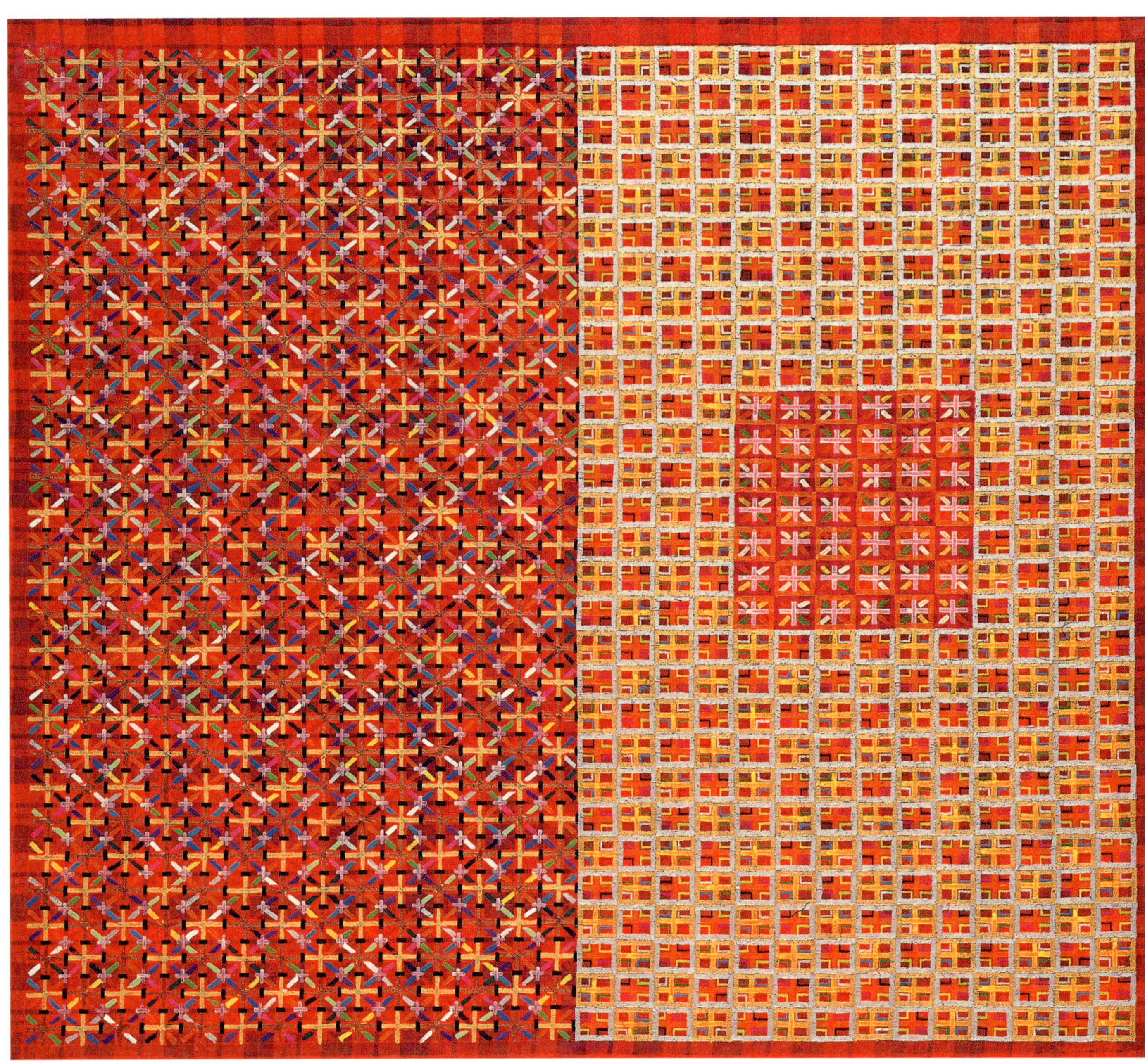

53. Appearance of Crosses 2000-3   2000

Acrylic on tartan
140 × 160 cm (55⅛ × 63 in)
Private collection

In 1998 the Canadian art historian Serge Guilbaut came to see Ding Yi in his studio. Guilbaut remarked that like other Shanghainese artists', Ding Yi's work did not actually reflect the increasingly vibrant life of the city – especially all the bright electric signs and adverts that now blazed in the streets and shopping centres. Ding Yi pondered this and decided he wanted to present this new Shanghai, so different from the grey city he had grown up in where only 'on political holidays would you see some red banners and flowers giving Shanghai some colour'.[1] Indeed, he wanted to embrace and celebrate it. If his work up to that point had been formalist, now he wanted to focus on Shanghai and society. A first step was to move from his studio in the suburbs to one in the heart of Shanghai – in M50 (fig.54).

Like the 798 district in Beijing, M50 is one of the artistic and creative zones that in recent years have appeared in many of China's major cities. Originally, these areas housed the state-owned factories that functioned as the backbone of the Chinese socialist planned economy, where millions of tonnes of iron and steel and kilometres of textiles were manufactured. But when China started to adapt to the global market after Deng Xiaoping's 'southern tour' of 1992, these factories together with the millions of workers whose lives were bound to their assembly lines were, as if overnight, silently washed away. M50 had been host to Shanghai's No.12 woollen and textile factory since 1966, but in 1999 the factory ceased production, the workers left and artists and gallerists took over the spaces. Ding Yi was one of the first artists to move into M50, in 2001. For several years it was a vibrant artists' neighbourhood but in recent years it has become more of a haunt for tourists and selfie takers, the grunginess of the old industrial buildings now being seen as radical chic. Some galleries have stayed but others, including Ding Yi's gallery ShanghArt, have moved out.

Ding Yi said in 2007:

I have lived in Shanghai for more than 40 years and I look at the city every day. Since the mid-1990s, I could clearly feel how the city has been changing and expanding at an alarming speed . . . Nothing is left of the city's Utrillo-like gloomy, elegant grace. Today, the cityscape is filled with bright neon lights, endless traffic flows, flocks of high-rise buildings and LED screens constantly updating the stock markets, and billboards advertising consumer products everywhere.[2]

Whereas earlier he felt he had been responding mainly to what was inside himself, his own development and his own ideas, since 1999, he said, 'I have been reacting

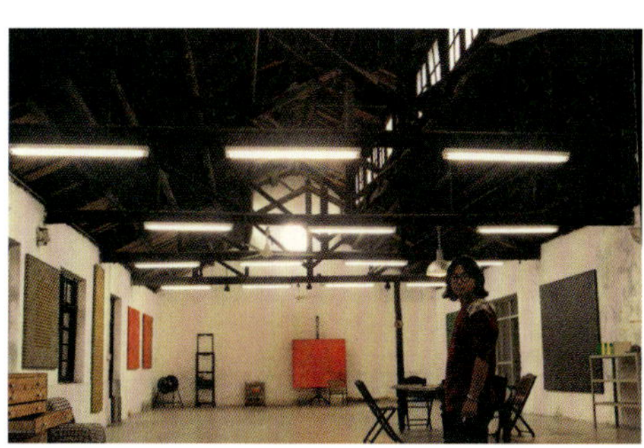

54. Ding Yi in his studio, M50, Shanghai, 2001

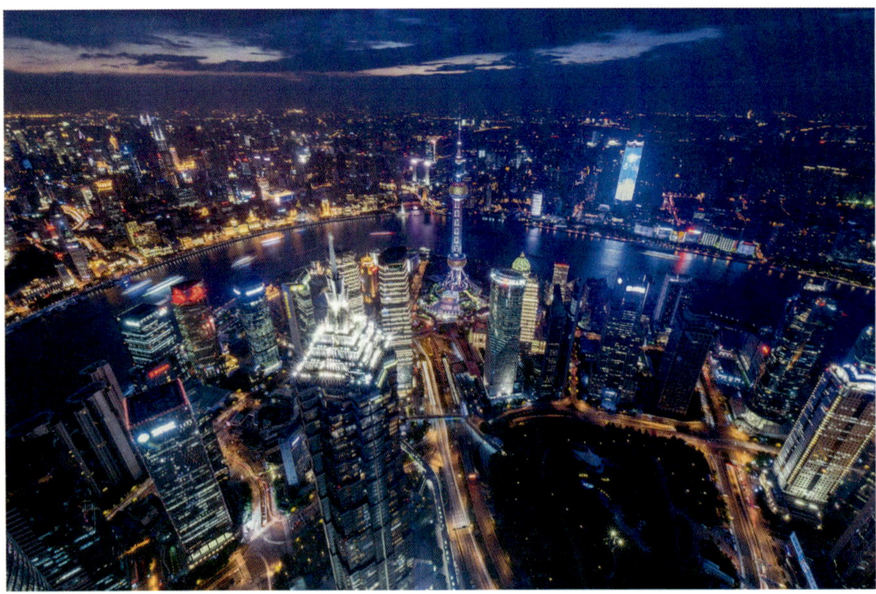

55. Bright lights of Shanghai

much more to my own environment, to things beyond me. In Shanghai the colours on the street, in advertisements and so on, are fighting all the time. This is not a peaceful city. There is shouting everywhere, giving rise to excitement, and now I want my work to express this kind of reality.'3 Though raised in the older part of the city and in a quieter era, Ding Yi embraced this moment of the city. Pudong and Lujiazui, China's financial centre, now represent one of the world's largest concentrations of skyscrapers. The LED lights that play on the facades of these buildings at night have become the new tourist attraction of Shanghai.

In response to these bright lights he began to paint with the fluorescent pigments that are used in advertising posters. He was also responding to video games, which were then a new thing in China, and more pixelated and clunkier than they are now. Compared with his early cross paintings, or even with the tartans, the actual mark making was also increasingly free and clearly handmade. One reason he gave for never using assistants in making paintings, as so many of his contemporaries were starting to do, was that he wanted to be responding always, consciously or subconsciously, to the world outside. He did not want painting to become a merely mechanical matter.

If we look at *Appearance of Crosses 2000-3* (fig.53) we can see that it has vivid lines, white, pink, lime green, purple, etc. that go diagonally in dashes like tracer bullets across the night sky. White and yellow squares seem to have been stamped across the right-hand side, dislocating the grid, syncopating its rhythms. Above all else, the colours are so bright, shiny and aggressive that they seem to move forward from the wall into the viewer's own space. The painting can no longer be seen as a window into recessive space. It is the visual equivalent of what jazz musician John Coltrane called a wall of sound. Everyone in the orchestra is playing simultaneously, loudly and at high

56. Appearance of Crosses 2000-3
2000 (detail)

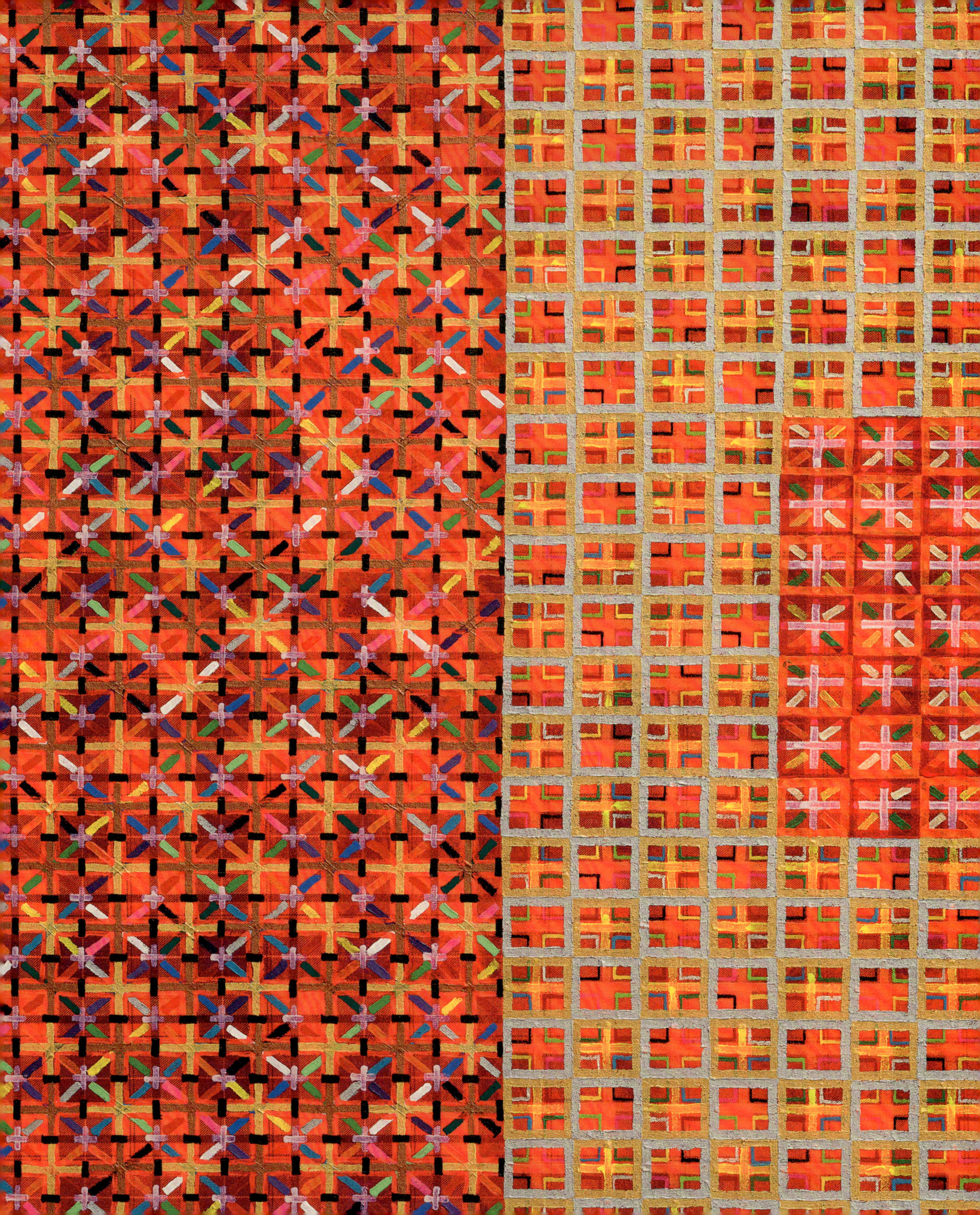

pitch. Once again, one could say of it as Huxley had earlier said of Shanghai: 'Nothing more intensely living can be imagined.' It feels almost delirious.

But as we get accustomed to this attack on the cornea, the smaller block of pink on white-crosses begins to seem like an island of serenity, and the boxes that fill out the right-hand side start to assert some stability. They are, if we look closer, much more evenly painted. At an atomic level, if we look at the colours within each square, there seems no consistency in how they are chosen. It is like looking down into the grass and seeing insects scurrying about willy-nilly.

Red, which as in many of these fluorescent paintings is the dominant colour, is of course seen as a happy and lucky colour in China. The base colour, that of the tartan, is actually quite a muted red but the effect of the fluorescent paints and the rhythmic complexity and intensity of the patterning make it seem intensely red – as if someone has illuminated it.

In *Appearance of Crosses 2001-4* (fig.57) again we see a smaller, enclosed block of paler, more blended colours on the left, sitting like an island of relative tranquillity in an agitated sea.

If there is an archetype of these fluorescent Shanghai paintings it is the diptych *Appearance of Crosses 2001-15, 16* (fig.58). The long vertical columns replicate the vertical LED signs so common in Chinese streets or the digital displays in the 1999 film *The Matrix*. It is easy to imagine they are moving up and down as the street signs do. The colours, especially the acid greens, are those of the city, definitely not of nature. The sense of flashing lights and pixelation and the hyperactive surface, also say something of his then interest in video games.

As he continued to work with fluorescent colours, optical patterns and contrasts, some paintings, *Appearance of Crosses 2002-9* (fig.59) for example, became closer to the Op art of Victor Vasarely (1908–97). However, as Ding Yi remarked later, 'I knew about Op art quite early, but it was not the direction I followed. I knew the works by Vasarely early on, but I always tried to avoid creating optical illusions in my works.'

From 2003 another change happened: the periodic abnegation of geometry. Until then all his paintings were structured by the geometry of the grid, even if that manifested itself as all-overness, but in paintings such as *Appearance of Crosses 2003-1* and *Appearance of Crosses 2004-2* (figs 60, 61) the structure seems, if not chaotic, then at least organic. The crosses resolve into clouds, blobs or clusters of particular colours. Now it was as if he was composing a picture much as a player of Go completes the board. With the accent no longer on verticals or diagonals, looking at the paintings feels more like scanning a flat area such as a map or an aerial photograph. As if to compensate for this new freedom, the marks in these paintings are more block-like, less obviously hand-painted.

He still wanted to make larger paintings, but the limited size of available textiles was a restriction. One solution was to gang several separate paintings together into a single, coherent unit. The first time he made such a 'constellation' was *Appearance*

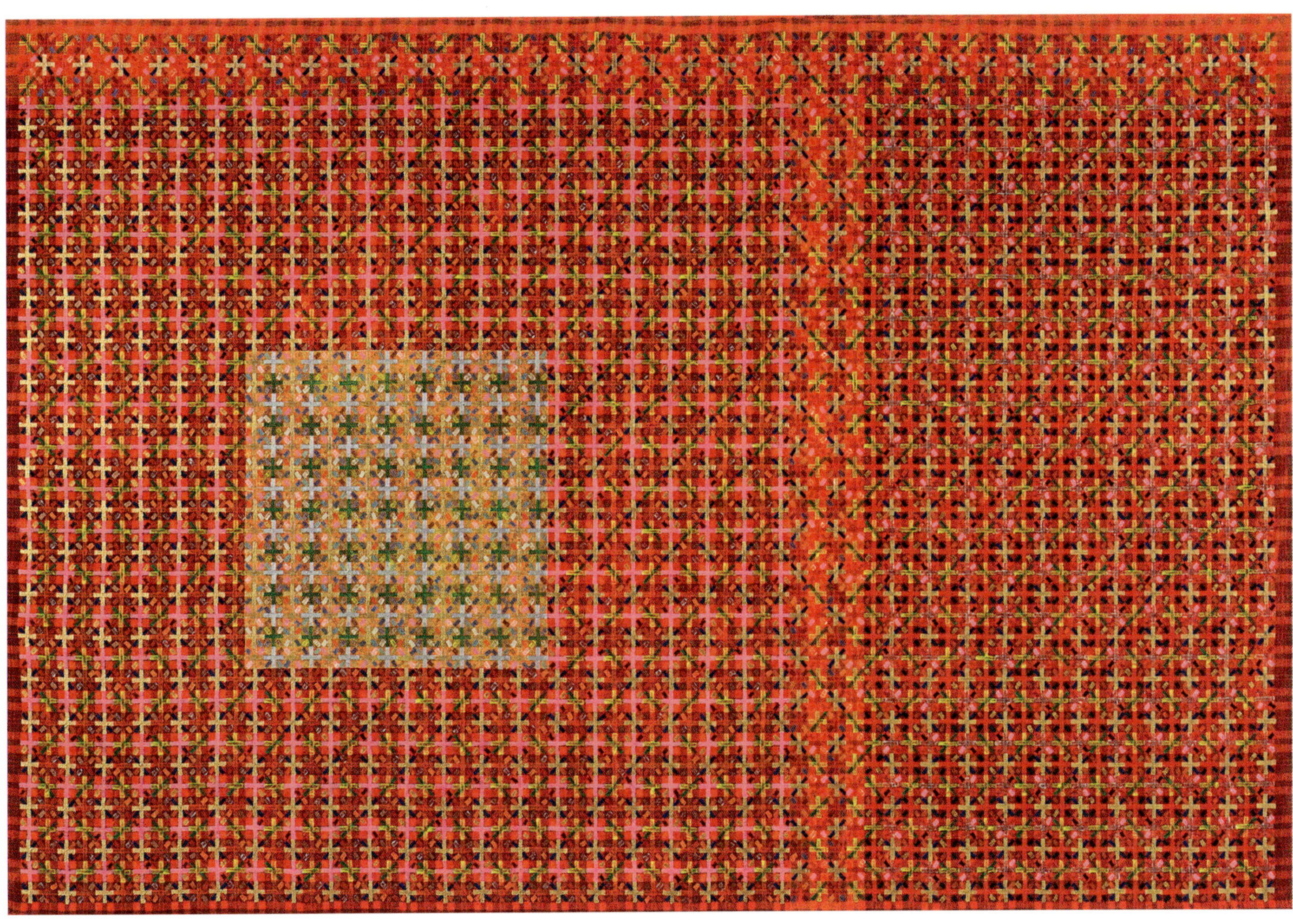

57. Appearance of Crosses 2001·4   2001

Acrylic on tartan
135 × 200 cm (53⅛ × 78¾ in)
Private collection

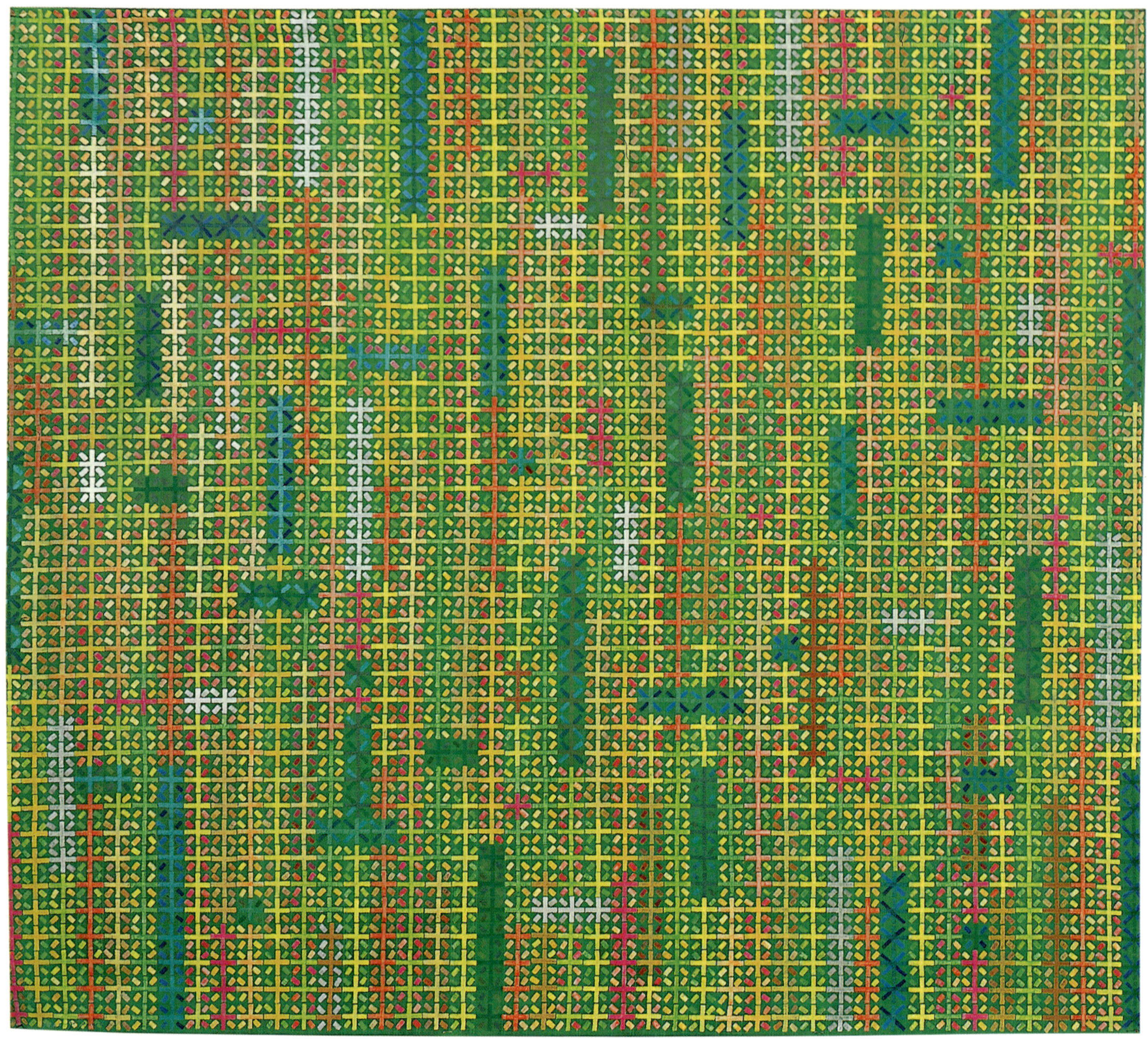

58. Appearance of Crosses 2001-15, 16   2001

Acrylic on tartan
In 2 pieces, each 140 × 160 cm (55⅛ × 63 in)
Private collection

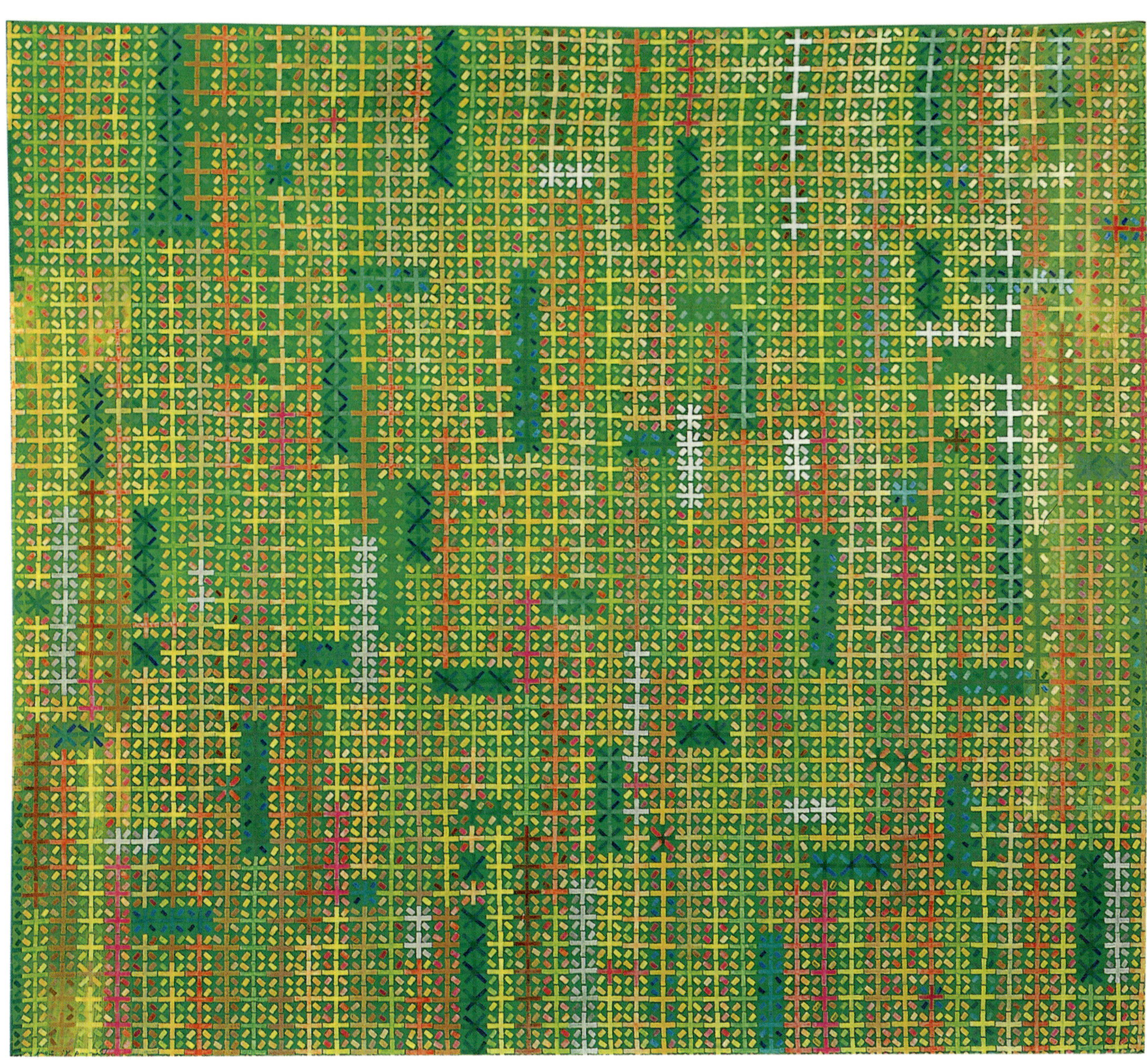

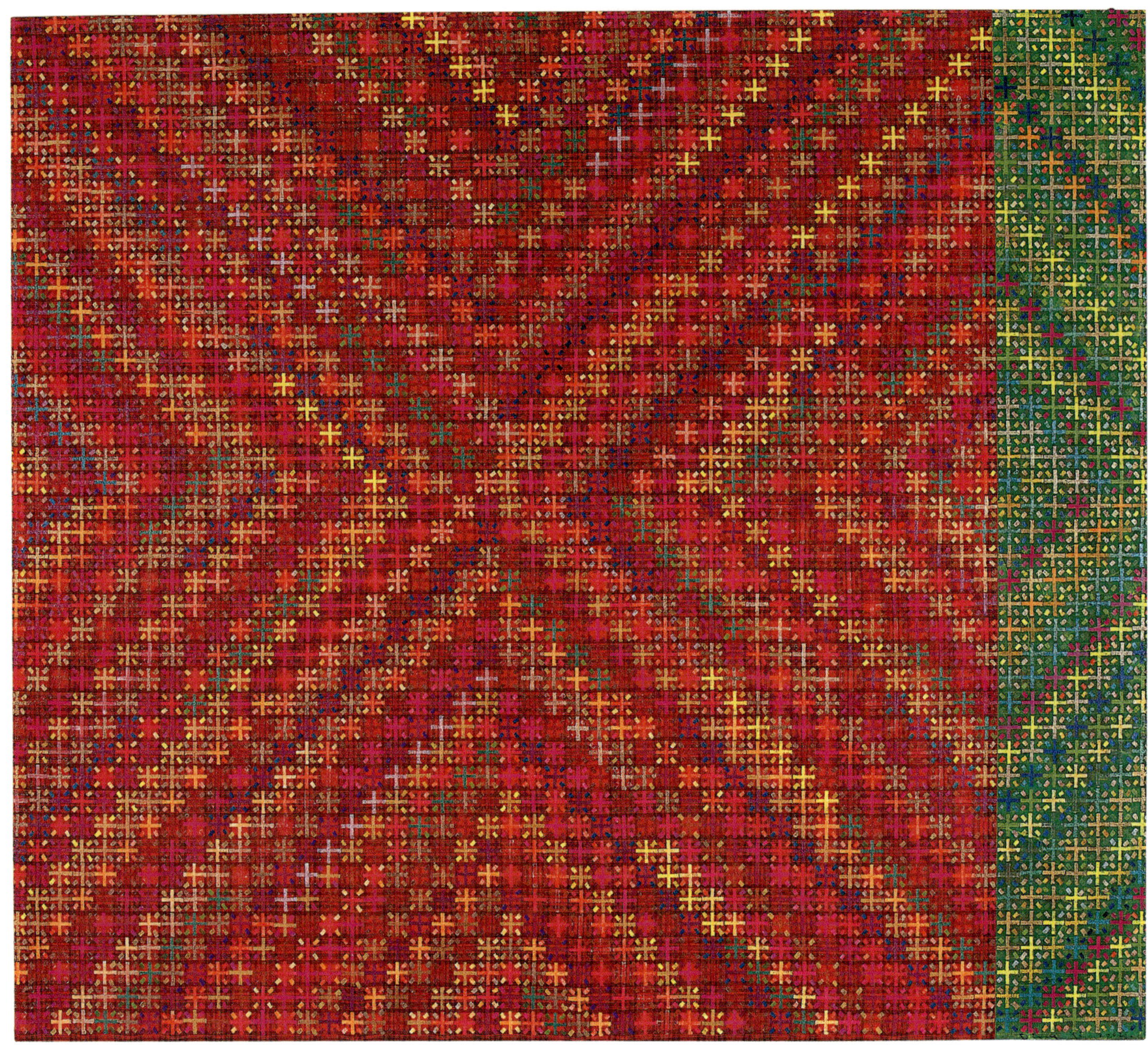

59. Appearance of Crosses 2002-9   2002

Acrylic on tartan
140 × 160 cm (55⅛ × 63 in)
Private collection

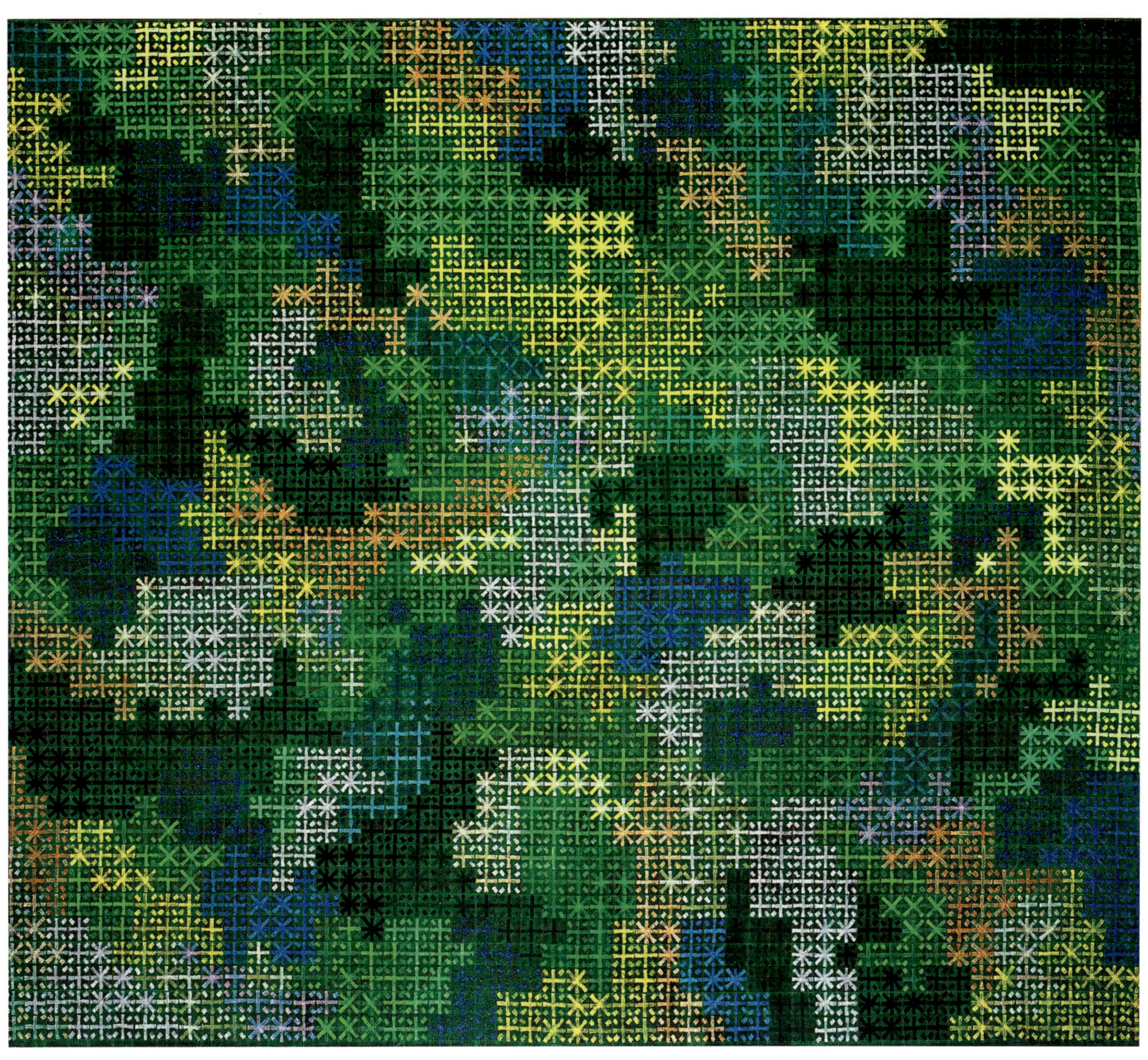

60. Appearance of Crosses 2003-1   2003

Acrylic on tartan
140 × 160 cm (55⅛ × 63 in)
Private collection, Shanghai

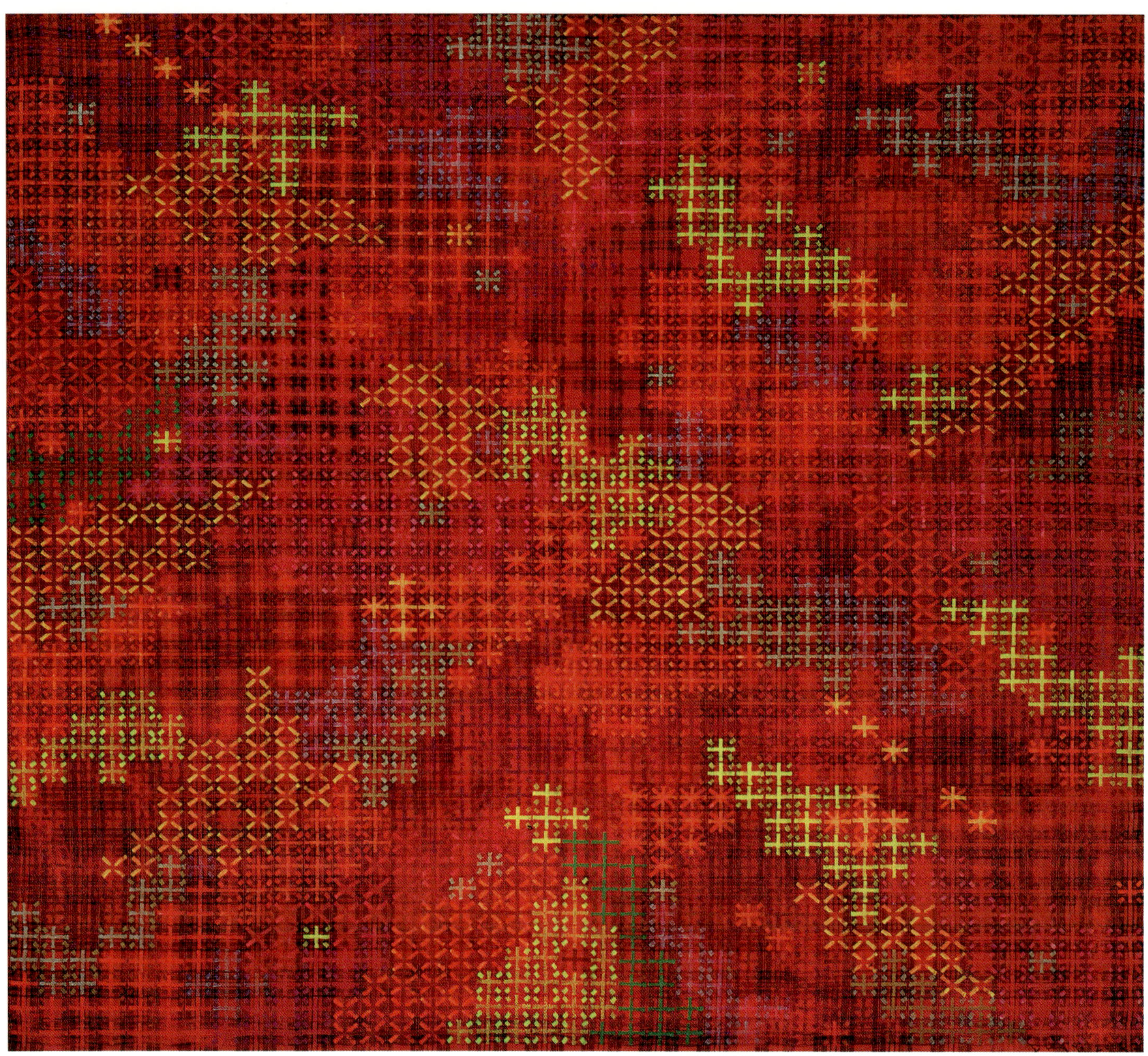

61. Appearance of Crosses 2004-2   2004

Acrylic on tartan
140 × 160 cm (55⅛ × 63 in)
Private collection

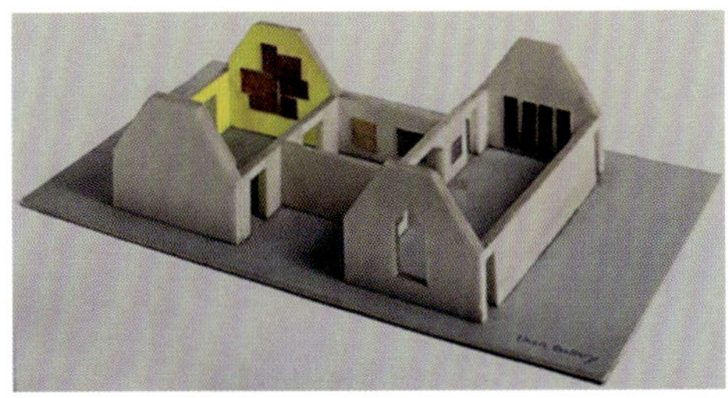

62. Ding Yi's model for the exhibition at Ikon Gallery, Birmingham, UK

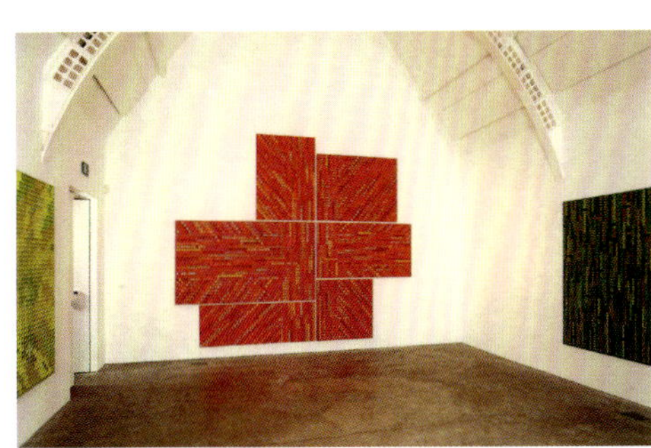

63. *Appearance of Crosses 2005-6*, shown at Ikon Gallery, Birmingham, UK, 2005

of Crosses 2005-6 (fig.64). Although he was happy to have it photographed against his rather battered studio wall – it made a nice contrast – this multi-panel painting was made specifically to fit onto a wall with a pointed ceiling at the Ikon Gallery in Birmingham in the UK (fig.63). As always, he wanted any exhibition of his to look right in a particular space. As was his practice by now, he made a model of the gallery and placed miniatures of *Appearance of Crosses 2005-6* and other works in it to make sure they would fit correctly on their particular wall and also relate to the other works in the exhibition. Ding Yi was always interested, obsessed even, in the process of painting, but also interested in how people experienced the work – hence this attention to installation.

It was the first, but not the last of such 'constellations' of paintings. Energising a wall by such a constructivist device appealed to his sense of design or architecture.

The Ikon exhibition was his first museum, or Kunsthalle, show outside China. The catalogue included an essay by the most internationally famous of Chinese curators, Hou Hanru, and an interview with the even more famous Hans Ulrich Obrist. These were signs Ding Yi had 'arrived' internationally. However, as Mathieu Borysevicz commented later,[4] Ding Yi had been accepted in China, and to an increasing extent abroad, as an important artist, yet critics had failed to produce much in the way of a critical or theoretical context to his work. His work was and remains profoundly anomalous in China, while in the West it does not fit with the normal preconceptions of what a Chinese artist makes.

His work has often been seen as Buddhist-like with its repetitions, and his use of the word 'spirit' in interviews and statements has fed such spiritualist readings. In 2005, for example, he was quoted as saying, 'In my paintings there is my spirit. My spirit influences my art as well as my attitude towards art determines my spirit.'[5] Again, in 2008 in the catalogue for an exhibition in the Netherlands that he was included in, an unacknowledged writer tells us that 'in his aspiration to go beyond conventional Chinese painting and to create a new spirituality for today, his aim was to return to the essence of the form in which he saw the soul'. The writer concludes that his work has 'an almost trance-like effect on the viewer'.[6]

What could the writer, and by inference Ding Yi, have meant by 'a new spirituality'? We must return to this later.

Given the preconceptions people have about 'oriental' artists, one can also see why a critic writing in 2004 would say, 'His work is calligraphy for the computer age.'[7] But of course Ding Yi does not do calligraphy nor give any characters, only reiterating the +, × and ✳ shapes, all resolutely ambiguous in what they may mean.

Perhaps the best way to find a more nuanced understanding of his work is to think firstly about this basic mark or motif, the drawn or painted cross. × can mean a signature or mark for an illiterate, or an erasure – a crossing out. If you bring the basic signs in Ding Yi's painting, × and +, together it creates the Chinese character ✳, meaning rice. So you could say the basic semiotic in Ding Yi's paintings is

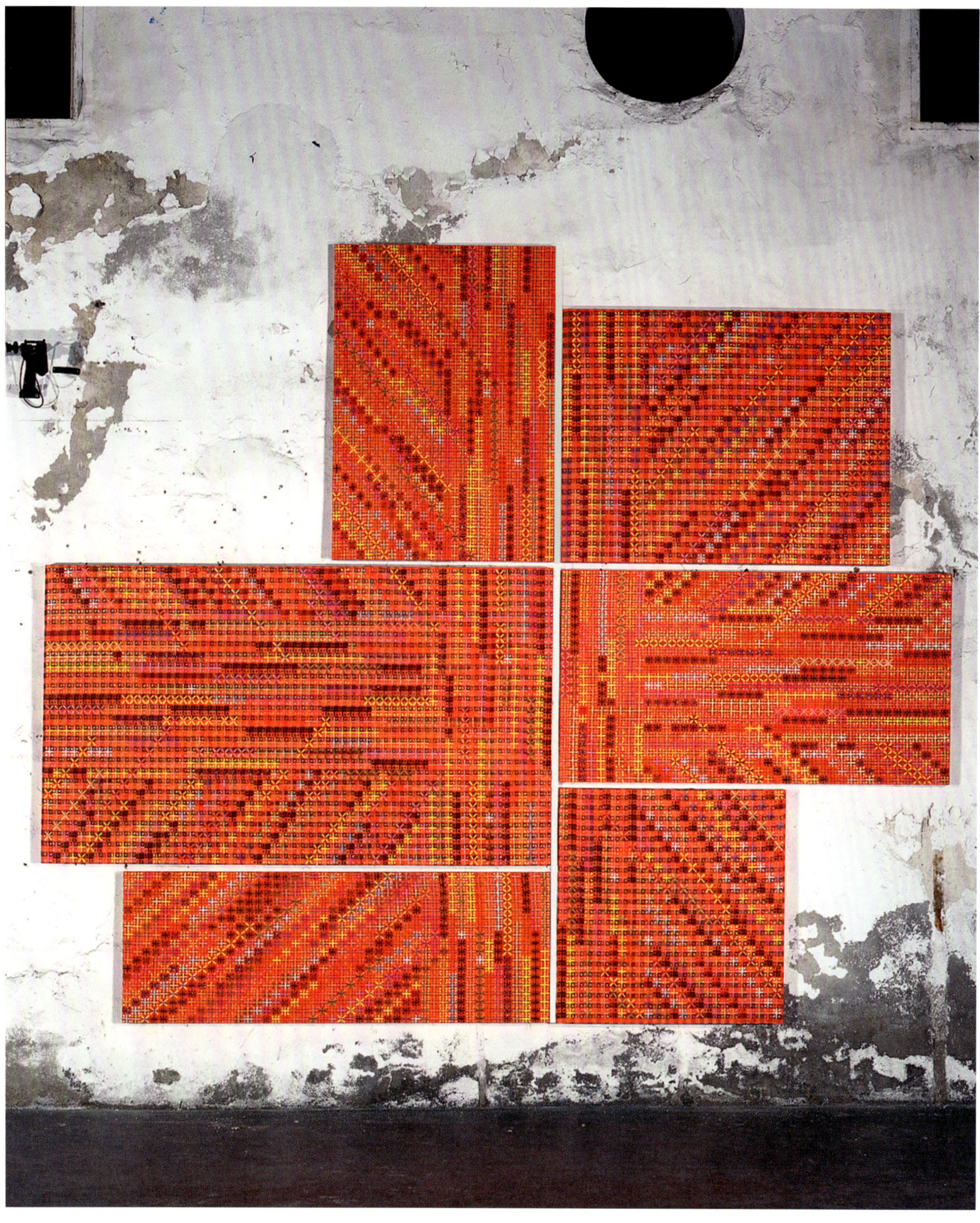

64. Appearance of Crosses 2005-6   2005,
in Ding Yi's studio

Acrylic on tartan
320 × 440 cm (126 × 173¼ in)
Private collection

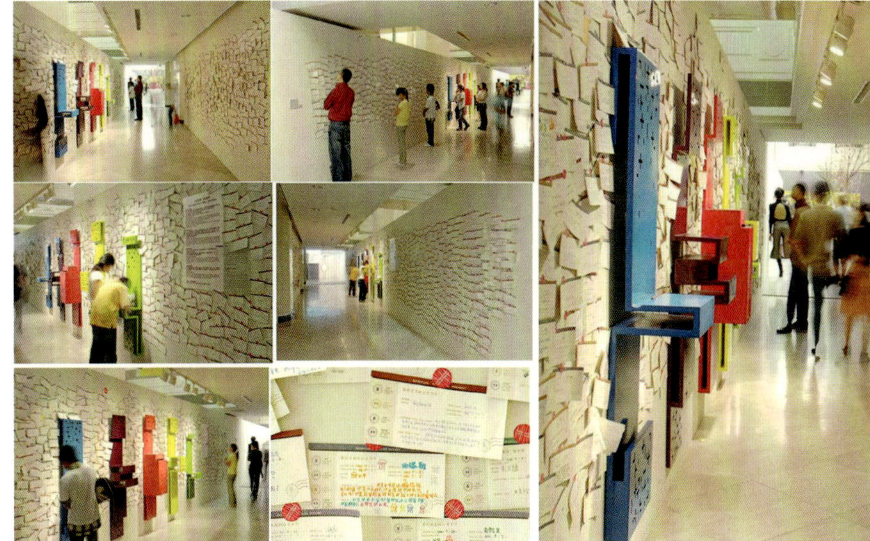

Participatory project at Shanghai Biennale 2006.
Afterwards shown in Ding Yi's solo exhibition at
Museo d'Arte Moderna, Bologna, 2008

also fundamentally Asian. Secondly and more importantly, we must continue to
think about our actual phenomenological experience of looking at and interacting
with the paintings. It also helps, thirdly, to look at how he has acted outside the
painting studio.

In 2001 he had wanted to leave his teaching job but was not allowed to. In the
People's Republic of China no one, including teachers, can leave their work brigade
without consent. The college was pleased to have an increasingly famous artist on its
faculty, especially one who was a serious and thoughtful teacher. However, in 2005
he finally managed to leave his job at the Shanghai Arts and Crafts College – but
only because he was offered a more senior position, a professorship, at the Shanghai
Institute of Visual Arts. In 2009 he became vice president of the School of Design
and the director of the Academic Committee.

Asked in 2018 how many of his students in his 25 years of teaching had gone on
to become successful painters, he said, 'None.' The most famous Ding Yi student is
Xu Zhen, a rising star in the international art market, a witty, dadaist artist who also
functions as gallerist and CEO of his art-production enterprise MadeIn Company. As a
teacher Ding Yi never wanted disciples and is contemptuous of those artists who want
their students to copy their style or work method. He has always wanted students to
be creative for themselves and to respond to particular sites and projects.

At the Shanghai Biennale of 2006 he displayed not paintings but a set of sculptures
which, unusually, played with cloud forms, auspicious symbols in Chinese tradition.
More intriguingly he also presented, attached to the wall, *Time Space Post Office*
(fig.65), five large metal boxes each with patterns of crosses and dashes cut into them
and a platform on which to fill in the questionnaires he provided. In these, visitors
were asked a series of questions about what made for a happy urban life. 'How big

should the city be?' 'What is more important: Environment, family, career, wealth, freedom or public services?' 'What should the role and function of contemporary art be?' 'Are you proud of the current condition of Chinese culture in areas such as politics, sport, soccer, cinema, theatre, architecture, design, painting, sculpture or cooking?' The addressee of the questionnaire could be another person or oneself in the future, as in the last question, 'If this was a letter for the future, what would your desire be?' These could then be posted in a central red mailbox. This filled up quickly during the event, so many hundreds of these completed forms were instead stuck to the wall so people could read each other's hopes for the future. This participatory project was repeated in 2008 when he had an exhibition in Bologna. Again, so many people filled in the questionnaire and posted it that the mailbox was soon chock-a-block and the responses were instead stuck to the wall, eventually covering several walls of the museum.

That he, a painter, should have made such a work is less surprising if we remember, firstly, how concerned he has always been about the experience of the audience and, secondly, how he wanted his paintings to be more than paint on tartan. He has always wanted more meaning, more significance than that.

These were also clearly designed objects, snappy; rather complex; and, of course, with everything at right angles. This too was unsurprising if we remember he studied initially as a product or interior designer and has normally taught design students rather than artists.

Since the late 1990s he has been making three-dimensional objects and installations – sometimes as art, sometimes as design. Some have been conceptual. As with a 2000 work where he put a '+'-shaped tile spacer in the wax and formed a solid cubic meter of it. It echoes earlier works by Robert Morris and Tony Cragg,[8] turning the materials and processes of making art into an inert cube. Others have been more sculptural: for example, a set of eight bronze crosses in 2008. He also participated in several public art projects in China. His trademark crosses and his concern with the relation of the individual to the city took on new forms in his designs for architecture, such as a bridge in Pudong (2001) and an internet cafe in Zhejiang (2004).

Asked in 2004 whether he was interested in working with commercial textile manufacturers, he said he was not: 'I'm mainly interested in the mass production of textiles and the way that fits in with contemporary culture.'[9] Some years later he did take on some more commercial design projects: scarves for Hermès, a unique suitcase for Louis Vuitton. In all these cases he was aware that though he might reach new audiences, his old audience would feel he had 'sold out'. He was careful therefore that any contract would still leave him in full control of his art and image.

The hard and somewhat impersonal feel of the later fluorescent paintings was accentuated by painting in the boxes or lines of the cells, in 2006, as we can see in *Appearance of Crosses 2006-14* (fig.67). The paint marks are determinedly chunky and box-like themselves. The rhythm is strident, like that of an insistent military march.

Subsequently, he has talked of how uncertain he felt at this time, that perhaps there was something wrong with the city's development, that he should paint chaos.[10] The tartan is dominated in this period, and barely visible – from early on in these fluorescent paintings, he rarely left the edges of the tartan unpainted as he had before.

In 2007 he published one of his longest statements, 'Deconstructing the Abstract'.[11] In it he talks, perhaps surprisingly, of his interest in traditional cultures:

Tradition and reflection

The integrity of traditional culture is challenged by the contemporary society. The meaning of traditional culture is deconstructed by globalization, multinational political systems, the competition for economic profit, computer networks and changes in society's framework, which as a result makes traditional culture 'unreal' in modern life so it gradually becomes a spiritual or memorial set of 'relics'. My paintings created by chalk and charcoals intend to focus on these vestige of traditional culture. Based on an archeological approach, I focus on the historical remains. They are either buried in the earth or eroded by wind and rain, naturally what they appear as today are broken, faded and fragments. I try to ponder over these unknown materials through my art pieces.

He talks also of the need to break away from habitual ways of working:

On the edge

I try to make my art on the edge, or in other words, make it appear artless. There is something about art in it, but there is also something from industry, design and everyday life. When art is fused with other areas, it nurtures some vitality. In fact, it is dangerous for an artist to stick to his 'individual pattern' as such a stereotyped pattern will often lead to repetition and empiricism. I frequently search for a painting technique that is on the edge to weaken those normative painting elements . . . The art that is on the edge has a kind of potentiality that broadens the vision and meaning of art, and it also pushes the artist to stand away from the traditional, idiomatic experience. Because of such adjustments, the narrative of Art is broadened with new propositions.

He presents self-discipline in making a work of art as the very opposite of a consistent personal style:

Methodology

This is a personal methodology. How can an artist retain self-discipline in his art piece during a long period of consistent personal style? Often I turn to some other technique to make the touch and management of my art pieces foreign, or strange, or awkward and unexpected. For an artist, the biggest obstacle is

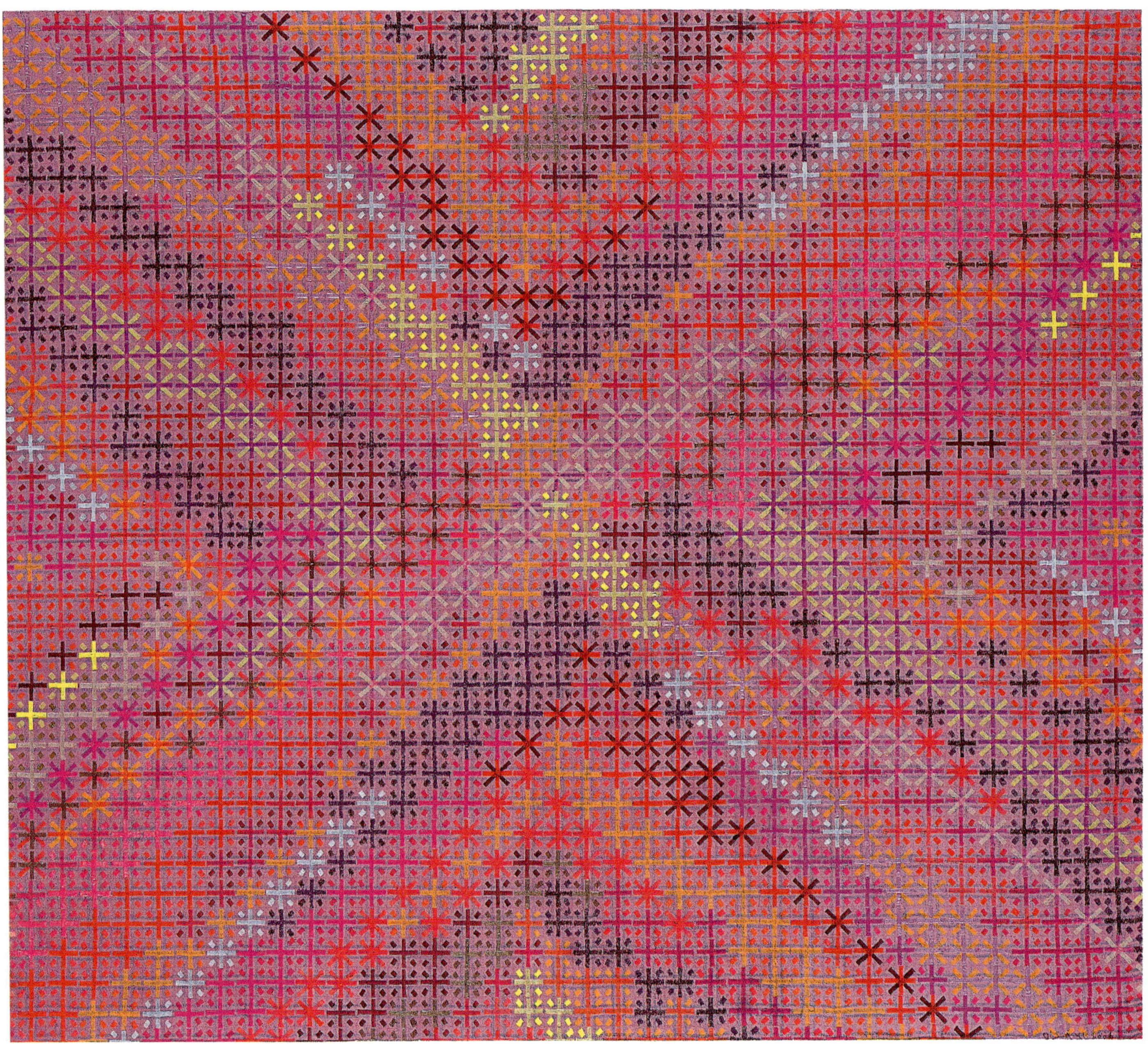

66. Appearance of Crosses 2006·9   2006

Acrylic on tartan
140 × 160 cm (55⅛ × 63 in)
Private collection

86

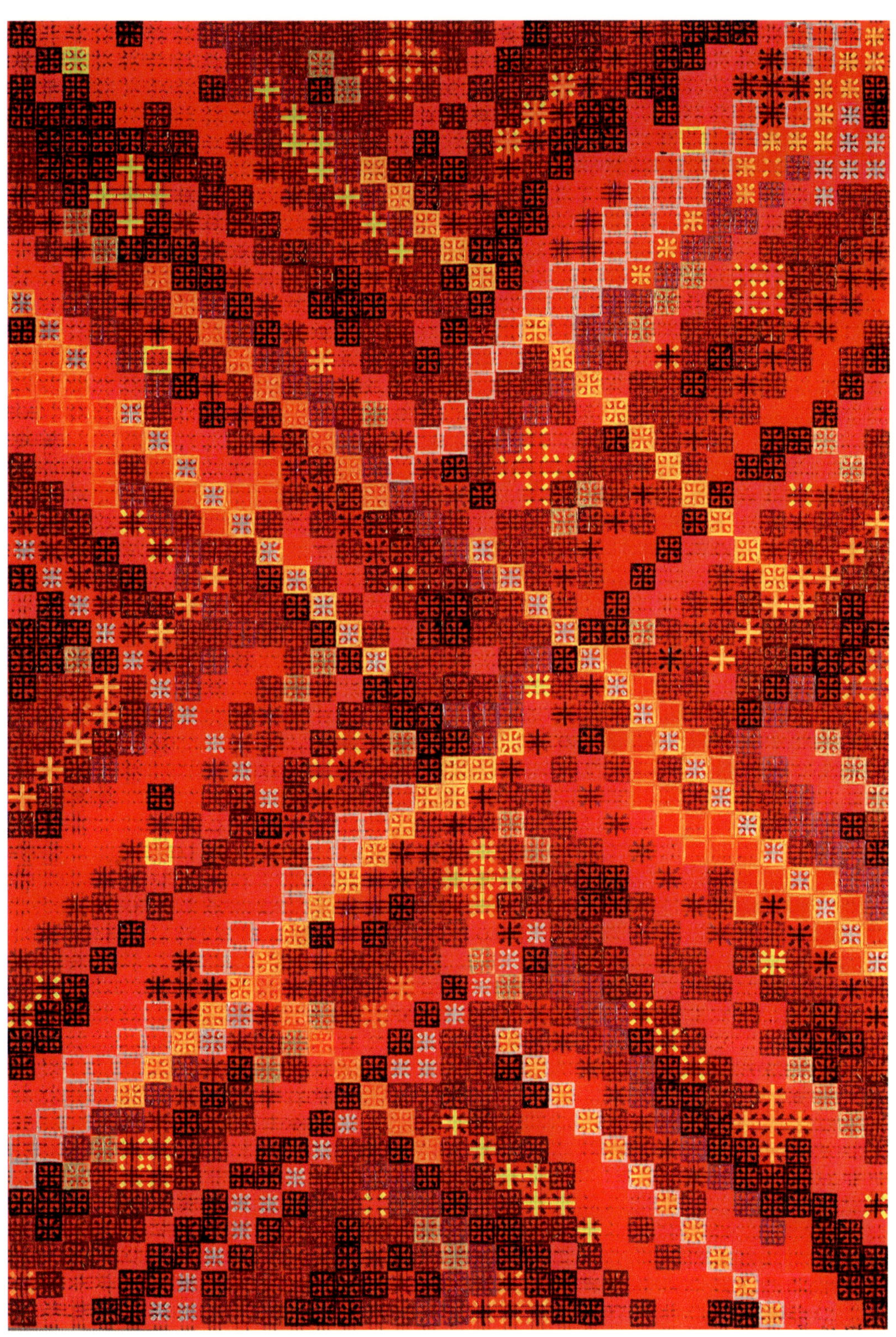

67. Appearance of Crosses 2006-14   2006

Acrylic on tartan
200 × 140 cm (78¾ × 55⅛ in)
Private collection

craftiness, or craftful-ness. Sometimes I purposely slow down my working pace
to add difficulty to my paintings. For example, I reduce the size of each cross
or paint layer by layer. My purpose is to make my technique unskilled and slow
down my judgments about the painting. Sometimes painting needs a different
kind of 'itinerary'. When the structure becomes more complicated and the
colours more intricate, it needs to be returned to the start, and simplicity. From
simplicity to complicatedness and then back to simplicity, or sometimes from
the colourful world back to the black-and-white world. I call this process 'self-
filtration' that enables me to clearly view the essential problems. Perhaps this
is the best methodology for an artist to keep or regain a clear mind.

By now he was trying to push his painting in different directions and create varying
moods or atmospheres. He was capable of making calmer fluorescent paintings.
Appearance of Crosses 2008-25 (fig.68), for example, is almost pastoral compared to others.
With black and dark green as dominant colours, the relatively few white and yellow
crosses shine out like stars in the night sky. This does not evoke the dynamic lights
of Shanghai; quite the contrary.

If we compare two paintings from 2009 we see the range of feelings he could
evoke. In *Appearance of* Crosses *2009-3* (fig.69) most of the squares are not outlined,
or just outlined sparingly in white paint. He is toning down the colour. The lines
are diagonal only and often meandering. The movement is slow. *Appearance of Crosses
2009-10* (fig.70) in comparison is like a rocket exploding in the night sky, except that
when we look harder we realise it is very much a painting of squares, and squares
within squares – like a very lo-res reproduction with big pixels. Formally he is
playing the circle off against the innumerable squares. This is a painting that shows
the extraordinary amount of apparent depth he can create just by the use of colour,
especially when the ground is dark.

In 2010 he launched a book on his fluorescent paintings (*Ding Yi, Flourescence*) at
the Minsheng Art Museum, Shanghai. It was, in the event, to mark the end of both his
tartan paintings and his fluorescent paintings. After that he began preparing for a large
exhibition at the same museum the next year which would include new and old works.
He did not want to call such a show a retrospective, rather a mid-career survey. It was
to be a matter of taking stock, of presenting a body of new work and moving on.

In two paintings made later that year, *Appearance of Crosses 2010-12* and *Appearance of
Crosses 2010-16* (figs 71, 72), he began using canvas again rather than tartan. Moreover,
he used a black anonymous ground, as if the glaring lights of downtown Shanghai had
been turned off and one could look at less strident manifestations of light and colour.

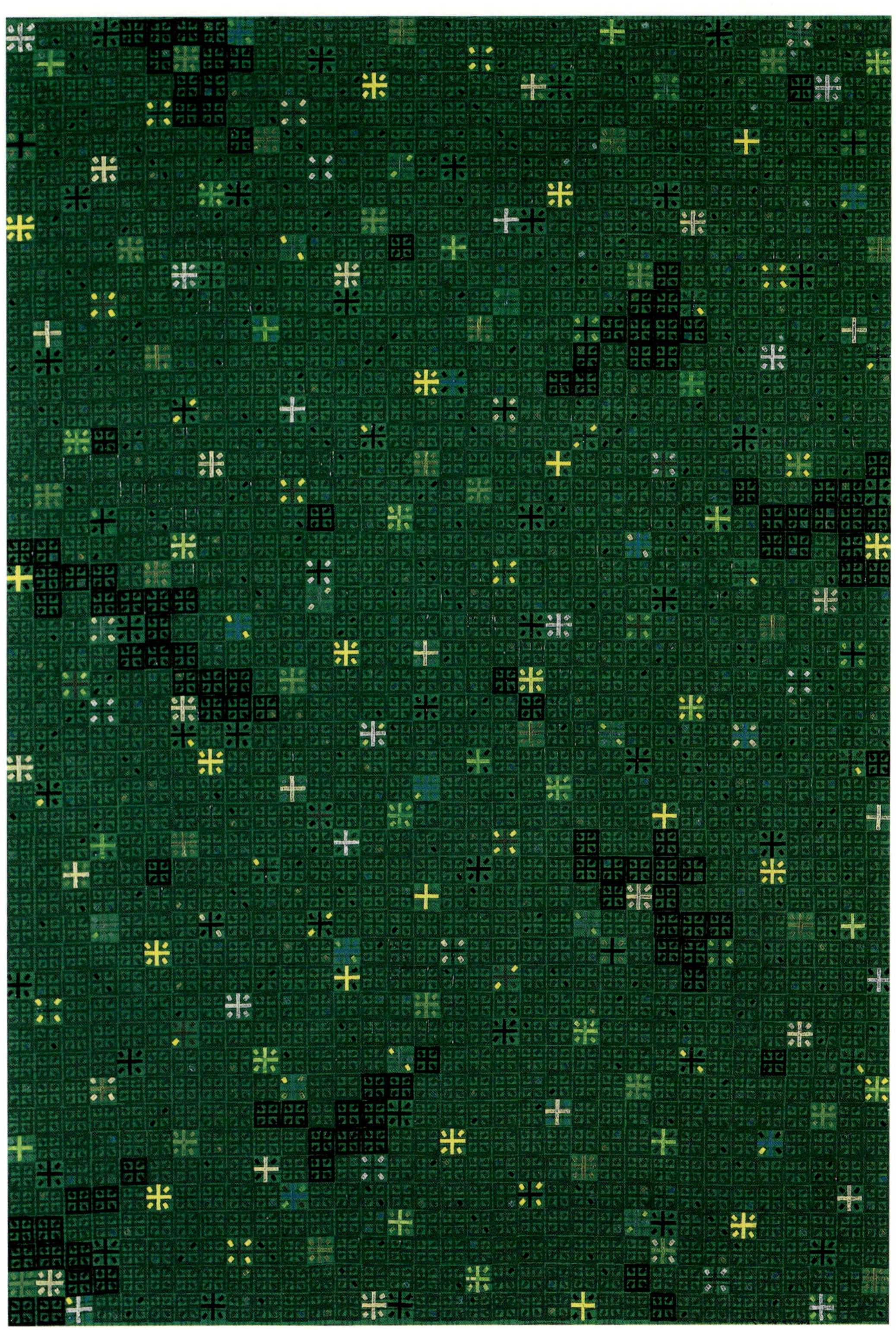

68. Appearance of Crosses 2008-25   *2008*

Acrylic on tartan
200 × 140 cm (78¾ × 55⅛ in)
Private collection

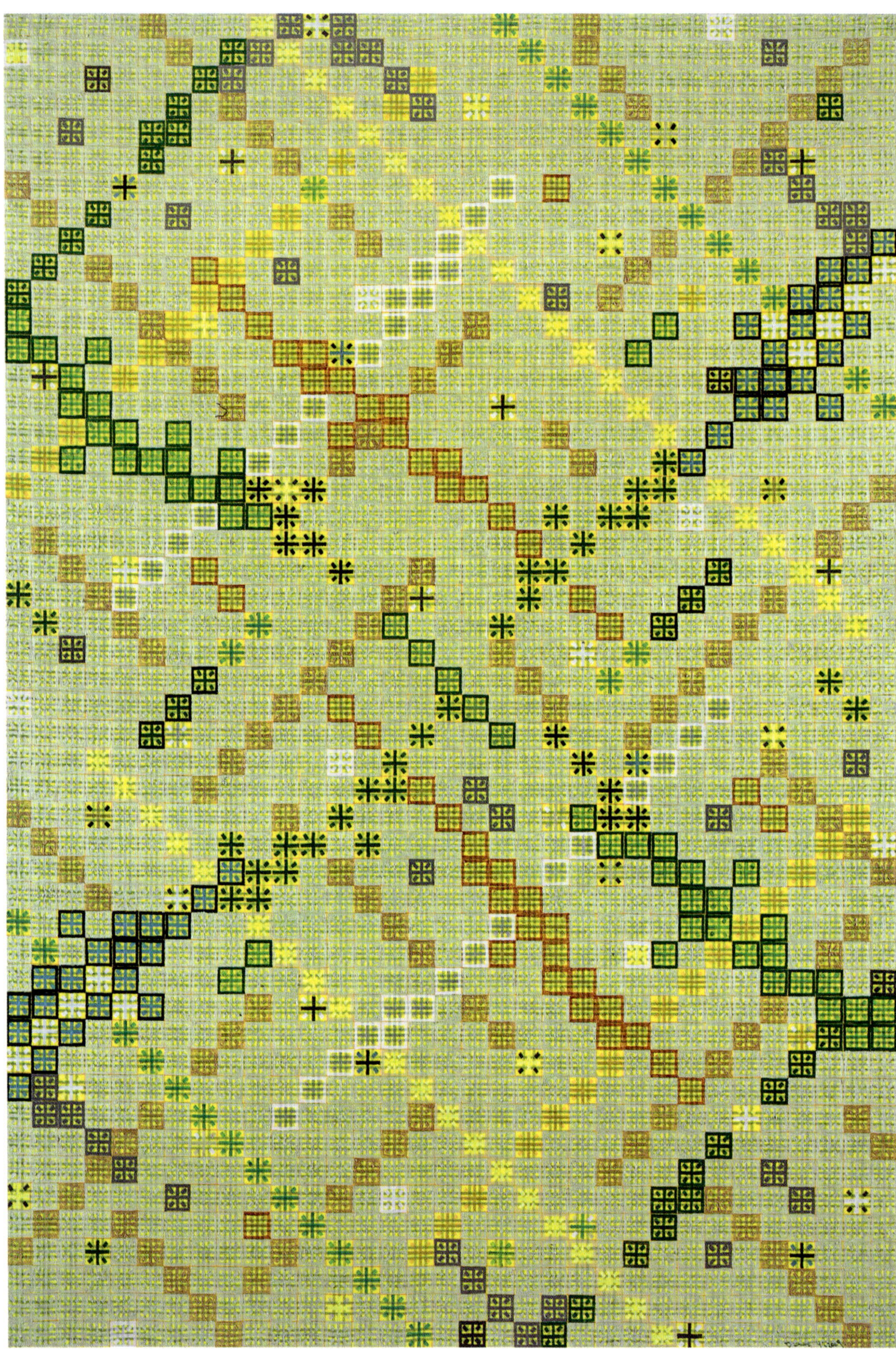

69. Appearance of Crosses 2009-3   2009

Acrylic on tartan
200 × 140 cm (78¾ × 55⅛ in)
Private collection

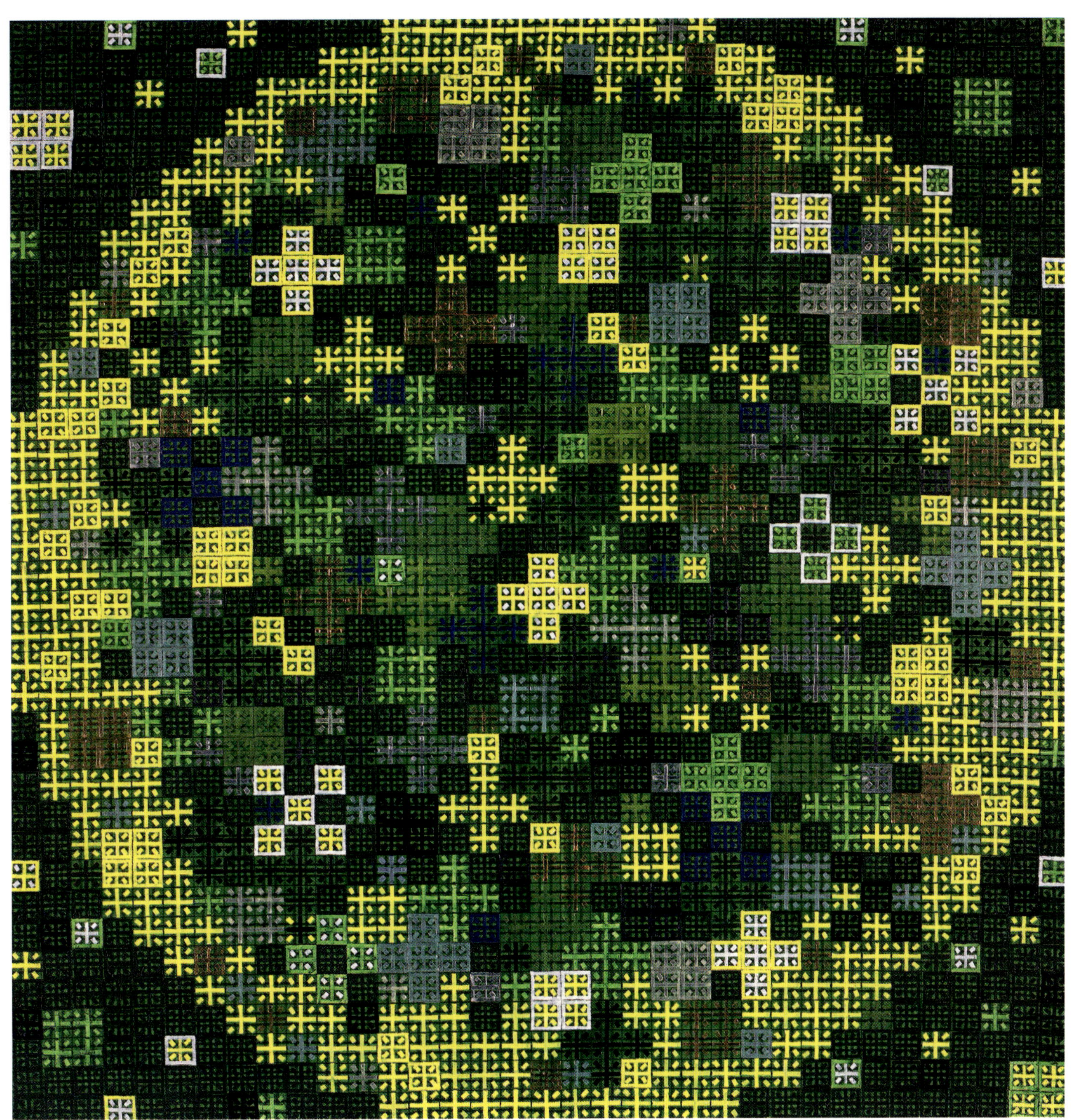

70. **Appearance of Crosses 2009-10**   2009

Acrylic on tartan
150 × 150 cm (59 × 59 in)
Private collection

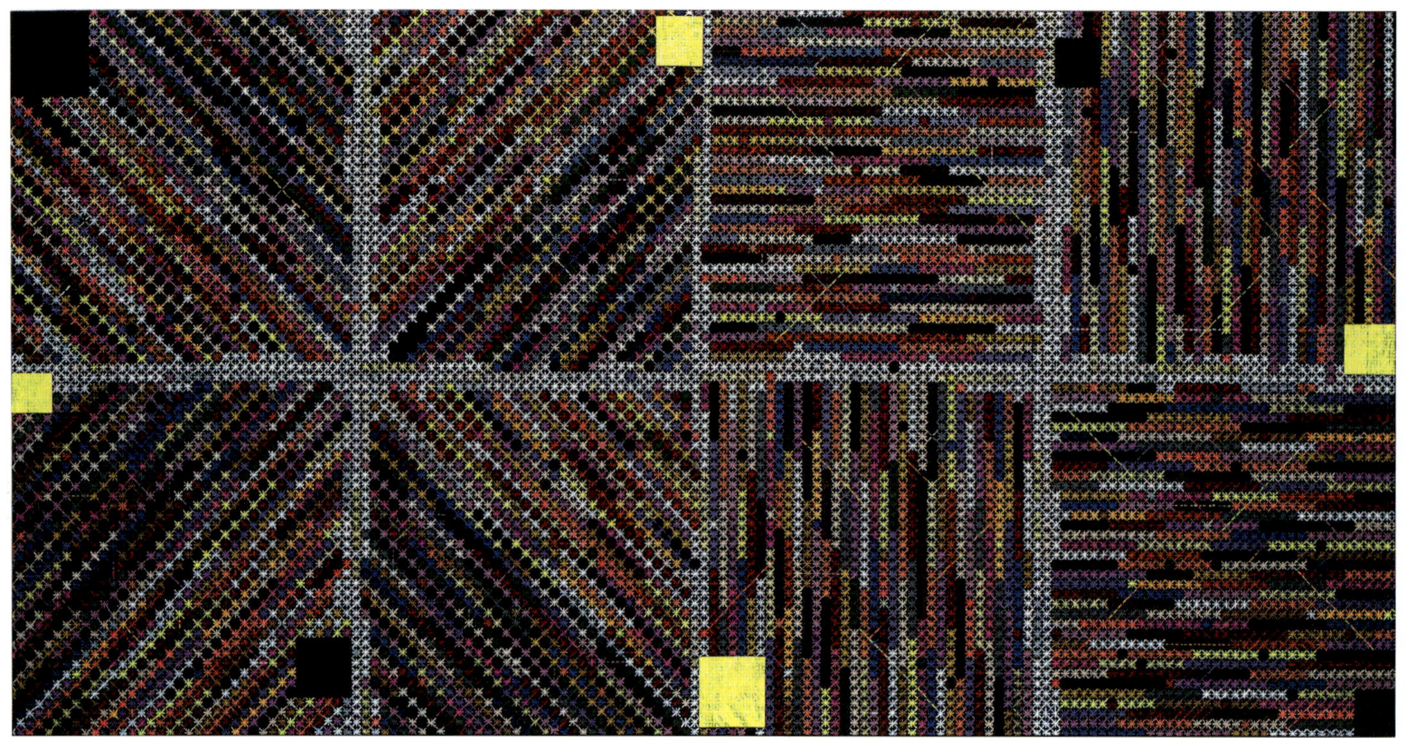

71. Appearance of Crosses 2010-12   2010

Acrylic on canvas
220 × 440 cm (86⅝ × 173¼ in)
Private collection

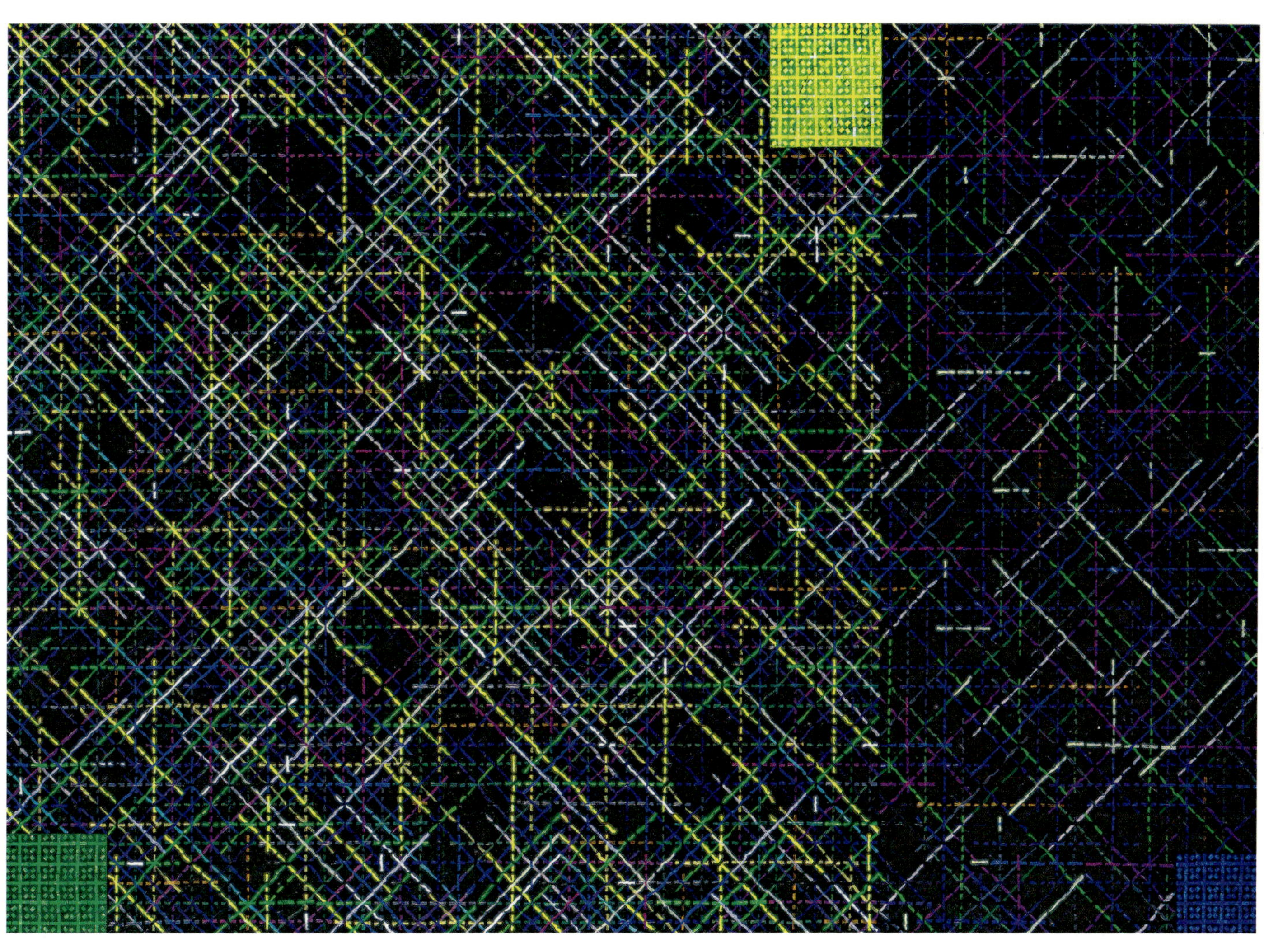

72. Appearance of Crosses 2010-16   2010

Acrylic on canvas
140 × 200 cm (55⅛ × 78¾ in)
Private collection

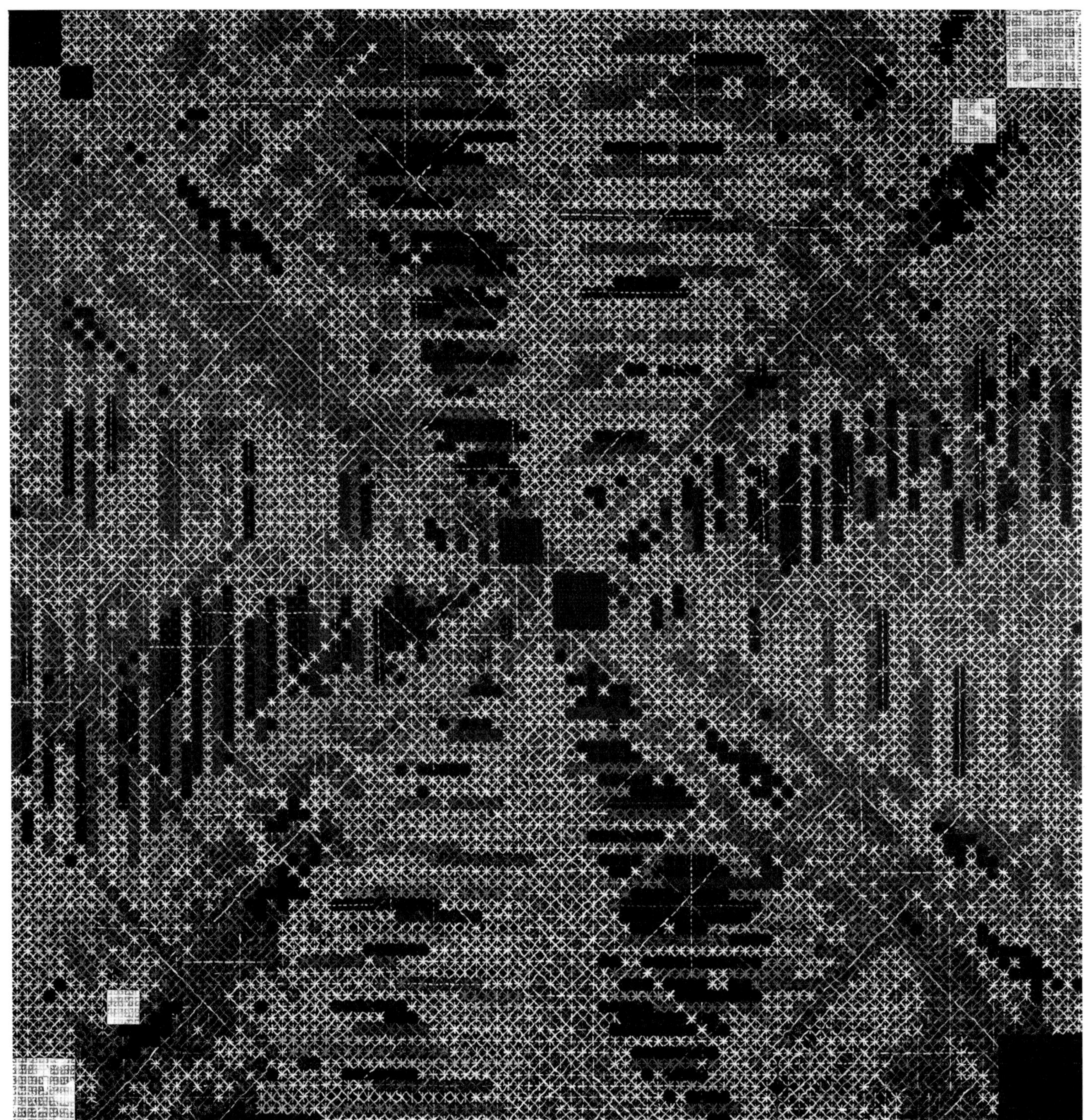

73. Appearance of Crosses 2011·7   2011

Acrylic on canvas
300 × 300 cm (118⅛ × 118⅛ in)
Private collection

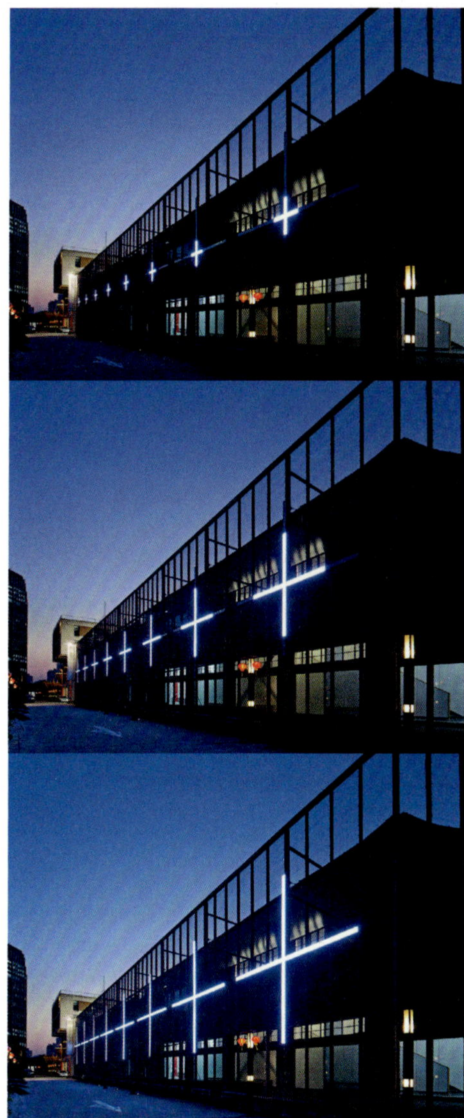

74. Flashing (Appearance of Crosses – Light)   2011

LED tubes
In 8 pieces, each 600 × 600 cm (236¼ × 236¼ in)
ShanghART Gallery, Shanghai

In 2011 Ding Yi was invited to have an exhibition at the Minsheng Arts Museum in Shanghai. He had recently stopped making the fluorescent paintings – partly because they were hurting his eyes but also, more importantly, because he wanted to progress. But to understand what to do next, he had first to consider and understand what he had done. The Minsheng show was to be the first of several exhibitions where he hung new works alongside his older works. Also, to a greater extent than before, it was an exhibition where he would work with the space. The Minsheng is a cold, hard, cavernous expanse – originally it was the Shanghai No.10 Steel Factory. He re-articulated the space, and made it less cavernous, by hanging some of his paintings like screens in the centre of the room. This emphasised the minimal 'thingness' or quiddity of his paintings.

At the same time, he installed eight LED crosses on the Minsheng Museum's exterior wall (fig.74). Each illuminated cross would expand in five computer-programmed stages, from 1.2 metres square to 6 metres square, then contract. As ever, he was interested in pushing his cross motif into architecture, not so much competing with the building as enlivening and transforming it.

Above all else, the paintings changed. Paintings such as *Appearance of Crosses 2010-12* and *Appearance of Crosses 2010-16*, though still highly dynamic, had not been so aggressively red and had been toned down by a black ground. Now in *Appearance of Crosses 2011-3* (fig.75) all vivid colours were banished, only a subtle infusion of muted reds and greens being allowed. In the ensuing series of large, dark square paintings, *Appearance of Crosses 2011-4* to *2011-7* (fig.77), colour was entirely absent. Like many painters who have wanted to get back to basics and start again, he confined himself to black and white.

Some people remarked on how these looked like aerial views, as if one were flying or floating above the world and its patchwork of fields, roads and towns. The crosses would gather into clusters or else be corralled into overpainted blocks. The clusters especially suggested a more organic world. Whereas the fluorescent paintings had seemed to pop away from the canvas and advance into the space in front of the viewer, these works had a greater sense of space either behind or within the painting. Compared with the preceding paintings they seemed meditative, their darkness suggesting the tranquil feeling of exploring or absorbing the night sky. In the Minsheng exhibition this sense of night, tranquillity and meditation was enhanced by having only these four paintings in the final room of the exhibition.

This and subsequent exhibitions were to be opportunities to restage, re-see and rethink his oeuvre. Each of his exhibitions is a conversation with other people as well

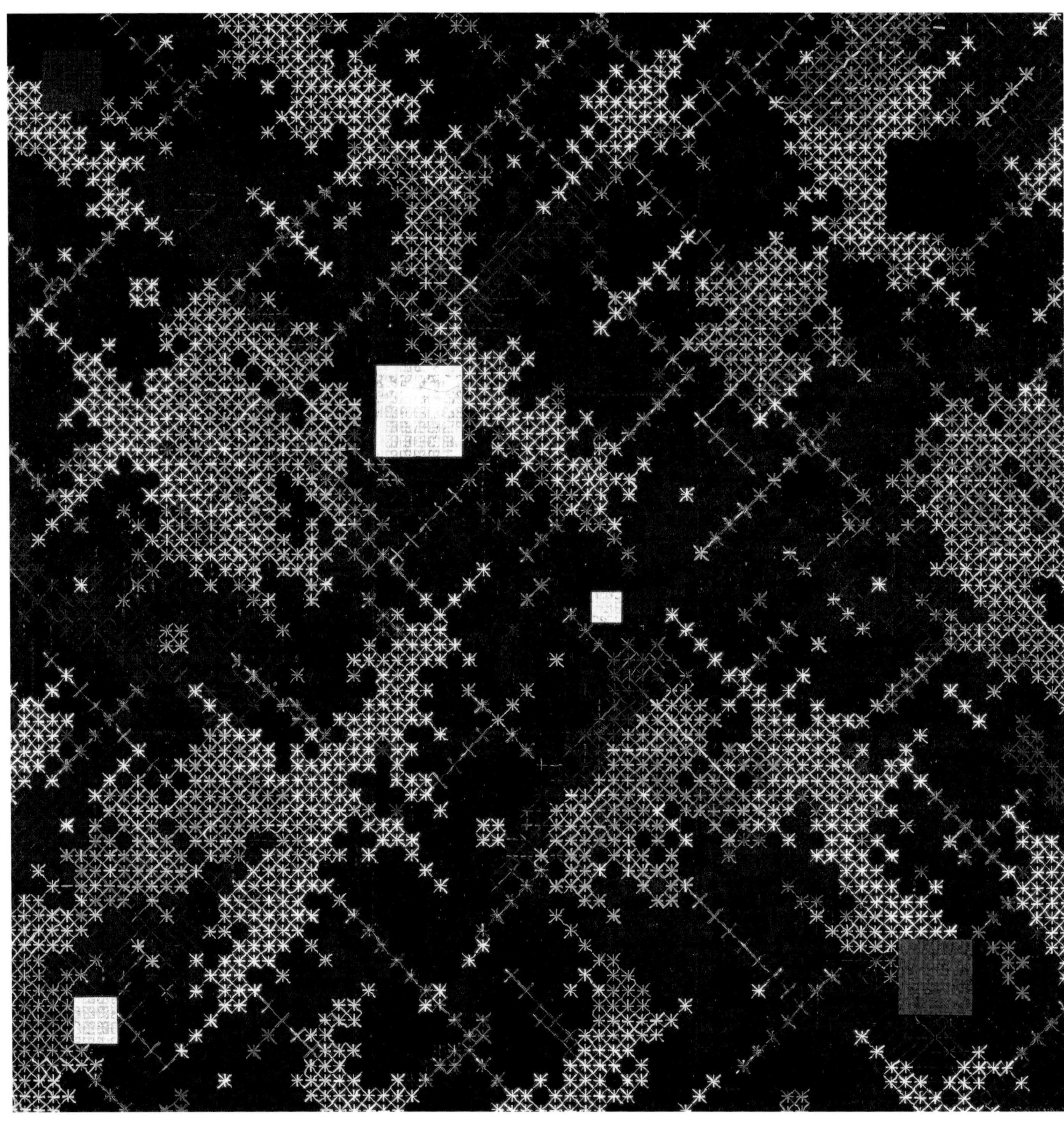

75. Appearance of Crosses 2011-3   2011

Acrylic on canvas
220 × 220 cm (86⅝ × 86⅝ in)
ShanghART Gallery, Shanghai

76. Appearance of Crosses 2011-3
2011 (detail)

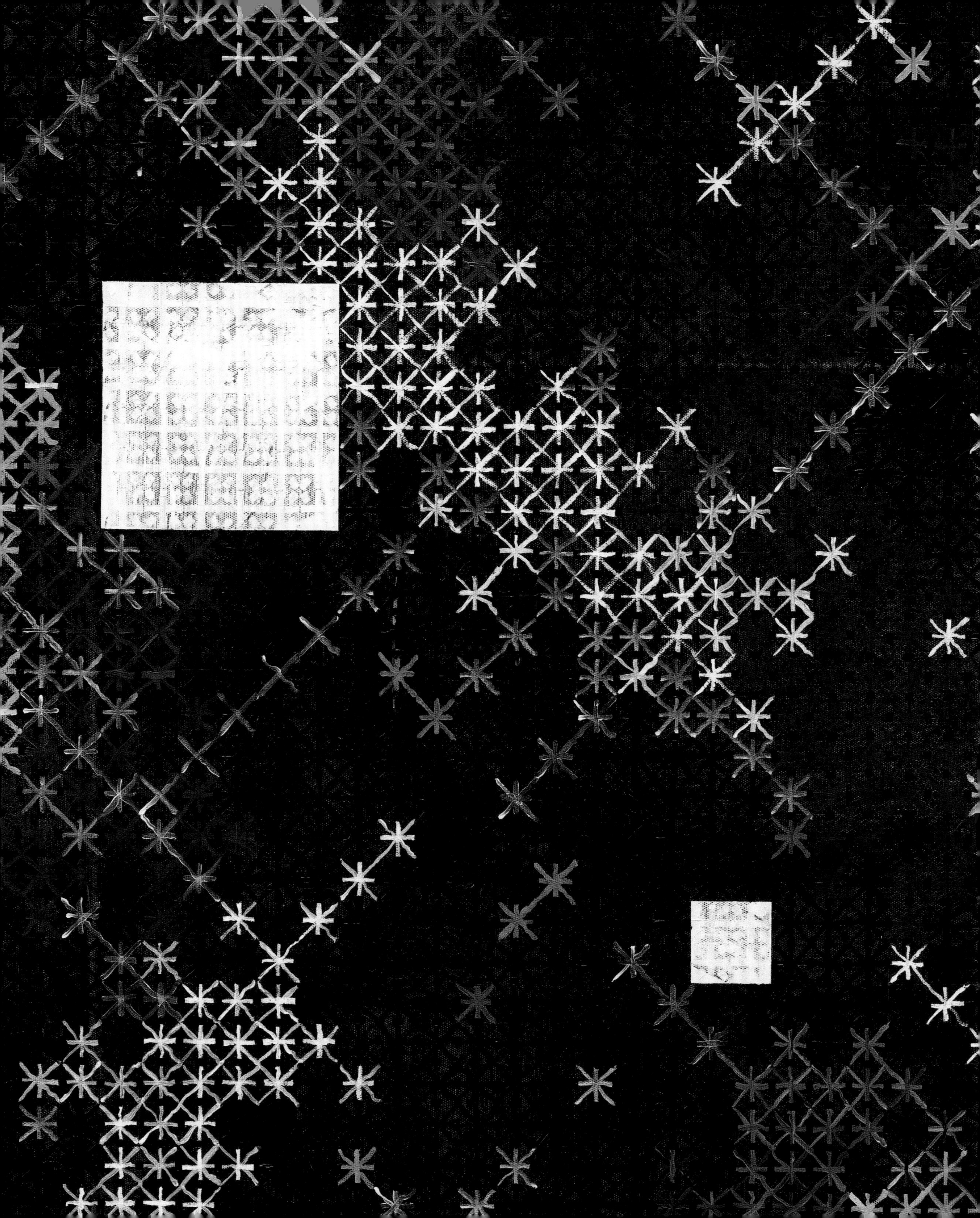

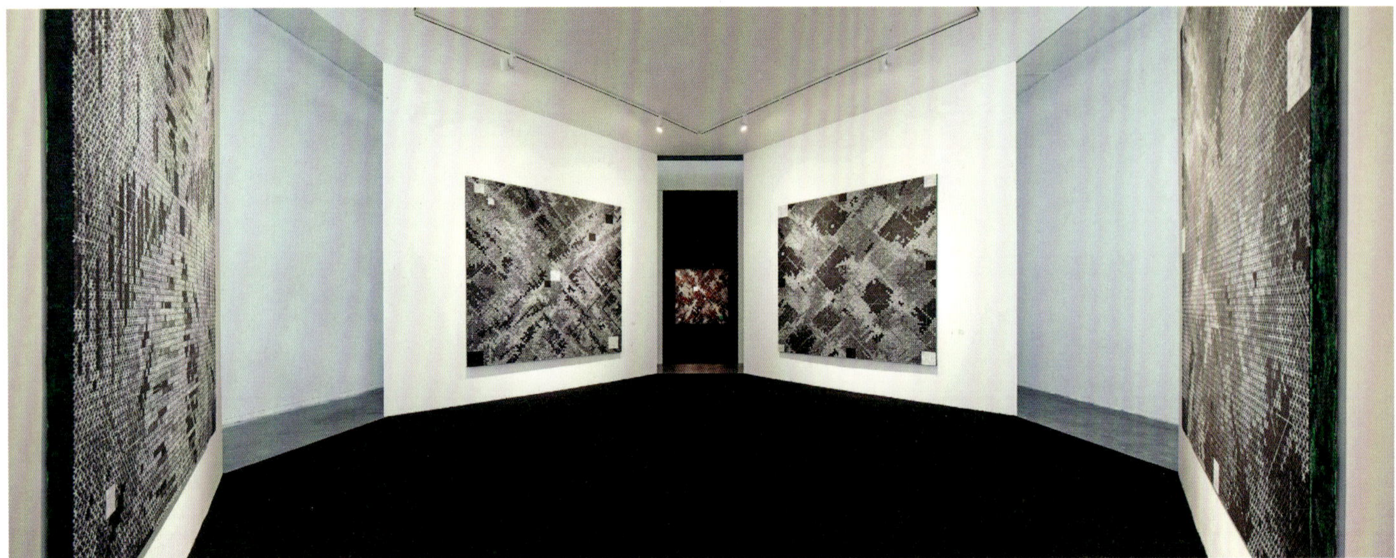

77. Ding Yi's solo exhibition at Minsheng Art Museum, Shanghai, 2011.

From left to right:
Appearance of Crosses 2011-7, 2011-6, 2011-3, 2011-5, 2011-4

as with his changing self. The catalogue for this exhibition, unusually, contained five essays, including one by ourselves.[1] It not only reproduced all 69 of the paintings in the exhibition, mostly one per page, but also included 41 mainly full-page details of those paintings. Ding Yi wanted the catalogue, like this book, to give some of that key experience of being close to the painting, of how it feels to be immersed in the intricacies and rhythms of the crosses. Similarly, emphasising the importance of the drawings to him, all 36 drawings in the exhibition were reproduced, again almost all full-page; there were also 16 full-page details of them. It is hard to think of another painter today who insists on having so many details of his works being included in publications. (His very first catalogue, for a 1994 exhibition in the Shanghai Art Museum, had comprised 25 full-page illustrations of works and four full-page details.) The ambition, scale and production values of this catalogue bore witness not only to Ding Yi's growing reputation, but also how support for art in Shanghai was growing exponentially.

In 2012 Ding Yi turned 50. It is a time when many artists have retrospective exhibitions, but also when many become averse to change, start to repeat themselves and become concerned with the subtleties within a narrow range of opportunities. Truly adventurous and creative late styles like those of Rembrandt or Hokusai or, in China, perhaps Qi Bashi and Huang Binhong are actually rare.[2] That Ding Yi has refused to call any of his museum exhibitions 'retrospectives' even though he has habitually included early works is indicative of how he wants never to stop, but to continue to experiment. Many of his contemporaries have been satisfied with their success and failed to develop. For Ding Yi, constantly reinventing himself is his driving strength.

In the 2013 *Art Changsha*, a sort of biennial in Hunan, four one-person shows were held, one being Ding Yi's. He exhibited, along with older work, eight new one-

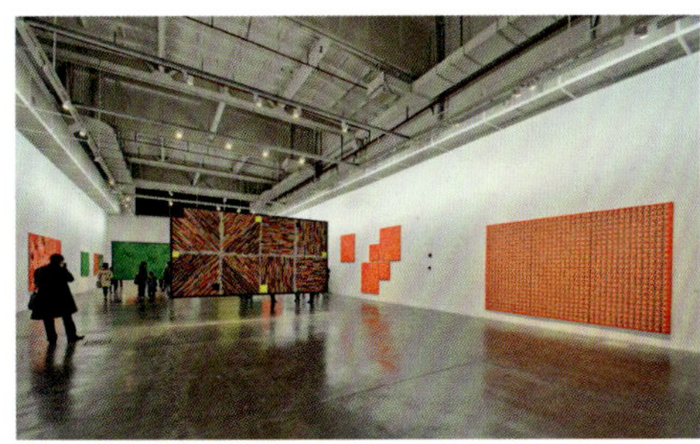

78. Ding Yi's solo exhibition at Minsheng Art Museum, Shanghai, 2011

metre-square paintings (*Appearance of Crosses 2013-3* to *2013-10*) in which colour was gradually reintroduced, firstly blue and green and eventually red, purple, pink and yellow ochre.

The square format was to become his go-to format when thinking through new ideas or moves. After the fluorescent works, the touch by which each dash, line or cross is made become more obvious and gentler. If in the earliest *Appearance of Crosses* paintings the crosses were dumb – mechanically applied, without nuance – and in the later fluorescent paintings often relentlessly assertive, what we see in the following years is an un-dumbing of the cross to the point where it becomes not an empty or demonstrative sign but a mark or breath. As he put it a few years later, 'I believe that when an artist is young and energetic, he/she tends to create very rational artworks. As we get older and experience more, our artworks employ more emotion and sentiments, even if we still use a very rational structure or framework.'[3]

As always, his explorations were conducted in parallel with drawing, or works on paper. The very large paper work *Appearance of Crosses 2013-B2* (fig.82) extended both this notion of floating and the sense of the clusters of crosses being more organic, like islands in a sea or, if we dare say it, water lilies in a pond. The colours are overtly soft and lyrical. He was exploring a particular mood or sensation made possible by the use of chalk on corrugated paper, not trying to emulate Monet or the all-over paintings of Jackson Pollock – although a viewer may see similarities. But unlike Monet or Pollock, the grid is always there, however muted or cloaked. By the ensuing year he was letting colour dominate his paintings again, not just tint the predominant black and white.

From the start of the millennium Shanghai had been undergoing a comprehensive facelift as it prepared to hold the 2010 World Expo. Old quarters disappeared under the bulldozers and new housing projects were scattered everywhere in the city. At the Shanghai Institute of Visual Arts Ding Yi was given the task of creating a new school of public art to meet the increasing demands of the booming real-estate firms. It was the first such programme to be founded in China. But in agreeing to head this new course he stipulated that he would stop after seeing the first intake of students through the four years. (As the programme started in 2011 this meant that when the first cohort graduated in 2015 he was finally able to cease teaching.) In the curriculum that Ding Yi designed, much emphasis was given to project-based research. Starting from thinking about space, the students were encouraged to develop their conceptual ideas into real-life practices. The hand-making process was an important part of learning in Ding Yi's classes. Instead of showing a 3D sketch model on a computer, he always asked his students to present their works with a handmade model, a practice that he brought with him from his years of teaching experience in the Arts and Crafts College. Projects were set in actual places whose history and ethos or spirit students had to explore and respond to. He also insisted that there should be no more than 50 students in each year – the days of classes of a select five students were long gone!

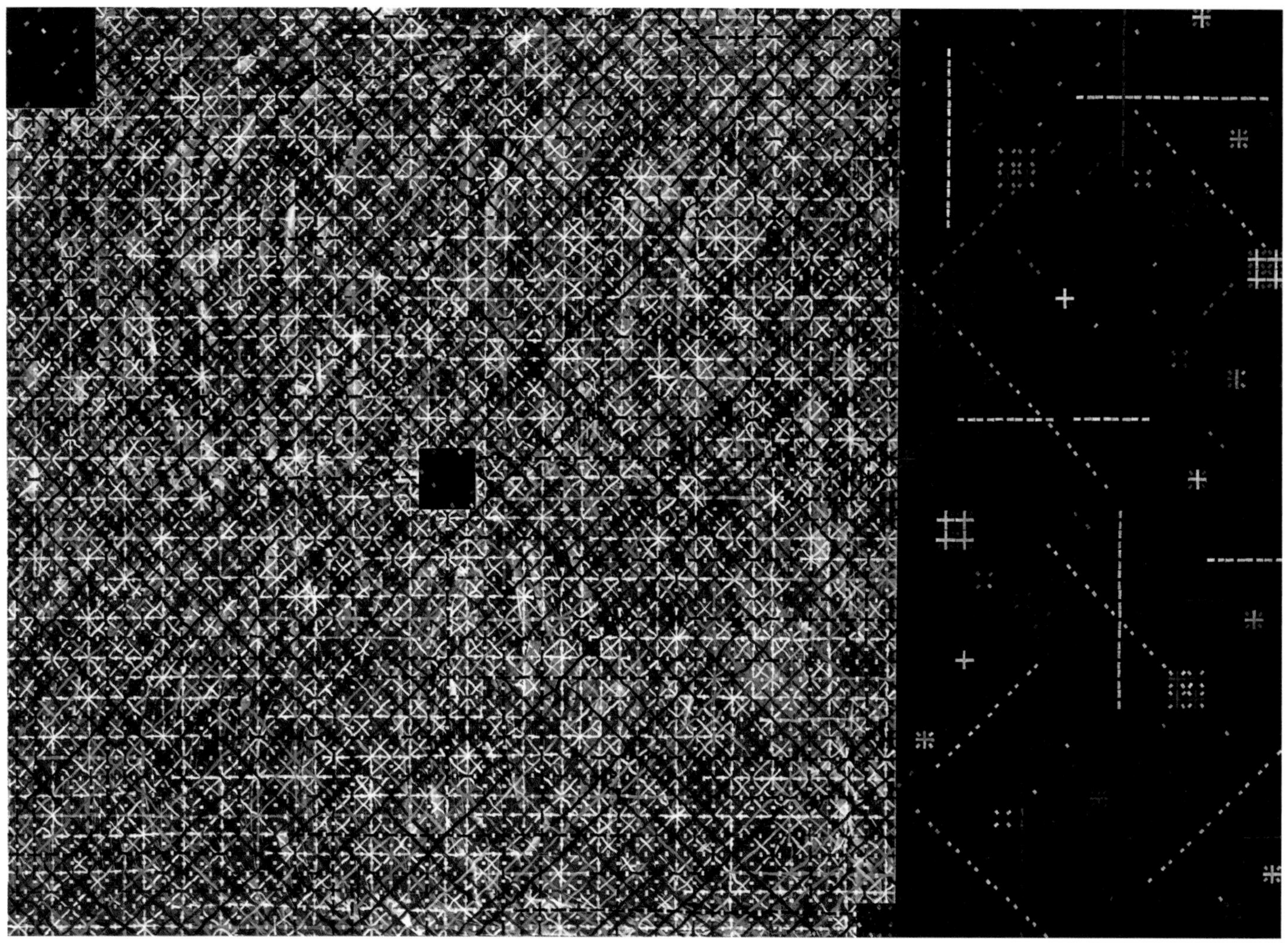

79. Appearance of Crosses 2012-13   2012

Acrylic on canvas
140 × 200 cm (55⅛ × 78¾ in)
Private collection, Beijing

80. **Appearance of Crosses 2012-B13**   2012

Acrylic on paper
32 × 43 cm (12½ × 17 in)
Private collection

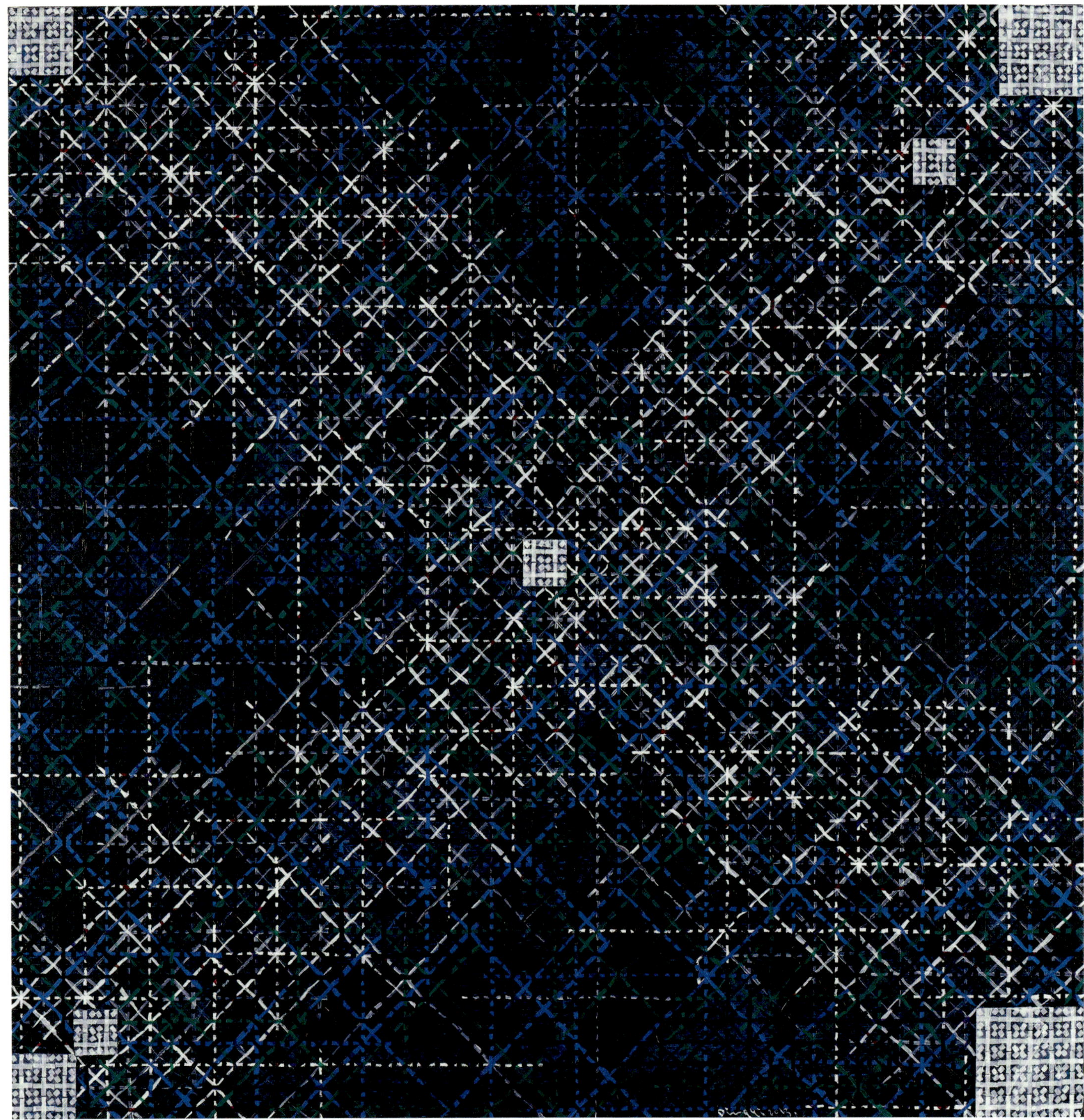

81. Appearance of Crosses 2013-7   2013

Acrylic on canvas
100 × 100 cm (39⅜ × 39⅜ in)
Private collection, Shanghai

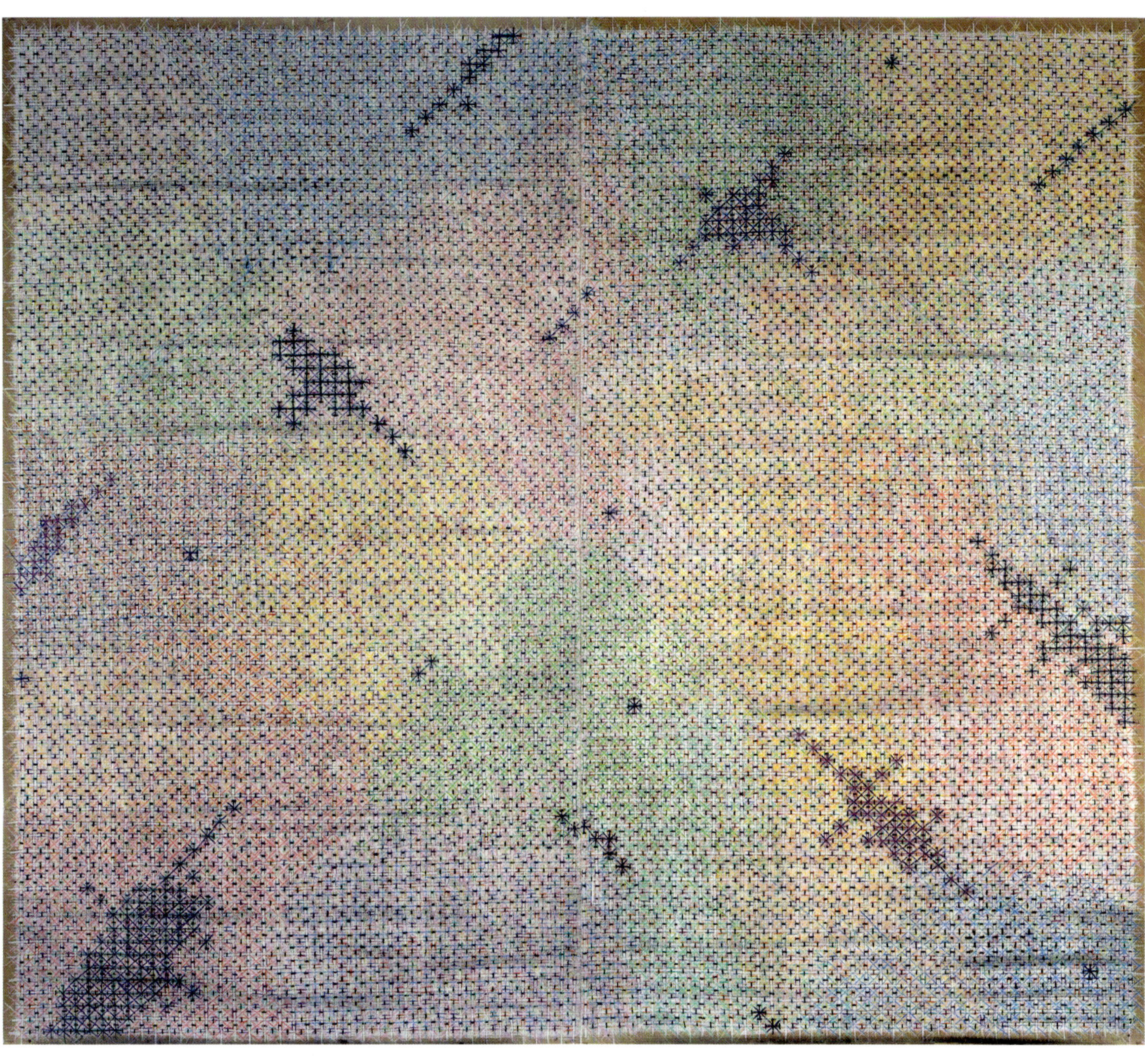

82. Appearance of Crosses 2013-B2   2013

Chalk, pencil and charcoal on corrugated paper
320 × 364 cm (126 × 143¼ in)
Private collection, Shanghai

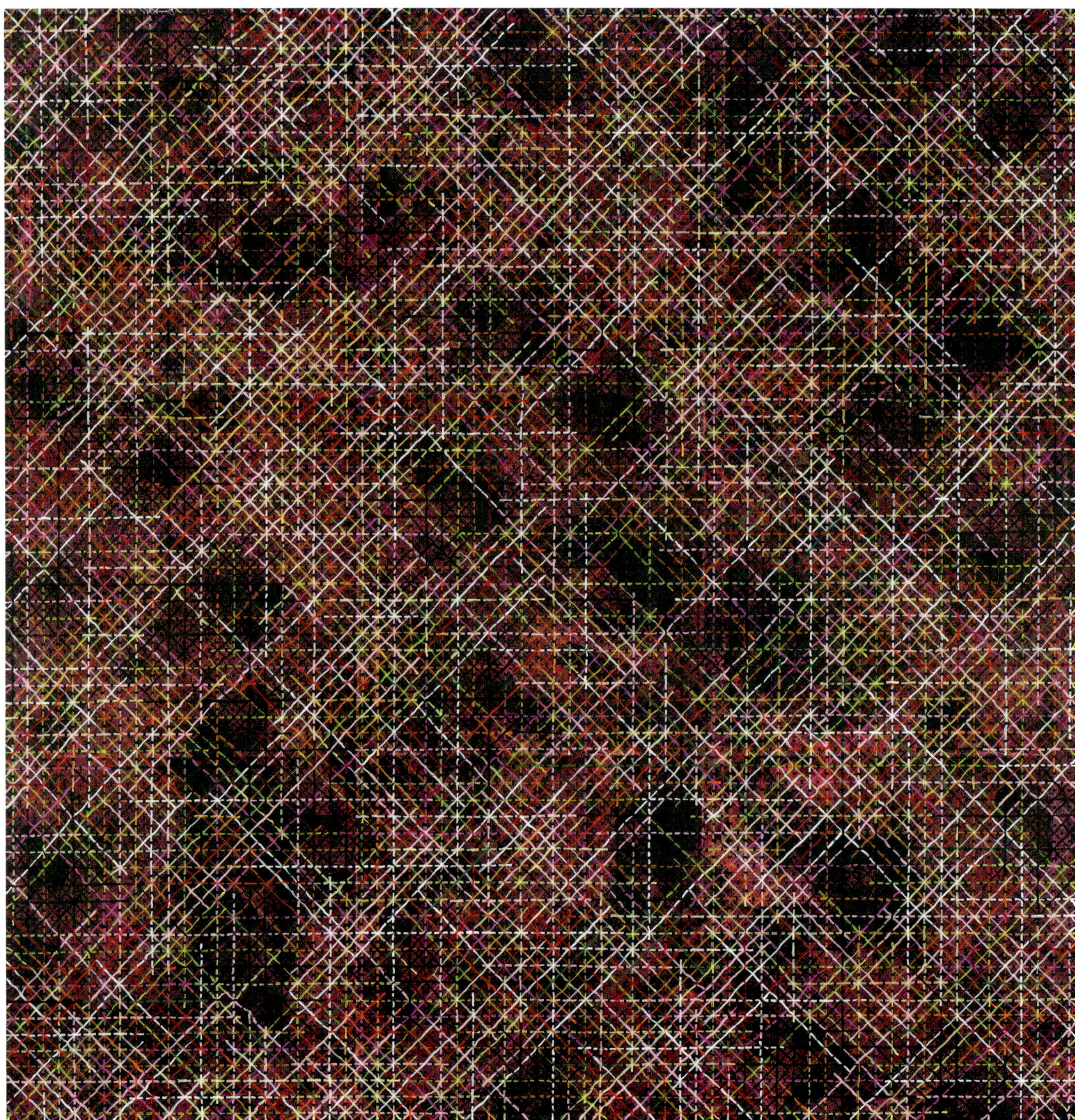

83. Appearance of Crosses 2014-2   2014

Acrylic on canvas
200 × 200 cm (78¾ × 78¾ in)
Private collection

84. Appearance of Crosses 2014·11   2014

Acrylic on canvas
200 × 200 cm (78¾ × 78¾ in)
Private collection

The 2010 World Expo was a high point in Shanghai's evolution as a world capital for trade and commerce. In the new post-Expo economy which followed, in 2012 the Shanghai municipal government initiated the new 'art and cultural corridor' along the Huangpu river (a tributary of the Yangtse), to be known as the West Bund. The initiative offered land to private museums, galleries and artists with an overall ambition to build China's equivalent of New York's Museum Mile. With a series of cultural endeavours from both private capital and government agencies – including the Long Museum West Bund, the Yuz Museum, the Shanghai Center of Photography and a Chinese outpost of Centre Pompidou – the West Bund Museum Mile is beginning to take shape as a major cultural hub for Asia. In 2015 Ding Yi moved into a new studio in the West Bund, close to his gallery ShanghArt and the Yuz Museum. Dating from when the area was the centre of Shanghai's marine and aviation industry, Ding Yi's new studio, which was the maintenance hangar for planes from the nearby domestic airport, is far larger than his previous one, and with much taller walls. Clean and airy, a mezzanine holds his library, with space for materials underneath.

In summer 2014 he met Frank Stella at the opening of Stella's exhibition in Switzerland. Facing the then 78-year-old pioneer of minimalism and the artist whose work had once had such an effect on him, Ding Yi was thrilled but also bewildered:

The whole exhibition felt for me like an exhibition of sculptures, not paintings. It is hard to imagine that this is the same Frank Stella, the rational and dynamic hero in my heart, who is now making art like a child playing with toys. They are free and spontaneous, but in my view, the lack of his original signature geometric forms and stripes is disheartening. His art work has become decorative. Does it mean that pursuing spirituality through minimal art is a mission impossible?[5]

It was a question that Ding Yi wanted to raise with Stella, but he posed it to himself and his peers first. For the past decades, Western art has been a strong influence on Chinese artists, but more and more Ding Yi feels the stimulation of Chinese society and the urge to reflect this dynamic time with a new imagery, an imagery that in his words 'might be able to preserve some kind of cultural ambition for the future'.

Ding Yi was invited to show in the Long Museum in 2015 (fig.85). He prepared a group of ten large (480 × 240 cm, 189 × 94½ in) double square paintings on wood. 'Why paint on wood?' one may ask. As always, just as he had suspended some of his paintings from the ceiling in the large austere space of Minsheng Art Museum to stop it looking like an aeroplane hangar, he was concerned to respond to and work with the space. The Long Museum has a beautiful, austere, elegant interior but its walls are high and made of concrete, hard and cold. He felt canvas did not have enough weight to compete. Using a new type of surface was also part of his programme of challenging himself, and part of his undiminished desire to work against different surfaces and textures. The fact he could carve back into the wood opened another area for him to explore.

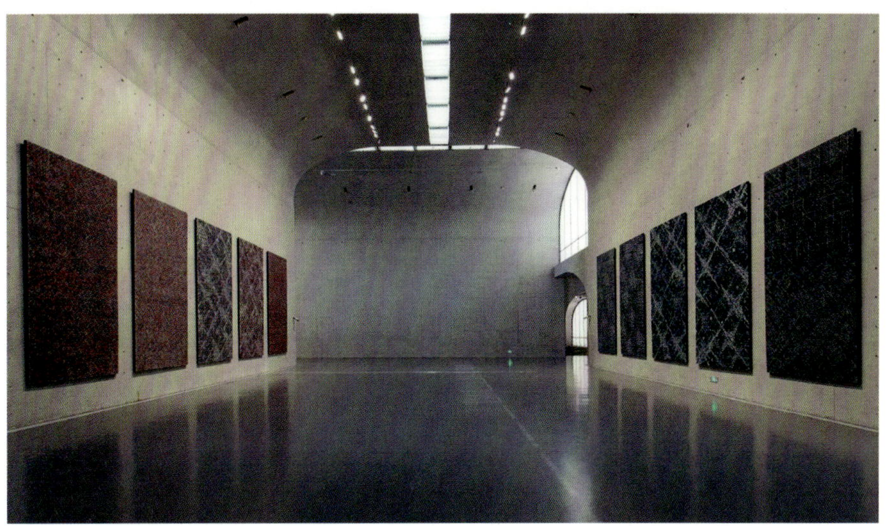

85. Ding Yi's solo exhibition at the Long Museum, Shanghai, 2015

Though painted together and related one to another the works were not one unit, and he could have no expectation that any one collector or museum would be willing to buy and house such a group. The pleasure of seeing such similar, related but different paintings was only for those who saw this exhibition.

In *Appearance of Crosses 2015-1* (fig.86) red underlay the black ground, while in others, such as *Appearance of Crosses 2015-8* (fig.88) with blue and green, two colours underlay the black. Digging in with his wood-carving tools was like excavating, exposing not only the lower stratum of red in the case of *Appearance of Crosses 2015-1* and blue and green in *Appearance of Crosses 2015-8* but in every case the yellowish wood beneath. As in the later Xi'an works each painting was completed by digging out the interstices, so that the whole panel seemed to shine forth. The grid as the star-filled night sky.

As with the exhibition at the Minsheng Art Museum, the catalogue for this exhibition was also important. It was a very large format with the ten paintings on one double-page spread and two fold-outs each showing four paintings. Full-page details of five of them were also included. As in this book, the paintings were reproduced with floor and surrounding walls shown so as to highlight their architectonic status. The details served to emphasise their immersive nature when viewed close to.

After this solo exhibition at Shanghai's Long Museum in 2015, Ding Yi announced ambitiously that he would make a solo exhibition each year in a different city in China. The first such exhibition was in the Hubei Museum of Art, Wuhan, in 2016, where he showed eight new square paintings on wood, each 240 cm (94½ in) square, including *Appearance of Crosses 2015-15* (fig.92). For this and all his subsequent exhibitions outside Shanghai, Shi Yong, himself an important avant-garde artist of Ding Yi's generation, who works as the art director of ShanghArt gallery, has taken on the role of exhibition designer. 'There are always unexpected space shortages or unsatisfactory layouts that need both smart solutions and quality control among many provincial museums', Ding

86. Appearance of Crosses 2015-1   2015

Mixed media on basswood
480 × 240 cm (189 × 94½ in)
Private collection, Hong Kong

87. Appearance of Crosses 2015-1
2015 (detail)

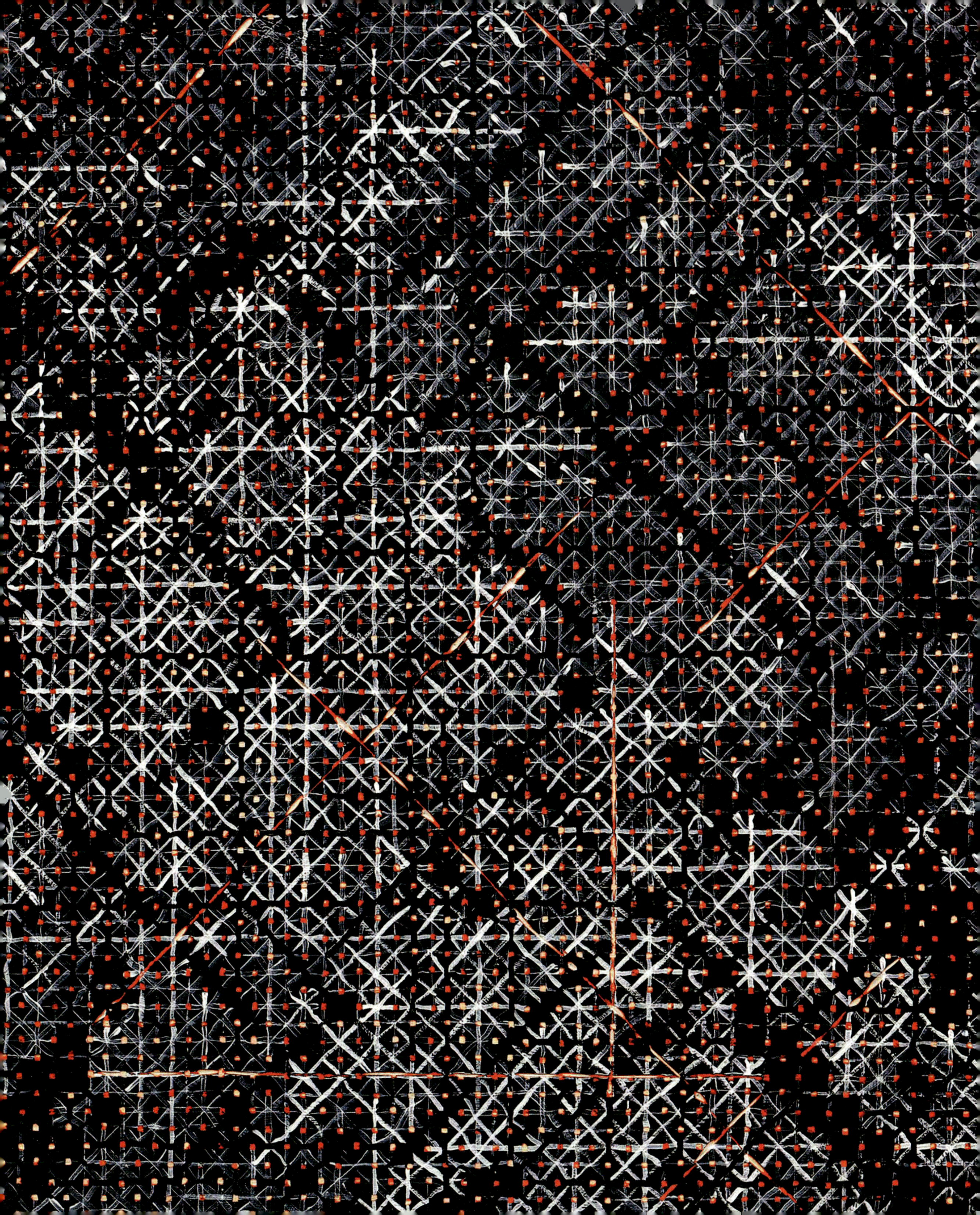

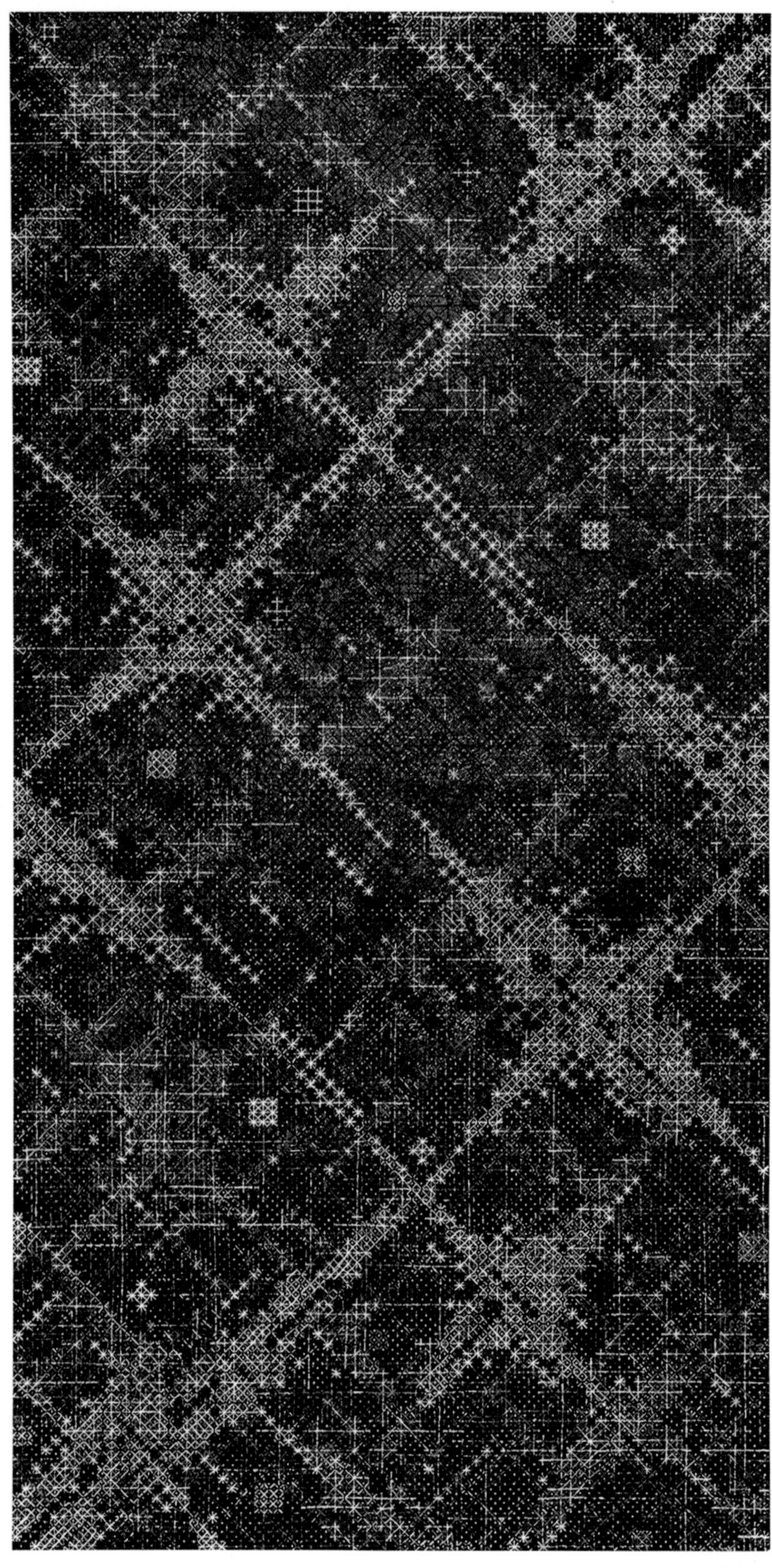

88. Appearance of Crosses 2015-8   2015

Mixed media on basswood
480 × 240 cm (189 × 94½ in)
Collection of Long Museum, Shanghai

89. Appearance of Crosses 2015-8
2015 (detail)

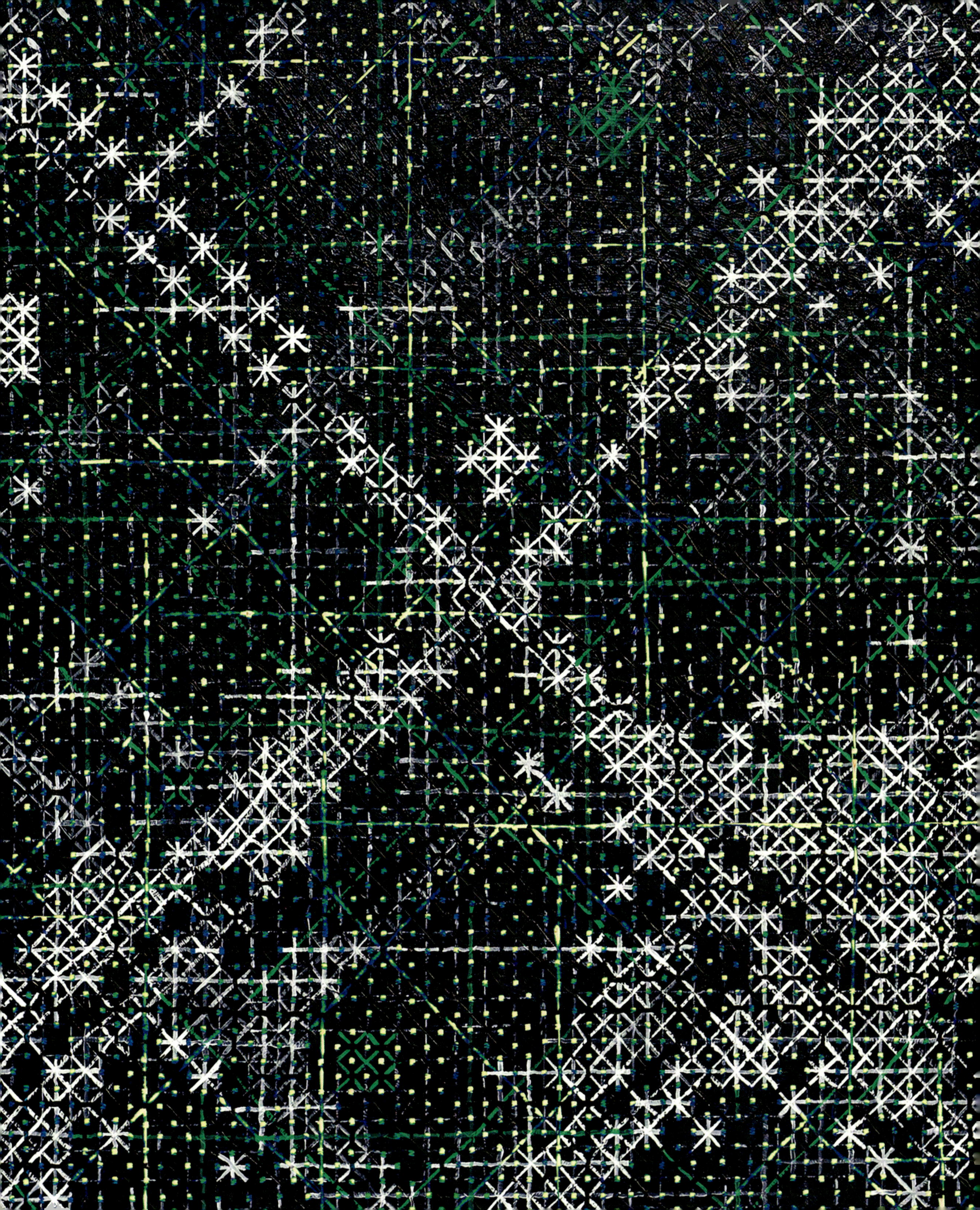

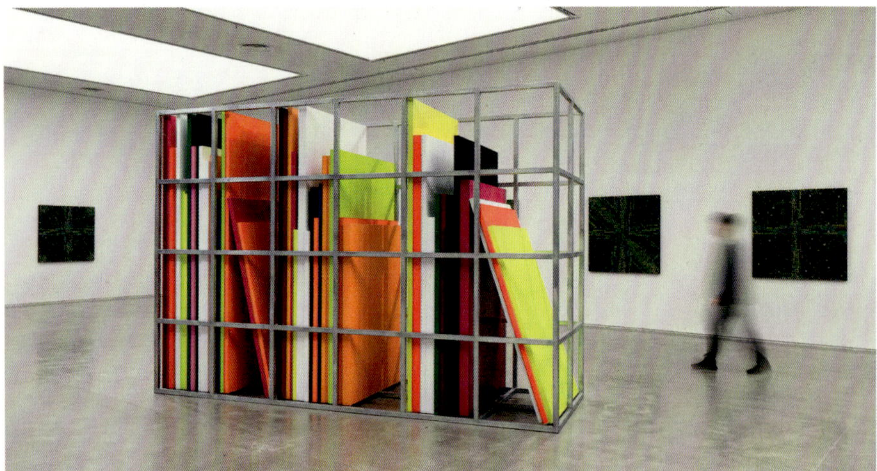

90. Painting Stand   2018 (42 pieces)

Aluminium alloy (painted aluminium 'honeycore' hex
panels), galvanised-steel frame, steel plate
Frame: 388 × 132 × 260 cm (152¾ × 52 × 102⅜ in);
plates (47 pieces in total): biggest 252 × 120 × 4 cm
(99¼ × 47¼ × 1½ in), smallest 146 × 120 × 4 cm
(57½ × 47¼ × 1½ in)

Yi told us. 'Shi Yong has initiated a concept of the installation: it always starts with
my newest works (always the monumental ones) in the main hall of the museum. In
Xi'an the entrance hall had three large pillars that Shi Yong had to connect together
with fake walls to create an entity. In Wuhan Museum the wall is not big enough for
my large paper work *2013-B1* (400 × 1267 cm; 13⅛ × 41½ foot) so Shi Yong has to
create a tilting wall to allow more space. As viewers we enter the inner part of the
museum and as the ceilings get lower, there are often works from earlier period and
of smaller scale. In Xi'an they even painted the walls with light yellow and green as
marks to separate works from different periods.'

All these new works were painted in black, white and grey, though inflected by
the yellowish brown of the exposed wood where he had cut through the paint. He had
set himself the challenge of creating eight different paintings without depending on
colour coding. He also showed 58 older paintings, beginning with *Breaking the Shrine*,
and nearly as many paper or small works, including *Appearance of Crosses 2013-B7*
(fig.91).

The Xi'an exhibition we discussed in Chapter 1 was the second outcome of this
annual commitment. The exhibition in Xi'an had the same format – new large works
and a selection of earlier pieces going back to 1986, when the cross first appeared in
his work. The paintings and drawings were hung not chronologically but thematically,
to show the contrasts and continuities in his work. As always, it is clear how
concerned Ding Yi was with the way the exhibition looked as a whole. He had the
rooms specially rebuilt, and designed the entrance to the exhibition, also placing a
sculpture outside the museum.

In 2018 when he exhibited the eight square paintings we discussed in Chapter 1
at ShanghArt he also exhibited a complex steel-and-aluminium sculpture (fig.90). It
was complex not so much in its box and stack of metal 'paintings' but in the colour
relationships that were set up.

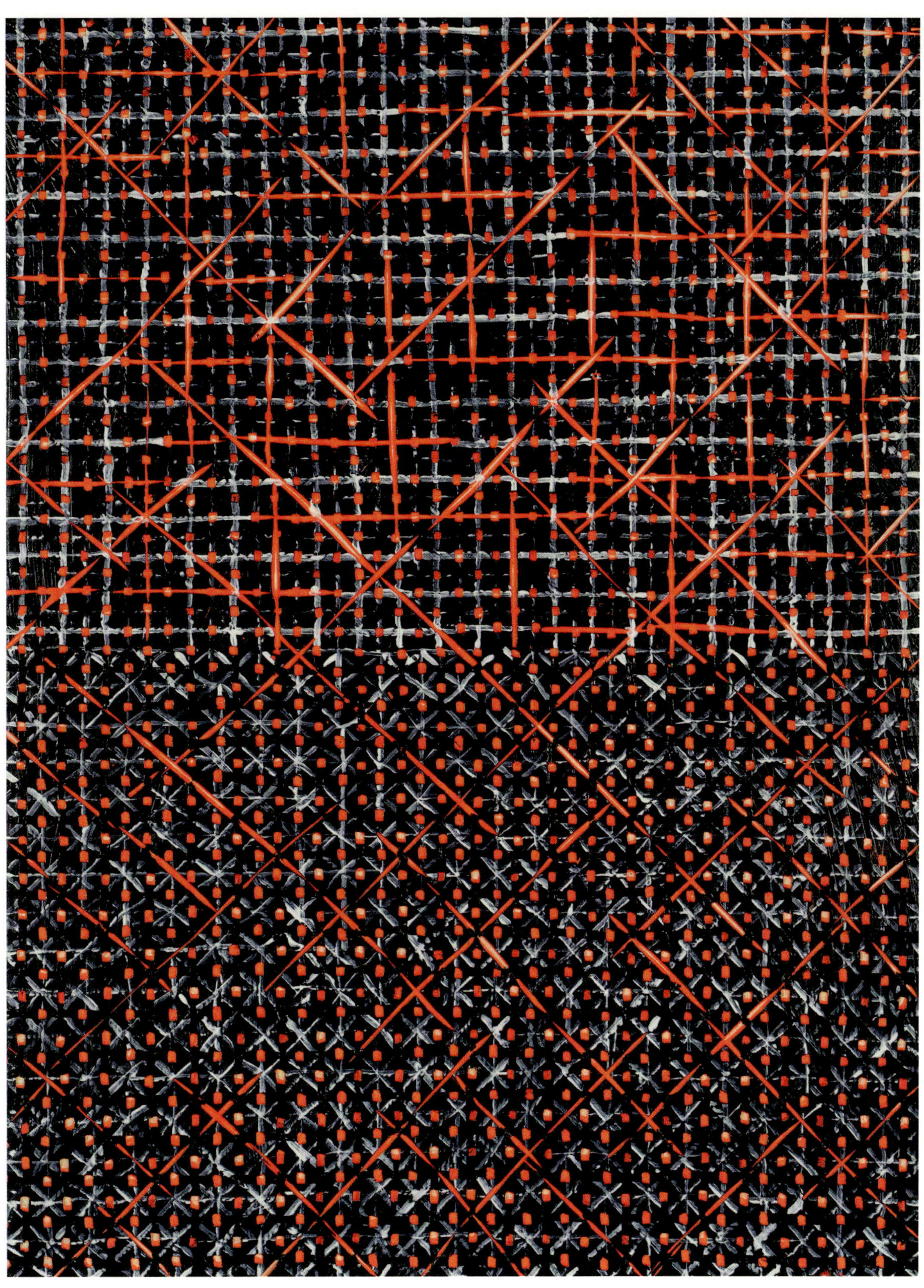

91. Appearance of Crosses 2015-B7   2015

Mixed media on basswood
60 × 45 cm (23⅝ × 17¾ in)
Private collection

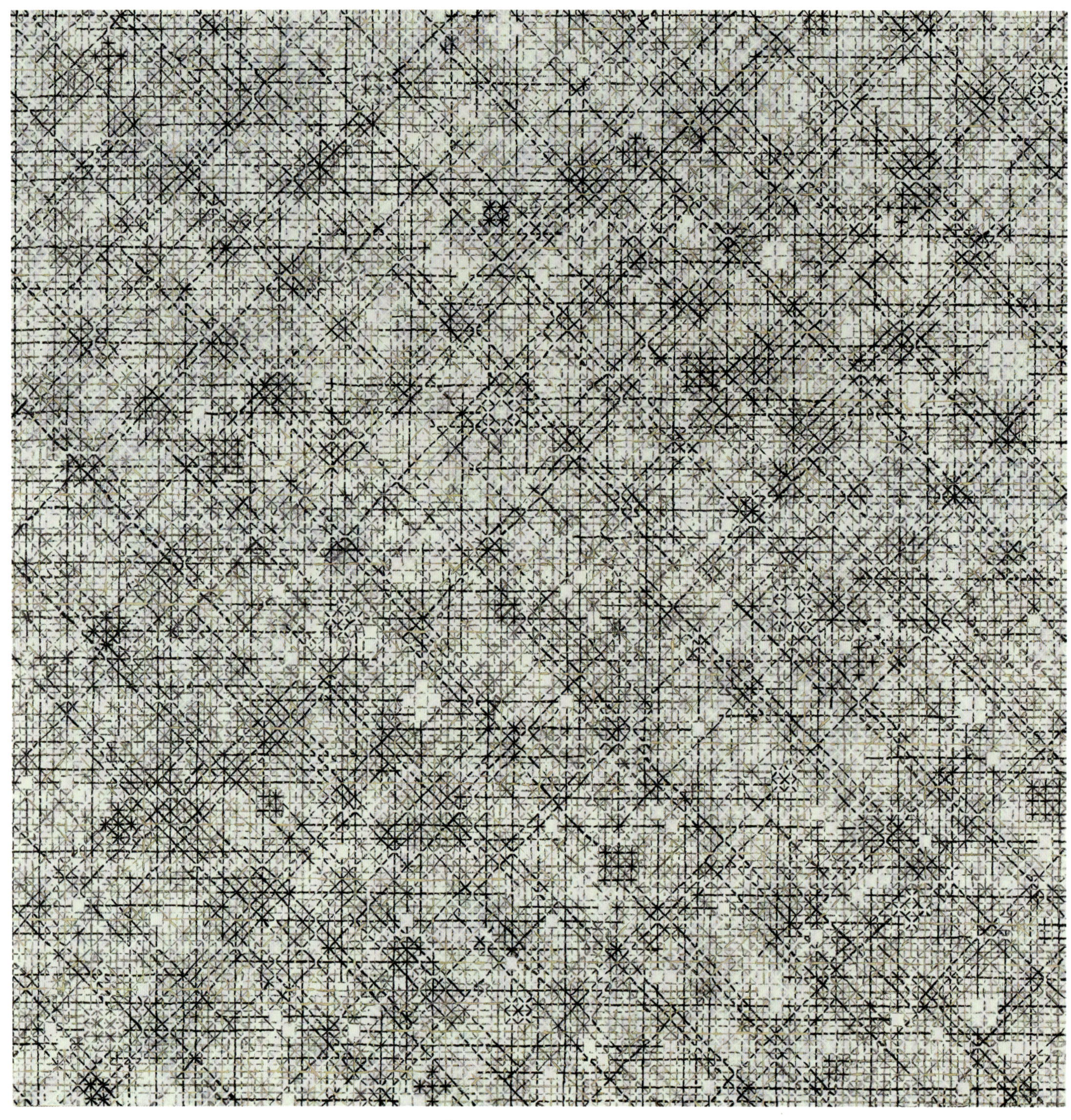

92. Appearance of Crosses 2015-15   2015   93. Appearance of Crosses 2015-15   2015 (detail)

Mixed media on basswood
240 × 240 cm (94½ × 94½ in)
Private collection, Hong Kong

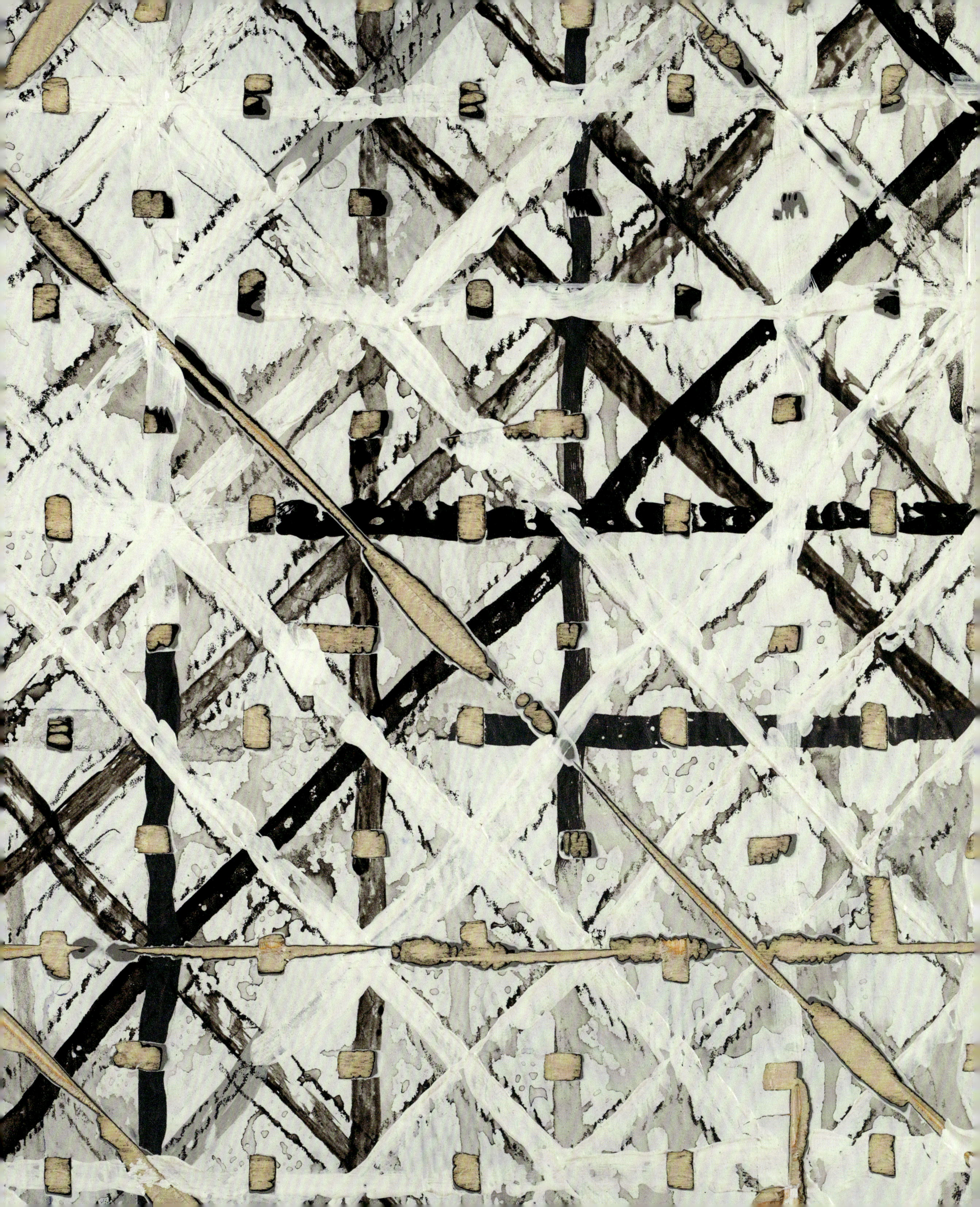

An architectural work in the same year was the *Mountain House* he designed for Chongqing, a mountainous megacity in south-west China (fig.95). From outside the house looks like an accumulation of precast concrete panels, but as one goes inside one becomes aware that the light leaking through the cross-generated windows and doors creates a dynamic rhythm. As we have discussed, Ding Yi's large paintings create a sense of both immersion and immensity, absorption and the architectonic; his architecture and its site here evoke similar sensations, in a rather surprisingly romantic way.

Whereas Ding Yi's two-dimensional paintings, whatever their different materials, are engaged in making a complex pictorial space – think, for example, of the sensation of vertigo we experience when facing a large painting such as *Appearance of Crosses 2018-2* (fig.96) – his three-dimensional works, whether they are architecture or sculpture, bring his crosses into an exploration of the world outside. If we consider Marcel Duchamp's notion of a two-dimensional projection as the shadow of the three-dimensional world, then the three-dimensional world as we know it can be seen as the projection of the four-dimensional universe. *Mountain House* most especially seems to suggest the existence of a fourth dimension.

In October 2018 Ding Yi's third annual exhibition opened in Guangzhou at the Guangdong Art Museum (fig.94). If Xi'an represents ancient China with its splendid culture, then the story of Guangzhou (formerly Canton) is about foreign trade. From the mid-18th century it was the only port open to Western traders, who did not just purchase tea, silk and local products but also brought Western-style artefacts to China, including glass paintings and oil paintings. From the 1860s painting schools and workshops started to appear in Canton where Western-style painting techniques were taught to the Chinese artisans. In this way we can say that Canton is the birthplace of Western oil painting in China. After the Opium Wars of 1839-42 and 1856-60, China was forced to open more ports to the foreign powers, but Canton continued to play an important role in China's foreign trade. During the Cultural Revolution, when China was isolated from the outside world, the Canton Fair was the only foreign trade fair that kept operating. When the open-door policy in the 1980s started the process of economic reform, Guangzhou once again attracted people from all over China to come and make money by trading. Guangzhou is close to Hong Kong both geographically and culturally (Cantonese is spoken in both), so it was always a place where fashionable clothes, movies and pop music could be imported. In the minds of the Chinese people, Guangzhou represents trendy fashion, Western influences and a business-driven mindset.

Guangdong Art Museum is located on Ersha Island in the centre of the Pearl River. On such islands, the British and French built their enclave after the Second Opium War. In modern times, many of these islands on the Pearl River have been turned into luxury residential areas with high-end, Western style buildings and lush parks surrounding them. On a fine day in mid-autumn, the island is filled

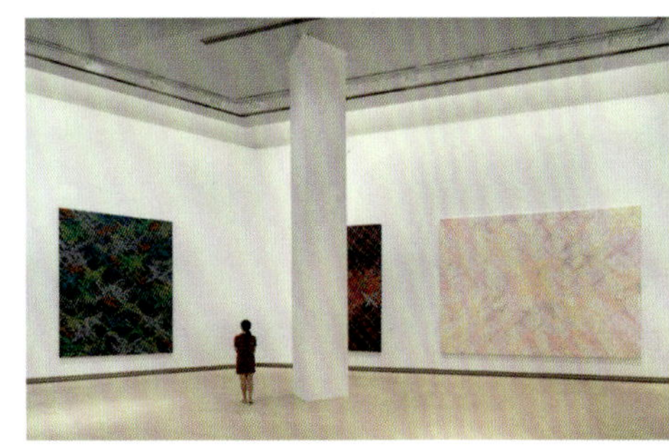

94. Installation shot of Ding Yi's solo exhibition in Guandong Art Museum, 2018

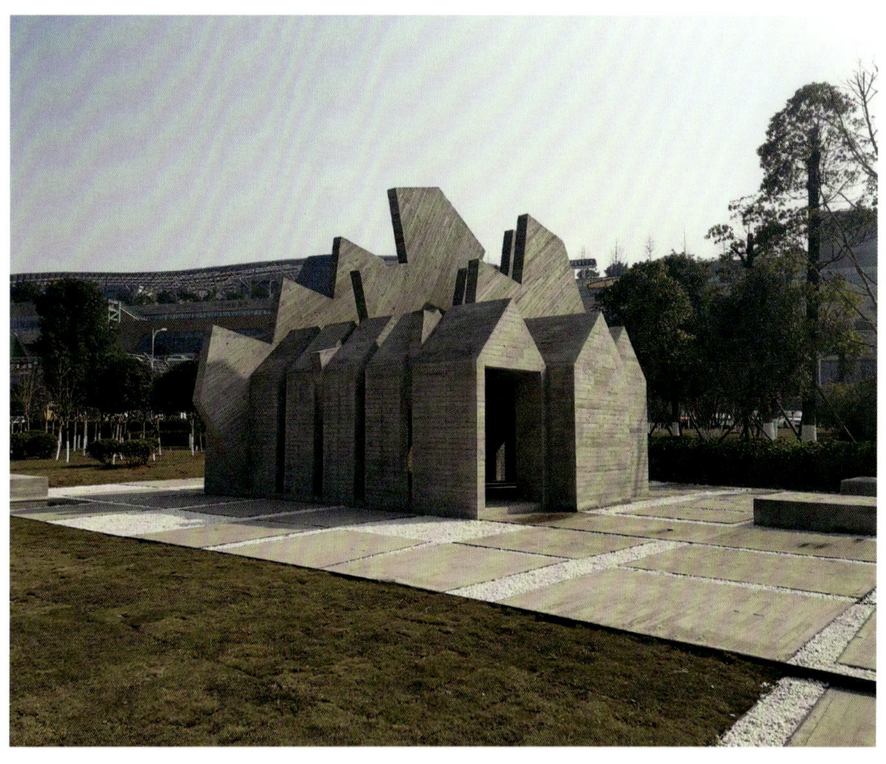

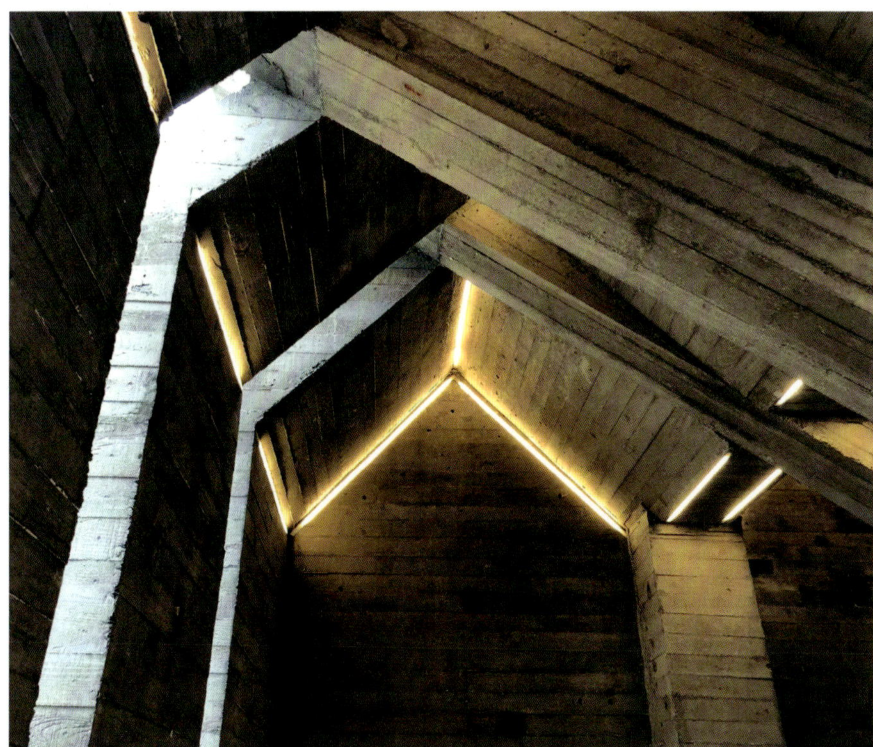

95. **Mountain House**, Yuelai New Town,
Chongqing, 2018

Concrete, LED light
Building: 7.5(L) × 8(W) × 6.3(H) m (24½ × 26¼ × 20½ ft)
Chongqing Yuelai Group

with tourists from all over China: newly-wed couples in Western wedding outfits pose for photos on these greens. In front of the Guangdong Art Museum a few curious tourists stop and stare at the large poster on the museum as if at some kind of secret code. In square block fonts, in yellow and black colours, it says 'Ding Yi + × 30'.

Interviewed for the catalogue of this show by He Jing, Ding Yi recalled, 'I've been working as an artist for thirty years . . . I've been in my studio daily, working on the canvas closely. What that means is, I think I've been totally immersed in my canvas. I think the process is best described as a kind of "enlightenment".'[6]

He does not go on to elaborate what this may mean, only adding, 'the only thing you need to think about is producing a good painting. And you need to fully live your own experiences and express or reveal them.' It is certainly not 'enlightenment' in the full Buddhist sense, but inevitably it has spiritual connotations. The word has appeared recurrently as we have seen: in his 2007 essay, 'Deconstructing the Abstract', he had claimed that 'form was the spirit,' and that the job of the painter was 'to reveal the general spiritual power about this living era'.[7]

What does this mean? Ding Yi is not a practising member of any religion, church or sect. In an essay for the 2009 Bologna exhibition Cao Weijun uses the term 'spirit' no fewer than 19 times: 'spirit of self-discipline', 'spiritual power', 'expression of spirituality', 'spiritual quality', 'the spiritual meaning of his works', 'pursuit of spirituality', 'the Chinese spirit.' It is a multivalent word that can mean the mood or character of an age, or a sense of something immanent or deeper.

A related question that Ding Yi has increasingly asked himself in recent years is, 'Where is the new spirituality in abstract paintings?' The references he uses in the discussion with He Jing are the leading figures of abstract painting, such as Kazimir Malevich:

> I keep thinking about Malevich's white-on-white work. When I compare my work with his, I can't help but feel my own is full of waffle. It's really difficult to attain that kind of absolute spirit, as he did. My reaction to that is to ask: where's the new spirituality? How do you express it? What method should you use? The answer of course, is to use your own method – not Malevich's – and use it to extract something more powerful for your painting.[8]

The exhibition started on the second floor inside the star-shaped museum building. The largest hall of the museum was given to the monumental-scale works including several new paintings made especially for the exhibition. The walls were bathed in even and bright lighting that allowed the paintings to float in a harmonious atmosphere. 'For the Guangdong museum the lighting in the main hall was specially adjusted to create a smooth environment without shadows', Ding Yi remarks. His exhibition designer, Shi Yong, adds, 'Every centimetre of those walls had been illuminated. That was perhaps the most expensive part of the installation.' The paintings, however, shifted through different colour zones. *Appearance of Crosses 2018-2* (fig.96), like its predecessor *Appearance of Crosses 2018-1* (fig.12), is predominantly red and black with scattered yellow, green, white and even pink colours used to mark crosses and draw lines. The clusters of red crosses seem magnetised so that they all face in one direction.

The 11th-century Chinese poet Su Shi alluded to the grand experience of a mountain hike, and the awe and wonder he felt at the spectacle of nature:

> Viewing the mountain peaks and valleys, horizontally and vertically
> Various shapes and forms from near and from far.

But the poem's inner meaning lies in the last two lines:

> I cannot grasp the complete truth about the Lu mountains
> Simply because I am amidst and surrounded by them.

Su Shi used the experience to illustrate how different ways of looking could bring different sensations in nature and thus, at the philosophical level, question the objectivity of beauty and truth. Although Ding Yi's paintings are far detached from any historical narratives that would relate to a Song Dynasty hike, nevertheless *Appearance of Crosses 2018-1* and *2018-2* could be seen as drawing on Ding Yi's visit a year previously to the National Geological Park at Yadan, near Dunhuang in western China, which is famous for multicoloured ridges and cliffs.[9] Ding Yi would only have been able to comprehend the valley in its entirety if he had possessed a drone to send flying above the rock formations to capture images. Nevertheless, some inner cognition led to abstract paintings which replicate the actual shapes of the rock formations.

> When I'd got two thirds of the way through *Appearance of Crosses 2018-1*, it suddenly occurred to me that the painting looked very much like the land formation I saw in Yadan in Dunhuang, where centuries of sand erosion has moulded the landscape in a particular way. I thought I should paint a similar piece but larger, with more going on in the picture. The new painting should also breakthrough in the sense of having more raised surfaces. A desire for the work to have an inclined impulse emerged. When I completed the larger *Appearance of Crosses 2018-2*, I began to wonder how I might alter the basic foundation of my paintings. That's why in the next piece, I began to reconfigure my colour scheme. In order to make the colours clearer, I thought some parts of the painting should be less saturated . . . So that's how my paintings began to link up and how each began to influence the next.[10]

96. Appearance of Crosses 2018-2   2018

97. Appearance of Crosses 2018-2
2018 (detail)

Mixed media on basswood
366 × 726 cm (144⅛ × 285⅞ in) (in 3 pieces)
Private collection

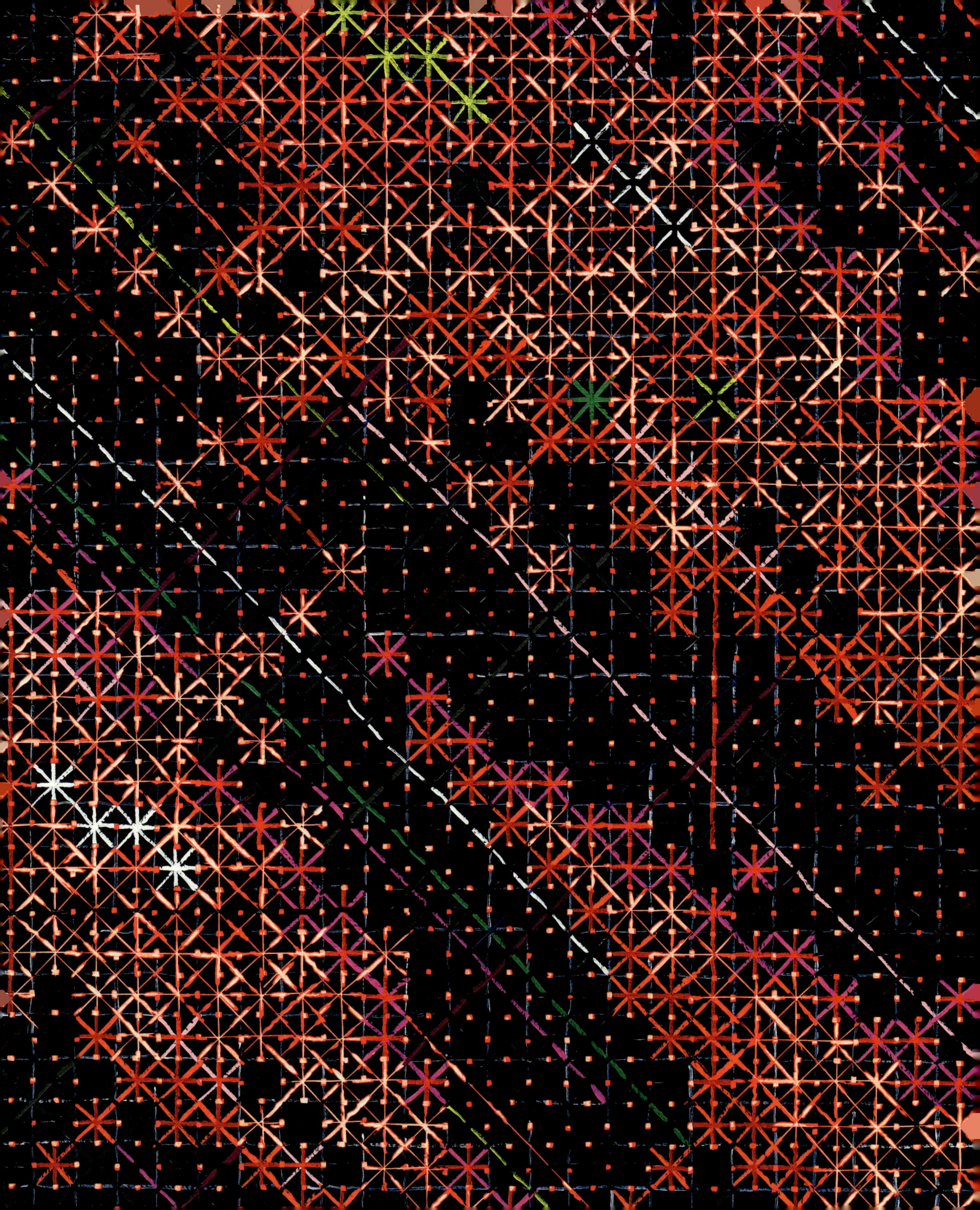

This linking, this way he moves from painting to painting, shows how his whole career can be seen as a game of Go. Take the centre! Take the corner! And it explains why at this late stage his work is as lively and varied as in the early 1990s: Do it differently! Use a different material!

The outcome of this thought was a group of works with less saturated colour, the largest of which was the 366 × 488 cm / 144⅛ × 190½ in *Appearance of Crosses 2018-8* (fig.98), specially made for Guangdong. The ground was now white, and by digging into it Ding Yi excavated reds and yellows, then overlaid them with yellow, blue, orange, greys, pinks, red and white again. After the muscular, powerful drive of a painting like *Appearance of Crosses 2018-2* this seems surprisingly pastoral. The lyrical, summery feel of these paintings is appropriate for the city of Guangzhou, which is known as the Garden City because its subtropical climate allows flowers to bloom all year round. Also in this opening room was the vast paper work *Appearance of Crosses 2017-B4* (350 × 792 cm / 137⅞ × 311¾ in) which was similar to the large paper work at Xi'an but far lighter in tonality and mood.

As always there was a section of the exhibition devoted to his drawings, including ones such as *Appearance of Crosses 2017-B20* (fig.99), where the colours had been toned down or minimised by a final application of white acrylic. Clearly, the drawings had paved the way for Ding Yi to lighten the paintings and make white, not red or black, the dominant colour. One way in which he has referenced his background in Chinese culture is in making a number of drawings in accordion books or scrolls. (They are exhibited in the same way as classical scrolls are exhibited in museums in China, spread out in a glass vitrine and viewed from above.) However, rather than the leisurely walk through a landscape of lakes and mountains that such scrolls traditionally provide they instead offer a set of formal variations on a circle form or, in *Variations on a Motif*, a square grid of about 16 by 16 crosses. Although the paper works never function as preparatory sketches for the paintings, we can see here he is working out configurations or clusters of marks that may emerge directly or indirectly in later works. 'I painted them at home, after dinner, on the dining table, under a reading lamp. Just a bit each day', Ding Yi remarked. Since 2009 he has used such accordion books to explore shapes and configurations in a series of themes and variations. They can be seen as creating a vocabulary of potential forms. They are also satisfying to look at, frame by frame, like listening to Bach work out and resolve a fugue.

In 2019 he postponed his intended annual exhibition outside Shanghai, as he had been invited to be part of a large exhibition in Shanghai Power Station of Art along with Yves Klein and Lee Ufan. Having secured the agreement of the Yves Klein Archives and Lee Ufan to participate, the curators had come to the conclusion that of all Chinese artists, Ding Yi was the best suited to show with these two masters. Of course, Ding Yi was very happy to exhibit with two such important artists of the 20th century, and he was interested to see what he would learn from the encounter.

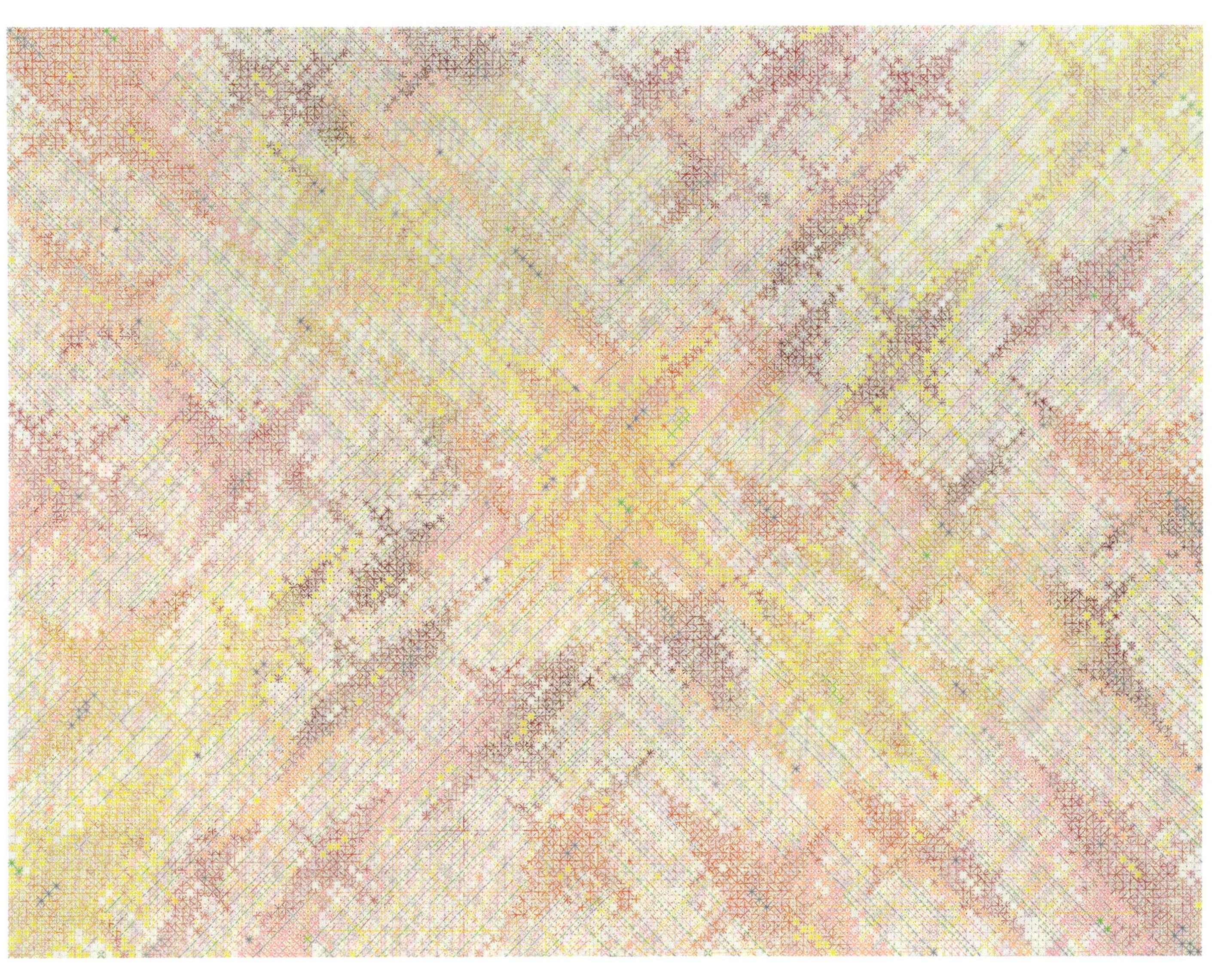

98. Appearance of Crosses 2018-8   2018

Mixed media on basswood
366 × 484 cm (144⅛ × 190½ in)
HEM (He Art Museum) collection, Shunde

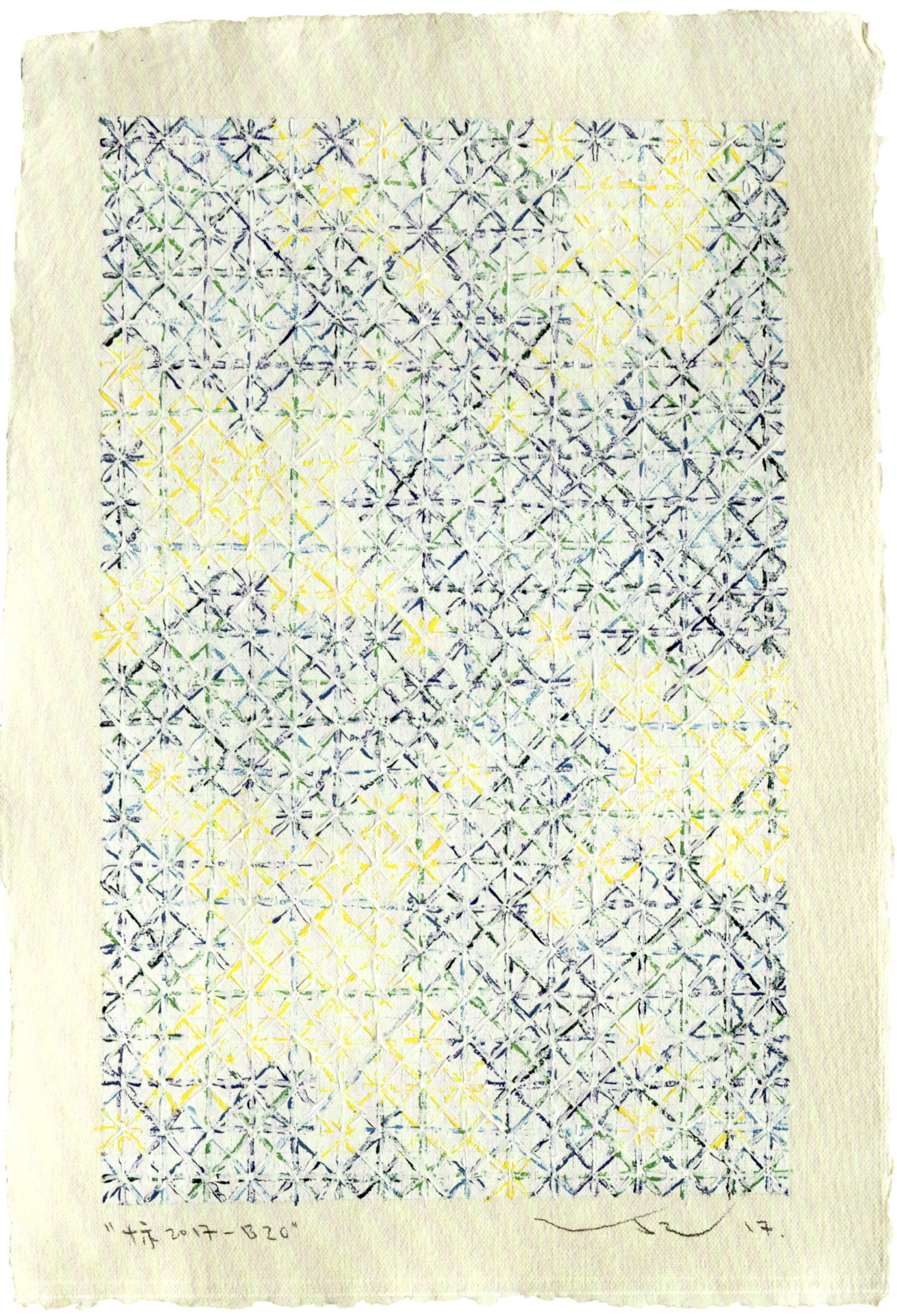

99. Appearance of Crosses 2017-B20   2017

Acrylic and colour pencil on paper
43 × 32 cm (17 × 12½ in)
Private collection

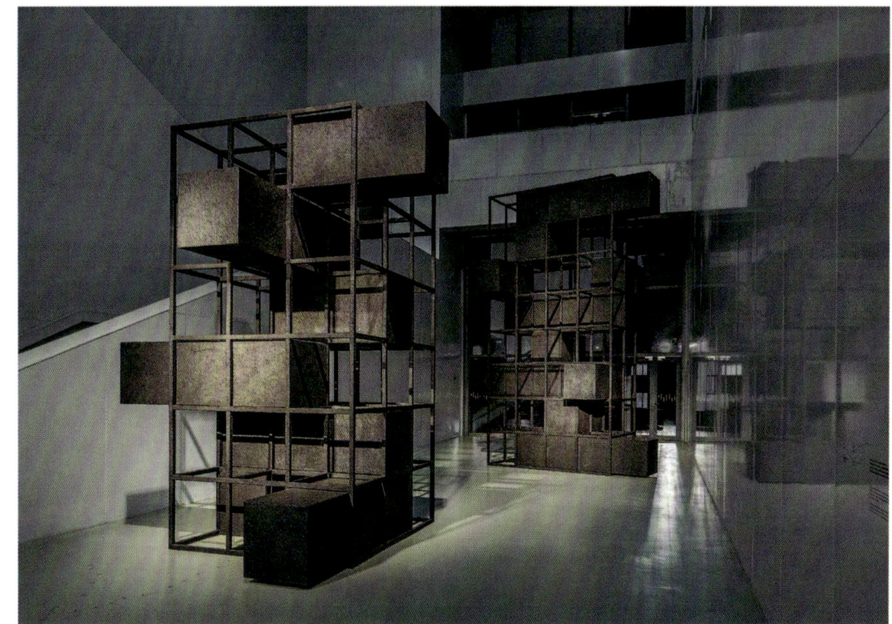

100. Installation view of *Object* at the exhibition *The Challenging Souls: Yves Klein, Lee Ufan, Ding Yi*, Power Station of Art, Shanghai, 2019
Cast aluminium, black patina, wax sealant
Two pieces: 388 × 196 × 196 cm (152¾ × 77⅛ × 77⅛ in); 512 × 132 × 260 cm (201½ × 52 × 102⅜ in)
Courtesy Power Station of Art

The exhibition was spectacular. The Yves Klein Archives allowed the re-creation of one of the artist's floor rectangles of International Klein Blue, the size of a large swimming pool. (The Power Station is, as the name suggests, an old power plant with some enormous spaces.)[11] A large room was given over to photo documentation of Klein's career: this fascinated the huge crowds that attended. Lee Ufan made sculptures and installations especially for the exhibition. Ding Yi made a new massive drawing, *Appearance of Crosses 2018-B3* (fig.101), utilising the boat shapes that had appeared in *Appearance of Crosses 2018-1*. As in most paintings subsequent to *Appearance of Crosses 2018-2*, the boat shapes orient themselves on both diagonals. Working thus in monochrome was an inevitable response to the monochrome nature of Klein's and Lee Ufan's paintings.

Ding Yi also showed some new paintings which expanded on those shown in Guangdong, each centred on a boat shape transformed into a cross. He filled one room with a survey of his drawings, and made his largest sculpture to date: *Object* (fig.100). With their grids, they seem something like Sol LeWitt's sculptures, but the module is far more complex with an emphasis on the craftsmanlike surface of the material, very different from LeWitt's.

The exhibition (and accompanying book) was entitled *The Challenging Soul*. 'Isn't the avant-garde an appeal to awaken souls rather than an ephemeral trend that appears and disappears anonymously?' the text at the start of the exhibition, entitled 'In the name of avant-garde', proposed. 'What should art challenge and be challenged by when the world is singing the fantasy of globalism, capitalism and the advent of technology-driven information society?'

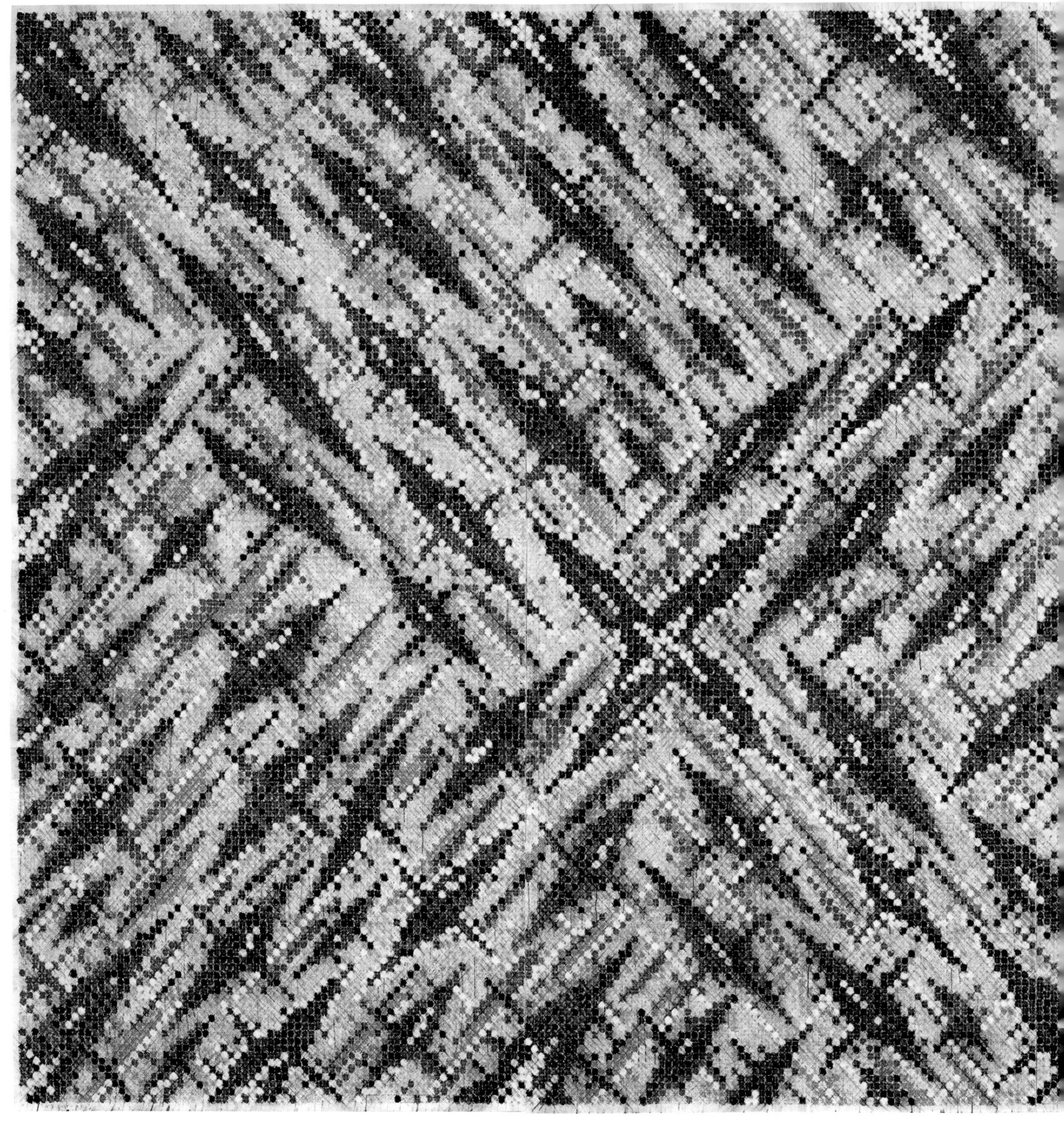

101. Appearance of Crosses 2018-B3   2018

Acrylic, pencil and chalk on ricepaper
450 × 936 cm (177⅛ × 368½ in)
Power Station of Art Collection, Shanghai

126

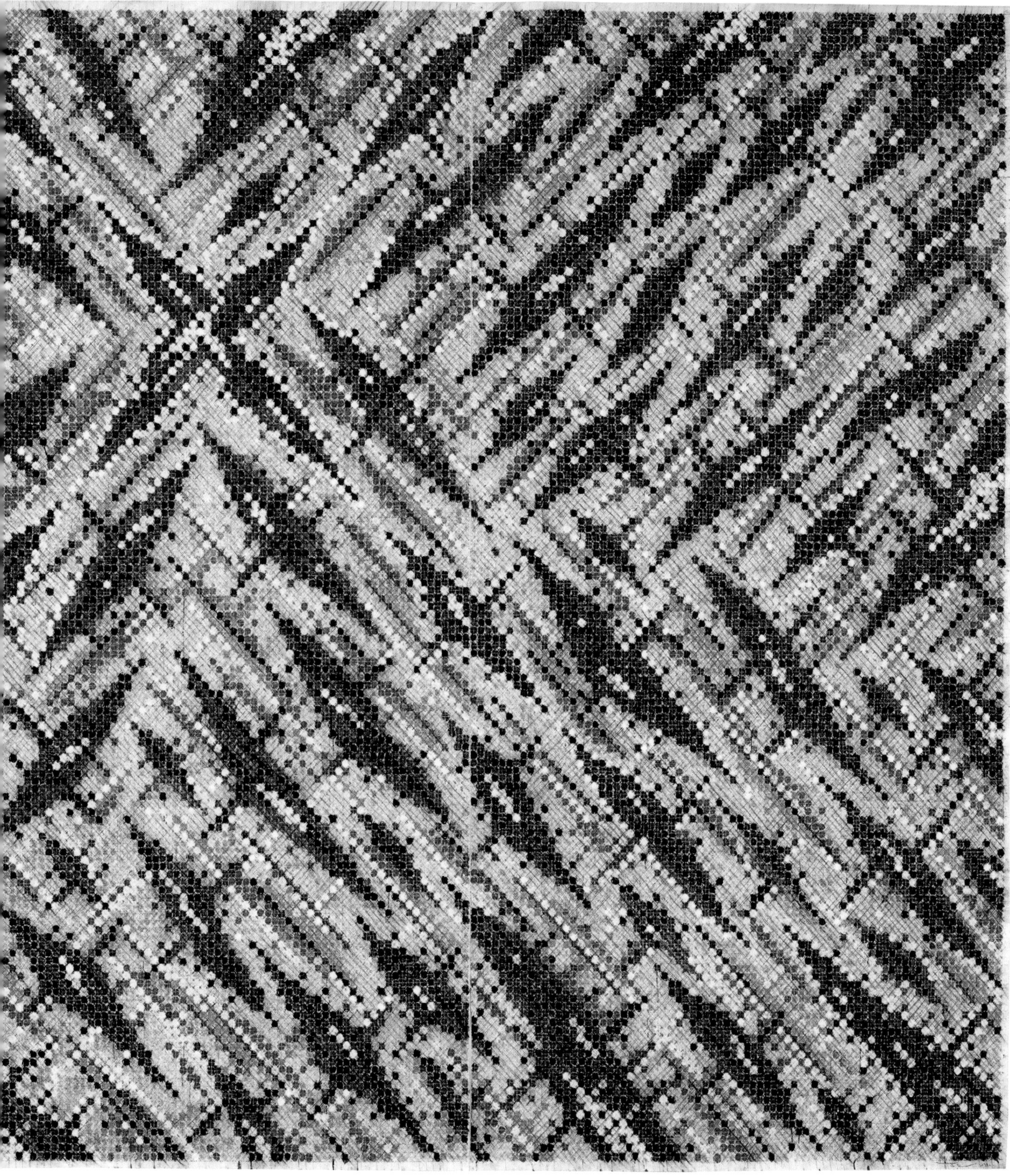

102. Appearance of Crosses 2019-1   2019

Mixed media on basswood
240 × 240 cm (94½ × 94½ in)
Private collection

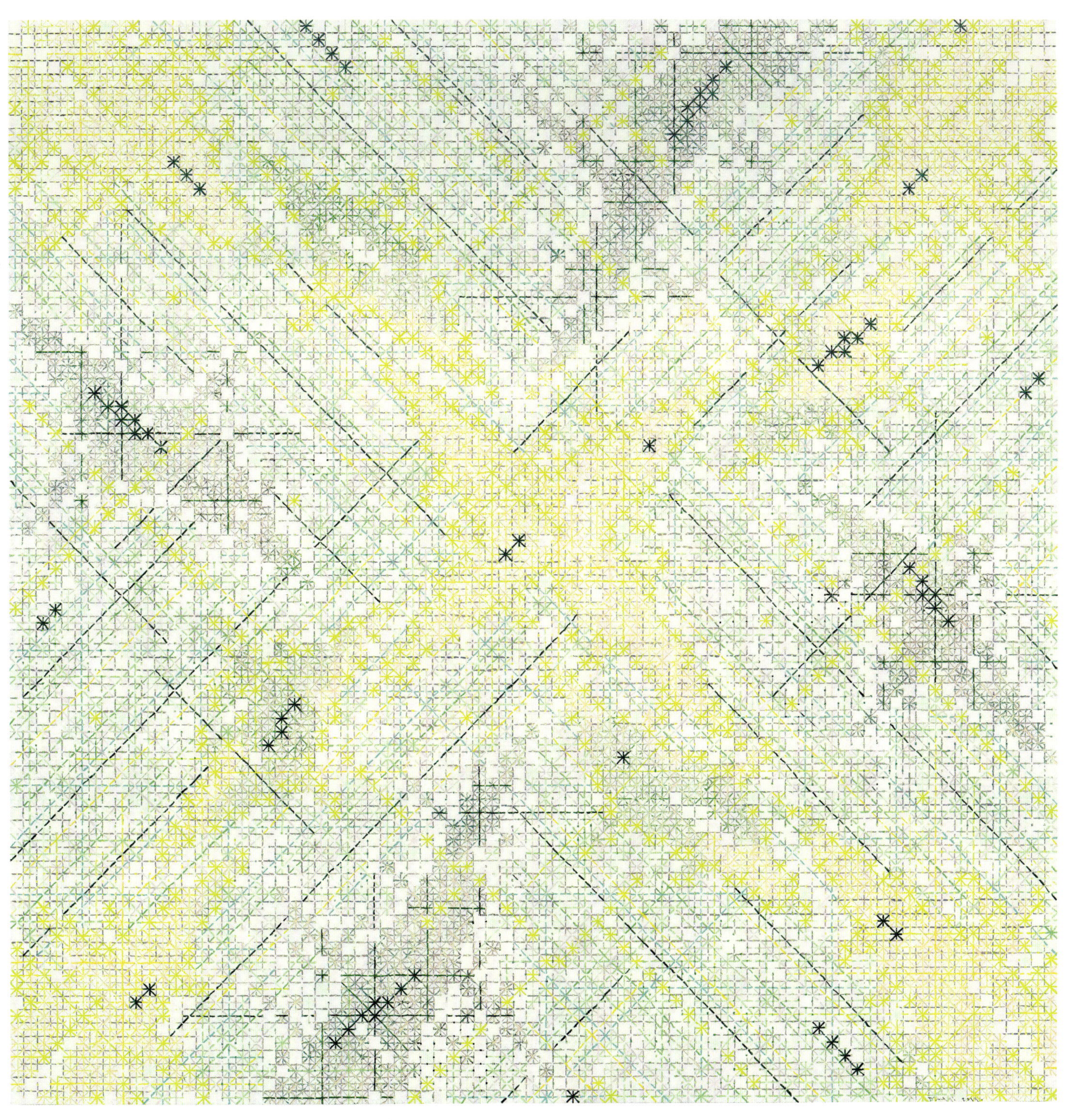

103. Appearance of Crosses 2019-2   2019

Mixed media on basswood
240 × 240 cm (94½ × 94½ in)
Private collection

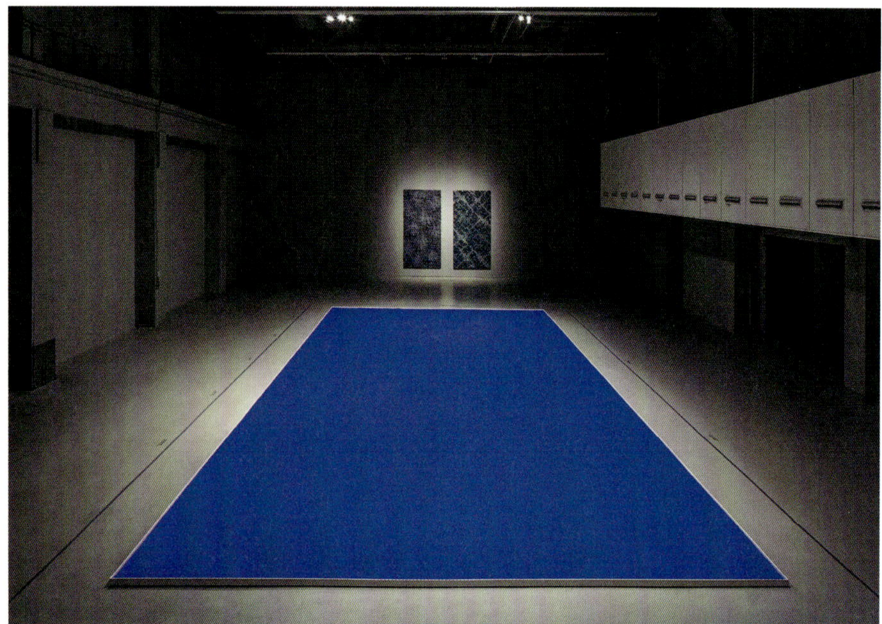

104. Installation of the exhibition
The Challenging Souls: Yves Klein, Lee Ufan, Ding Yi, Power Station of
Art, Shanghai, 2019.
Works shown: Ding Yi, *Appearance of Crosses 2015-6*, *Appearance of
Crosses 2015-7*; Yves Klein, *Dry Blue Pigment*
Courtesy Power Station of Art

All three artists certainly started their careers with a radical statement and body
of works. Each, by the complexity and autonomy of the work they created, presents
some sort of challenge to everyday ideology – past, present and future. But what do
they have in common?

Both Lee and Klein deal with the notion of the void. Ding Yi is more likely to be
accused of *horror vacui*. He gives us many highly worked details, whereas Klein gives
us monochrome or single-minded performances and Lee's paintings often consist of a
solitary brush mark, albeit perfectly formed. (Ding Yi is more taken by Lee's signature
single brush-mark than his recent many small brush marks in colour. He thought them
decorative.)

Although Lee and Klein have both made important contributions to painting,
these have been in the nature of anti-painting gestures, a rejection of all that went
before. Though when Ding Yi started he expressed his intention of 'making painting
not seem like painting', that didn't mean doing away with making things well. His
background as a graduate of an arts-and-crafts institute and over 25 years teaching
design students have been important for him. He was, and is, an artist who enjoys
the physical engagement in making things. For Ding Yi, the word 'craftsmanship',
which many contemporary artists deliberately try to avoid, is never a problem. The
execution of his works involves and celebrates meticulous technical skills.

Asked if he felt close to either Lee or Klein, Ding Yi said, 'Neither.' He felt Klein
was the bravest, although he liked the early works of Lee Ufan. He described both
artists as being consciously oriental – whereas he was not. He felt he used a global
language. He did not want to be exotic. Although Ding Yi's earliest paintings were, as

he claimed, not dependent on either Chinese traditional art or Western modernism but an attempt to go back to basics, and although his earliest work was a conscious attempt to make art that didn't look like art, his work soon developed into a dialogue with abstraction and its history.

Asked if he would have preferred to have exhibited with Mondrian, he replied, 'That would have been like grandfather, grandson.'

The previous year in a discussion with Sean Scully he had been asked how he saw Mondrian's *Broadway Boogie Woogie*. He replied:

This Mondrian painting is very important for me. It is not just a painting about New York City or Broadway, it is a very influential painting in the history of abstract art. I was still quite young when I first saw it. At that time people in China had not been much exposed to modernism and contemporary art. This painting opened a complete new world for me, one vastly different from that of the Chinese tradition and Chinese culture. I was deeply moved by it and in my early days my style was very much influenced by Mondrian – his highly rational constructionism in particular. Today I do not look at paintings like this any more. As an artist, at some point I have to start looking at my own issues rather than Mondrian's.

What we think he means here is that he no longer needs to look to Mondrian for influence or guidance. His own work is what he looks at most. As he pointed out to us while preparing the Guangdong exhibition, a small painting plants a seed for a larger painting and then each new painting contains some element that was unfinished in the previous work. 'One painting resonates with another, but eventually each new painting deals with a new issue. This is how the paintings are paired, developed and processed into new territory constantly.'

On our last visit to his studio, just before we left he invited us to have a drink in the mezzanine above the studio. There were paintings there by Sean Scully, Yu Youhan and Victor Vasarely plus a work by Ai Weiwei. Like many successful artists he had realised he could buy examples of the artists who he had respected or who had once influenced him. He has bought, for instance, a painting by Maurice Utrillo (fig.19).

We talked of his contemporaries. Who did he respect? He mentioned Liu Wei and Yu Youhan, though the latter is very old now. In Ding Yi's view, art is always about pushing the limit and challenging oneself. Among his contemporaries, such an aspiration is rare. Within the Chinese contemporary art world, there is a clear hierarchy or ranking. A male artist of Ding Yi's age and status could sleep comfortably with his achievements and fame. Instead, he keeps pushing. As for those artists who are not painters, 'Ai Weiwei,' he said, 'is a super clever artist and a very good friend.' He also admires Huang Yongping.

As we left we looked around at a studio already half filled with works made in the weeks since the opening of the exhibition at the Power Station of Art. On one wall

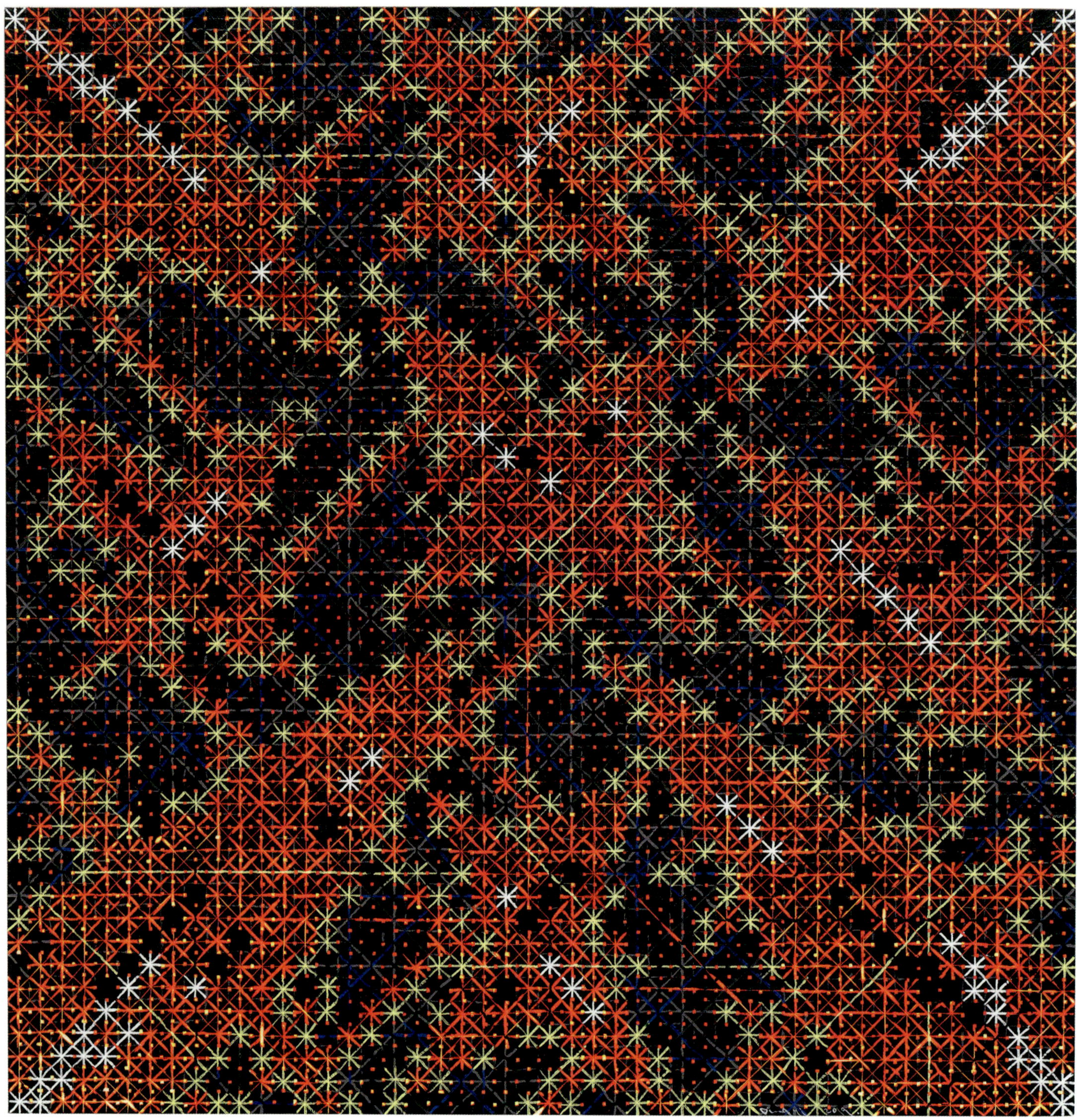

105. Appearance of Crosses 2019-14   2019

Mixed media on basswood
120 × 120 cm (47¼ × 47¼ in)
Private collection

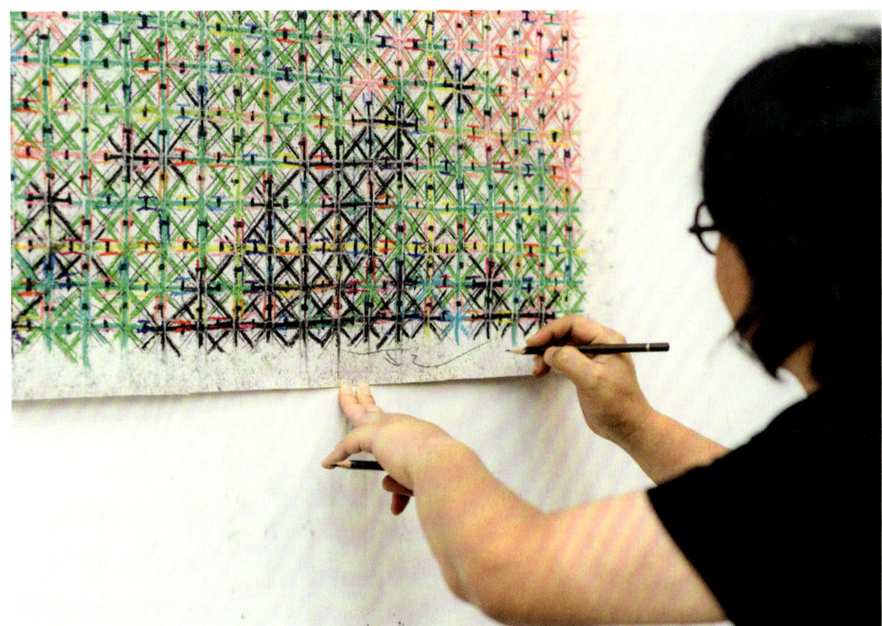

were three 1.2 by 2.4 metre (4 × 8 foot) paintings, two with dark grounds, one with light, all working around his boat shape but now morphed into a diagonal cross. On another, seven 1.2 metre (4 foot) square wood panels were set up. Four were now completed, two with light grounds, two with dark. Each treats the boat or crossed-boat shape differently – as a negative, as a row, as a foursome, as a grid of nine (*Appearance of Crosses 2019-14*; fig.105); those in the corner are larger. He had started on the fifth panel. Underneath it there were trays already half filled with slivers of paint and wood he had carved out of the painting. In it the boat shapes had become thin and elongated. On the table was a model of Galerie Rüdiger Schöttle in Munich where he will exhibit these works. After that he will start preparing for his next annual exhibition, probably in Chongqing.

One cannot but be impressed at his energy and his drive for constant change and renewal. 'It is very difficult to replace the interaction and solitude of viewer and painting', he said in 2013.[12] He has been an avant-gardist, a designer, a teacher of public art, but always a painter. He is a sharp, sophisticated voice within the world of Chinese contemporary art, but a global artist. He has developed a unique and personal body of work from the most rudimentary of signs, + and x.

Notes

Unless otherwise indicated, all quotations from Ding Yi are from interviews with the authors, 2017–19.

1: In Xi'an

1. Interviewed by Hans Ulrich Obrist, *Ding Yi*, exh.cat., Ikon Gallery, Birmingham, 2005, p.40

2: Early Work

1. Quoted in Jonathan Fenby, *The Penguin History of Modern China*, London, 2008, p.185
2. Ding Yi recalls, 'They wore gowns or robes like a doctor's robe but a dark blue colour. In the seventies the technicians in the factories often wore them. It was a status symbol for the technicians: the long robes distinguished them from the workers who wore uniforms. They were better off than the workers.'
3. Quoted in Michel Nuridsany, *China Art Now*, Paris, 2004, p.91
4. ibid.
5. Quoted in 'The Magician of Crosses' by Cao Weijun in *Ding Yi*, exh.cat., Museo d'Arte Moderna, Bologna, 2009, p.67 (quoted from Zhao Chuan, 'Yu Youhan and his Students' in *The Story of Shanghai Abstraction*, Shanghai, 2006, p.49)
6. Britta Erickson, *On the Edge: Contemporary Chinese Artists Encounter the West*, Stanford, 2005, p.23
7. Huang Ke, 'Abstract Paintings, New Form and National Conditions', *Liberation Daily*, 1983. Quoted in *A History of Exhibitions, Shanghai 1979–2006*, edited by Biljana Ciric, Centre for Chinese Contemporary Art, Manchester, 2014, p.38
8. Guang Liang suffered greatly during the Cultural Revolution. He destroyed many of his artworks by soaking them in water and flushing them down the toilet. The retrospective in 1982 demonstrated his artistic achievement as the pioneer in fusing the Western art style with the spirit of Chinese painting. He died in 1986.
9. Xiao Kaiyu, 'Ding Yi – Constant Negation' in *Ding Yi*, exh.cat., ShanghArt, 1998

10. Interview with Ding Yi in *A History of Exhibitions, Shanghai 1979–2006*, edited by Biljana Ciric, op.cit., p.101
11. ibid., p.56
12. Thomas Berghuis, *Performance Art in China*, Hong Kong, 2006, pp 63–4
13. ibid.
14. ibid., p.95
15. Statement by Carl Andre in *16 Americans*, exh. cat., MOMA, NYC, 1959. Quoted in James Meyer, *Minimalism*, London, 2000, p.47
16. Ding Yi, 'On Frank Stella', unpublished essay, October 2018
17. Interview with Hans Ulrich Obrist 2005, op.cit.
18. Michael Sullivan, *Art and Artists of Twentieth Century China*, London, 1996, p.259
19. Li Xiaofeng, interview with Ding Yi, *Yishu* 4 (2001), p.22
20. Quoted in Cao Weijun, 'The Magician of Crosses', op.cit., p.71
21. Li Xu, 'Appearance of Crosses of Ding Yi' in *Ding Yi*, exh.cat., Shanghai Art Museum, 1994, unpaginated.
22. Quoted in Karen Smith, *The Real Thing: Contemporary Art in China.*, exh.cat., Tate Liverpool, 2007, p.145
23. An exception was the presentation in Queensland where seven of the eight artists chosen were from Shanghai, including Yu Youhan who also showed abstract paintings.
24. Interview with Hans Ulrich Obrist, 2005, op.cit., p.34
25. 草图 as 'draft' in Chinese characters. In Chinese the same characters are used for both 'draft' and 'sketch'.
26. Marianne Brouwer, *Hans van Dijk/Dai Hanzhi: A Life with Art in China, 1986–2002*, Ullens Centre for Contemporary Art/ Witte de With Centre for Contemporary Art, 2018, p.138
27. Statement by Ding Yi in *Contemporary Chinese Oil Painting, from Realism to Post-modernism*, exh.cat., Galerie Theoremes, Brussels, p.128. Re-translated from the Chinese 2019

3: The Tartans: 1997 onwards

1. This is essentially a fake tradition fabricated around 1800. See Hugh Trevor-Roper, 'The Highland Tradition of Scotland' in *The Invention of Tradition* edited by Eric Hobsbawm and Terence Ranger, Cambridge, 1983, pp 15–42. The McPherson tartan for instance was only adopted in 1824 by Cluny MacPherson. Before then it had been woven under the name pattern No. 155 and then Kidd's – Mr Kidd having used it to clothe his slaves in the West Indies.
2. Quoted by Nataline Colonnello in *Mahjong: Contemporary Chinese Art from the Sigg Collection*, exh.cat., Kunstmuseum Bern, 2005, p.288
3. Interview with Hans Ulrich Obrist, op.cit.
4. Rosalind Krauss, 'Grids', *October* 9 (Summer 1979); reprinted in Rosalind Krauss, *The Originality of the Avant-garde and Other Modernist Myths*, Cambridge, MA, 1985, pp 8–22
5. Quoted in *Louise Bourgeois*, exh.cat., MoMA, NYC, 1982, p.43
6. Lawrence Alloway, 'Sol LeWitt: Modules, Walls, Books', *Artforum* vol.13, no.8 (April 1975); reprinted in Adachiara Zevi (ed.), *Sol LeWitt Critical Texts*, Rome, 1994, p.198
7. Robert Rosenblum, 'Notes on Sol LeWitt' in *Sol LeWitt*, exh.cat., MoMA, NYC, 1978; reprinted in Zevi (ed.), *Sol LeWitt Critical Texts*, op.cit., pp 313–14
8. More mundanely, it also gave him something to start with. This is nothing new: painters as diverse as Gerhard Richter and Ross Bleckner have employed assistants to create patterns or surfaces against which they can react.
9. Monica Dematté, 'Theorization of Casualness' in *Ding Yi*, exh.cat., ShanghArt Gallery, 1998
10. Quoted in Carter Ratcliff, 'American Sublime', https://www.tate.org.uk/art/artists/barnett-newman-1699/american-sublime
11. For the record, although we are using musical analogies to his work, he has no especial interest in music.

4: The Fluorescents: 2000–2010

1. Ding Yi interviewed by Mathieu Borysevicz, *Art Changsa, Ding Yi*, exh.cat., Hunan Provincial Museum, Changsha, 2013, p.142

2. Quoted in Cao Weijun, 'The Magician of Crosses'

3. Interview with Hans Ulrich Obrist, op.cit.

4. Mathieu Borysevicz '(In) Congruity, Universality, Ding Yi' in *Art Changsa: Ding Yi*, op.cit., p.37

5. Quoted by Nataline Colonnello in *Mahjong: Contemporary Chinese Art from the Sigg Collection*, op.cit., p.288

6. *Writing on the Wall: Chinese New Realism and Avant-garde in the Eighties and Nineties*, exh. cat., Groninger Museum, Groningen, 2008, p.120

7. Nuridsany, *China Art Now*, op.cit., p.98

8. Robert Morris, *Box with the Sound of Its Own Making*, 1961; Tony Cragg, *Stack*, 1976

9. Interview with Hans Ulrich Obrist, op.cit.

10. Ding Yi interviewed by Mathieu Borysevicz in *Art Changsa: Ding Yi*, op.cit., p.152

11. Subsequently pub lished in English in *Ding Yi*, exh.cat., Karsten Greve Gallery, Cologne, 2008. The English translation is, however, as so often, unsatisfactory. A much better translation was made later by Wang Jie and is available at http://www.shanghartgallery.com/galleryarchive/texts/id/1046. Please note we have adjusted this translation for greater readability and clarity.

5: Recent Work: 2011–2019

1. 'Ding Yi and the Impossibility of Abstraction', *Ding Yi*, exh.cat., Minsheng Art Museum, 2011. Under Tony Godfrey's name solely, but based on an interview conducted jointly.

2. Asked to name a Chinese master with a late style, Ding Yi remarked, 'It is difficult to give such an example. Traditional Chinese painting was taught by copying the masters. Many artists only had their own style when they get old. Many times, the changes of style, if there are any, are still quite subtle.'

3. Unpublished discussion with Sean Scully, 2017

4. Actually, *Appearance of Crosses 2012-B1* is even bigger. It consists of seven parts and measures 400 × 1270 cm (157½ × 500 in). *Appearance of Crosses 2013–B2* was made on the biggest wall at the M50 studio. It was first exhibited at the China 8 group show in Germany. https://www.shanghartgallery.com/galleryarchive/exhibition.htm?exbId=8462

5. Ding Yi, 'On Frank Stella', op.cit.

6. Quoted in He Jing, 'A Conversation with Ding Yi: In Quest of a New Spirit in Painting' in *Ding Yi + x 30 Years*, exh.cat., Guangdong Museum, Guangzhou, 2018, p.24

7. The earlier translation in the Karsten Greve exhibition catalogue ran, 'I wanted to take painting back to its innate quality of form, the form being the spirit.' As in Chapter 4 we have used the later translation by Wang Jie. http://www.shanghartgallery.com/galleryarchive/texts/id/1046.

8. Quoted in He Jing, 'A Conversation with Ding Yi', op.cit., pp 39–40

9. He was there to design a proposed cylindrical duplex bridge to the caves on the west cliff of the Yulin Grottoes. It seems this project will not be realised.

10. Quoted in He Jing, 'A Conversation with Ding Yi', op.cit., pp 32–3

11. The Power Station of Art is the first state-run museum dedicated to contemporary art in mainland China. It is also home to the Shanghai Biennale. Repurposed from the former Nanshi Power Plant, it was the Pavilion of the Future during the 2010 Shanghai World Expo. It now occupies an area of 42,000 square metres (452,000 square feet). Its 165-metre (540-foot) high chimney, also an independent exhibition space, has also become an integral part of Shanghai's world-famous skyline.

12. Ding Yi interviewed by Mathieu Borysevicz in *Art Changsa: Ding Yi*, p.148

Select Bibliography

Art Changsha: Ding Yi 2013, exh.cat., Changsha City Museum, Hunan Fine Arts Publishing House, 2013

Azure Wu, 'Ding Yi: Specific·Abstracted', *LEAP* 13 (Feb. 2012), pp 180–3

Daniel Baillon, 'On the New Crosses of "15 x Red"', ShanghART website, 1996, https://www.shanghartgallery.com/galleryarchive/texts/id/10

Bo Xiaobo, 'A Series of Paintings Shown in Crosses by Ding Yi', trans. by Zhao Zhengxin, ShanghART website, 1992, http://www.shanghart.com/texts/dingyi5.htm

Marianne Brouwer, *Hans van Dijk/Dai Hanzhi, A Life with Art in China 1986–2002*, exh.cat., Witte de With Center for Contemporary Art, Rotterdam; Ullens Center for Contemporary Art, Beijing, 2018

Cao Weijun, 'Interview with Ding Yi', *ShanghArt*, issue 3 (2007), pp214–19, https://www.shanghartgallery.com/galleryarchive/texts/id/1090

Monica Dematté, *Ding Yi*, exh. cat., ShanghART Gallery and NAAC, Shanghai, 1997

Ding Yi: opere su carta, exh.cat., Edizioni Salarchi Immagini, Galleria degli Archi, Cosimo, Italy, 1995

Ding Yi, 'Deconstructing the Abstract', ShanghART website, 2008, https://www.shanghartgallery.com/galleryarchive/texts/id/1046

Ding Yi, exh.cat., Museo d'Arte Moderna di Bologna, Bologna, Italy, Skira Editore S.p.A/MAMbo, 2009

Ding Yi, Flourescence, Shanghai People's Fine Arts Publishing House, 2010

Ding Yi, exh.cat., Minsheng Art Museum, Shanghai, 2011

'Ding Yi: Dialogue with Sean Scully', *Art China* (June 2014), p.17

Ding Yi, exh.cat., Timothy Taylor Gallery, London, 2017

Ding Yi, 'Artists' Artists: Frank Stella, *Die Fahne Hoch!* (Hoist the Flag!), 1959', *Frieze*, 2 Oct. 2017

Feng Boyi, *Ding Yi: + × 30 Years*, exh.cat., Guangdong Art Museum, Shanghai People's Fine Arts Publishing House, 2018

Paul Gladston, 'A Conversation with Ding Yi' in *Contemporary Art in Shanghai: Conversations with Seven Chinese Artists*, Blue Kingfisher, 2012

Tony Godfrey, *Painting Today*, Phaidon, 2009, p.165

Gong Yan, 'National Conditions', Interview with Xu Zhen and Ding Yi, *Flash Art* 3–4 (2016), pp 98–103

Rachel Gould, 'Ahead of Several New York Exhibitions, an Interview with Chinese Artist Ding Yi', *Culture Trip*, 1 Sept. 2017

Julien Guerrier, *Louis Vuitton City Guide: Shanghai*, 2018

Lorenz Helbling, '15 x Red by Ding Yi', ShanghART website, 1996, https://www.shanghartgallery.com/galleryarchive/texts/id/11

Magdalena Kröner, 'Ding Yi, Das Zeichen als Weltkondensat', *Kunstforum* (Feb. 2007), pp 108–15

Lin Weiguang and Yao Di, *Ding Yi: Fluorescence*, People Publishing House, Shanghai, 2010

Shane McCausland, *Ding Yi: What's Left to Appear*, exh.cat., Long Museum (West Bund), Shanghai Calligraphy & Painting Publishing House, 2015

Christopher Moore, 'Ding Yi: a User's Manual', *RanDian*, 17 June 2017, http://www.randian-online.com/np_feature/ding-yi-a-users-manual/

Michel Nuridsany, *China Art Now*, Flammarion, 2004, pp 90–7

Hans Ulrich Obrist, 'Resembling the World Outside', Interview with Ding Yi in *The Appearance of Crosses*, ed. Jonathan Watkins, Ikon Gallery, Birmingham, 2005, pp 32–41

Demetrio Paparoni, 'Ding Yi, La nuevas fronteras de la abstracción', *Art Global* (Sept.–Oct. 2012), pp 78–85

Re-appearance of Crosses: Ding Yi, exh.cat., Hubei Art Museum, Heibei Fine Arts Publishing House, 2016

Olivia Sand, 'Ding Yi', *Asian Art Newspaper* (March 2019), pp 2–4

Ulrike Schick, *Out of Shanghai*, exh.cat., Museum Gegenstandsfreier Kunst, Otterndorf, Germany, Snoeck Verlagsgesellschaft mbH, 2010

Barry Schwabsky, *Vitamin P: New Perspectives in Painting*, Ding Yi introduced by Hou Hanru, Phaidon, 2002, p.84

Colin Siyuan Chinnery, 'Ding Yi', *Frieze* 174 (Oct. 2015)

Minh An Szabó de Bucs, 'Das Kreuz mit der chinesischen Kunst', *Neue Zürcher Zeitung*, 13 June 2016

Caroline Turner, *The First Asia-Pacific Triennial of Contemporary Art*, exh.cat., Ding Yi introduced by Li Xu, Queensland Art Gallery, Brisbane, Australia, 1993

Hans van Dijk, *Mondrian in China: A Documentary Exhibition with Chinese Originals*, exh.cat., Ding Yi introduced by Cao Weijun, Art Gallery of Beijing, 1998, pp 35–7

Jonathan Watkins (ed.), *Ding Yi*, exh.cat., Ikon Gallery, Birmingham, 2006

Jonathan Watkins and Jo Spark, *Every Day: 11th Biennale of Sydney*, exh.cat., Ding Yi introduced by Huang Du, 1998, p.82

Wu Liang, '"Shishi" as a Mark Organization', ShanghArt website, 2004, https://www.shanghartgallery.com/galleryarchive/texts/id/8

Yang Chao, *Ding Yi: Appearance of Crosses: A Chronicle*, exh.cat., Xi'an Art Museum, 2017

Yu-Chieh Li, 'From Performance to Abstraction: A Conversation with Ding Yi', MoMA, 23 September 2015, https://post.at.moma.org/content_items/693-from-performance-to-abstraction-a-conversation-with-ding-yi

Biography

1962
Born 2 April in Shanghai. Named Ding Rong.

1969
Enters Kongjiang No. 2 Primary School in Yangpu District, Shanghai.

1973
Begins making cartoons and political posters for the class blackboard.

1975
Enters Kong Jiang Middle School in Yangpu District, Shanghai. Begins his first art foundation training.

1978
Enters Kong Jiang Senior High School. Visits exhibition of French nineteenth-century landscape painting in Shanghai. Encounters original works of Impressionism and Fauvism for the first time.

1980
Enrols in Shanghai Arts and Crafts College, majoring in product design.

1981
Meets Yu Youhan. In October visits exhibition *Artworks from Boston Museum of Fine Arts* in Shanghai. Encounters original works of Western abstraction for the first time.

1982
Starts painting street life in the style of Maurice Utrillo.
Visits exhibition *Guan Lian Retrospective* at Shanghai Art Museum.
Visits exhibition *250 Years of French Painting* at Shanghai Art Museum.

1983
Graduates from Shanghai Arts and Crafts College. Starts working at Shanghai No. 12 Toy Factory as toy and package designer.
Visits exhibition *Original Works of Picasso* in Shanghai.

1985
Fails the entrance exam for the oil painting department of the Fine Arts Department of Shanghai University.
Starts to use the name Ding Yi.

1986
Enrols at the Chinese painting department of the Fine Arts Department of Shanghai University.

1988
Makes his first cross painting: *Appearance of Crosses 1*.

1989
Participates in *China/Avant-Garde* exhibition at the National Art Museum of China, Beijing. (4 June student demonstration in Beijing ends in bloodshed on Tiananmen Square.)

1990
Graduates from the Chinese painting department of the Fine Arts Department of Shanghai University. Starts working at Shanghai Arts and Crafts College.

1993
Leaves China for the first time to participate in the Venice Biennale. Travels in Italy.

1996
First solo exhibition at ShanghArt Gallery in Shanghai.

1998
Marries Wang Yiwu.

1999
Only child, daughter Ding Yun, born.

2000
Exhibits at *Uncooperative Approach (Fuck Off)*, a protest exhibition organised by Ai Weiwei.

2001
Visits Germany for three months with family as artist in residence at Künstlerhäuser Worpswede Foundation.

2004
Receives China Architecture Award for his design of *Mountain House* in Helan Mountain, Ningxia Hui Autonomous Region in western China. Starts collecting art deco-style Shanghai old furniture.

2005
Becomes Professor of Fine Art at Shanghai Arts and Crafts College.

2006
Starts teaching at Shanghai Institute of Visual Arts.

2008
Buys a 1926 art deco-style apartment in downtown Shanghai and shows his furniture collection there.

2009
Becomes a member of the jury of M50 Young Artists Awards and the vice dean of Shanghai Institute of Visual Arts.

2011
Takes charge of Public Art department at Shanghai Institute of Visual Arts.

2013
Joins the academic advisory board of the Museum of Contemporary Art in Shanghai and the Power Station of Art.

2015
Leaves teaching job at Shanghai Institute of Visual Arts.

2016
Works as chief curator for Shanghai Design Biennale
Awarded 'Artist of the Year' by China Art Power 100.

2018
Joins the council of the 9th National Congress of the China Artists Association.

Exhibitions

Selected Solo Exhibitions

2019
Rim Light, Galerie Rüdiger Schöttle, Munich, Germany
Grids, Galerie Karsten Greve, Paris, France

2018
+ x 30 Years: Ding Yi, Guangdong Museum of Art, Guangzhou, China
Interchange, ShanghArt Gallery, Shanghai, China

2017
Appearance of Crosses: A Chronicle, Xi'an Art Museum, Shanxi, China
Ding Yi: Appearance of Crosses, Timothy Taylor, New York, USA
Ding Yi, Sean Scully Studio, New York, USA
Ding Yi, Timothy Taylor Gallery, London, UK

2016
Re-appearance of Crosses, Ding Yi Solo Show, Hubei Museum of Art, Wuhan, China

2015
DING YI: What's Left to Appear, Long Museum (West Bund), Shanghai, China
Ivory Black, ShanghArt Singapore, Singapore

2014
Scintillement, Galerie Karsten Greve, Paris, France

2013
Art Changsha: Ding Yi, Changsha Museum, Hunan, China

2012
Appearance of Crosses, Galerie Karsten Greve AG, St Moritz, Switzerland

2011
Ding Yi, Specific-Abstracted, Minsheng Art Museum, Shanghai, China
Ding Yi, Appearance of Crosses, Galerie Waldburger, Brussels, Belgium

2008
Ding Yi, Recent Works, Galerie Karsten Greve, Cologne, Germany
Appearance of Crosses 1989-2007, Solo Exhibition of Ding Yi, Museo d'Arte Moderna di Bologna, Bologna, Italy

2007
Ding Yi, Galerie Karsten Greve, Paris, France

2006
Graticule: Ding Yi's Works from 1989 to 2006, ShanghArt H-Space, Shanghai, China

2005
Appearance of Crosses, Ikon Gallery, Birmingham, UK

2004
Crossed Vision, Works by Ding Yi, China Art Archive and Warehouse, Beijing, China

2003
Ding Yi: Appearance of Crosses, Galerie Urs Meile, Lucerne, Switzerland

2002
Ding Yi: Appearance of Crosses, Galerie Waldburger, Berlin, Germany

2000
Ding Yi: Fluorescent Paint on Tartan, China Art Archive and Warehouse, Beijing, China

1998
Ding Yi: Crosses '89–'97, International Art Palace, Beijing, China

1997
Ding Yi: Crosses '97, Shanghai Art Museum, Shanghai, China

1996
15 x Red, New Works on Paper by Ding Yi, ShanghArt Gallery, Shanghai, China

1995
Ding Yi: Opere su Carta (Paper Works of Ding Yi), Galleria degli Archi, Comiso, Italy

1994
Exhibition of Ding Yi's Abstract Art Works, Shanghai Art Museum, Shanghai, China
Ding Yi's Work on Paper, Guangzhou Fine Art Academy, Guangzhou, China

Selected Group Exhibitions

2019
The Challenging Souls: Yves Klein, Lee Ufan and Ding Yi, Power Station of Art, Shanghai, China

2018
Art and China after 1989: Theatre of the World, Guggenheim Museum Bilbao, Spain/San Francisco, Museum of Modern Art, USA

2017
Bye Bye De Stijl, Contemporary Artists Respond to De Stijl, Centraal Museum, Utrecht, Netherlands
Last Night's Fortune Teller: The Third Part of an Exhibition Series with New Acquisitions of Chinese and International Contemporary Art, Daimler Contemporary, Berlin, Germany

2016
Permanent Abstraction, Epiphanies of a Modern Form in Escaped Totalities, Red Brick Art Museum, Beijing, China
Holzwege, ShanghArt West Bund Opening Exhibition, ShanghArt West Bund, Shanghai, China
An/Other Avant-garde China–Japan–Korea, 7th Edition of Busan Biannual, Busan Museum of Modern Art, Busan, Korea

2015
Une histoire: art, architecture, design des années 1980 à nos jours, Musée National d'Art Moderne, Paris, France
Image and Text, Chinese Contemporary Art in Greece, Castiglia di Saluzzo, Saluzzo, Italy
Calligraphic Time and Space: Abstract Art in China, Power Station of Art, Shanghai, China
China 8, Contemporary Art from China at the Rhine and Ruhr, MKM Museum Küppersmühle, Duisburg, Germany

2014
Hans van Dijk: 5000 Names, Ullens Centre for
   Contemporary Art, Beijing, China; Witte
   de With Centre for Contemporary Art,
   Rotterdam, Netherlands
Myth/History: Yuz Collection of Contemporary Art,
   Yuz Museum, Shanghai, China

2013
Revel, Celebrating MoCA's 8 Years in Shanghai,
   Museum of Contemporary Art, Shanghai, China
*Insightful Charisma, Inaugural Exhibition of
   Shanghai Himalayas Museum*, Himalayas Art
   Museum, Shanghai, China

2012
*Through All Ages, New Style: Invitation Inaugural
   Exhibition of Long Museum*, Long Museum,
   Shanghai, China
*Great Way Prevailing: Chinese Contemporary Public
   Art Exhibition*, Kassel, Germany
*The Seventh Shenzhen Sculpture Biennale–Accidental
   Message: Art is Not a System, Not a World*, OCT
   Contemporary Art Terminal, Shenzhen, China
Ai Weiwei, Wang Xingwei and Ding Yi: Persona 3,
   Chambers Fine Art, New York, USA

2011
*CHINA: The Art of a Nation, Outdoor Exhibition:
   Landscape in Mind*, The Kennedy Center,
   Washington, DC, USA
Verso Est – Chinese Architectural Landscape, MAXXI
   Museo nazionale delle arti del XXI secolo,
   Rome, Italy
Chinese Abstract Slow Art, Singer Laren Museum,
   Laren, Netherlands

2010
*The State of Things, Contemporary Art from China
   and Belgium*, National Art Museum of China,
   Beijing, China
*Thirty Years of Chinese Contemporary Art: Painting
   (1979–2009)*, Minsheng Art Museum,
   Shanghai, China
Shanghai, Asian Art Museum, San Francisco, USA

2009
*Collision, Experimental Cases of Contemporary Chinese
   Art*, CAFA Art Museum, Beijing, China

Out of Shanghai, Museum gegenstandsfreier
   Kunst, Otterndorf, Germany

2008
*Avant-Garde China: 20 Years of Chinese
   Contemporary Art*, The National Art Centre,
   Tokyo; The National Museum of Art, Osaka;
   Aichi Prefectural Museum of Art, Nagoya,
   Japan
*Writing on the Wall, Chinese New Realism and
   Avant-Garde in the Eighties and Nineties*, The
   Groninger Museum, Groningen, Netherlands
*Red Aside, Contemporary Chinese Art from the
   Sigg Collection*, The Joan Miró Foundation,
   Barcelona, Spain
La Escuela Yi, 30 Years of Abstract Chinese Art, La
   Caixa, Barcelona, Spain

2007
*85 New Wave – The Birth of Chinese Contemporary
   Art*, Ullens Centre for Contemporary Art,
   Beijing, China
The Tale of Silk, A Hermès Exhibition, Shanghai Art
   Museum, Shanghai, China

2006
Art in Motion, Museum of Contemporary Art,
   Shanghai, China
6th Shanghai Biennale – Hyper Design, Shanghai
   Art Museum, Shanghai, China
*The Blossoming of Realism, The Oil Painting of
   Mainland China Since 1978*, Taipei Fine Arts
   Museum, Taipei, Taiwan, China

2005
*Mahjong, Contemporary Chinese Art from the
   Sigg Collection*, Kunstmuseum Bern, Bern,
   Switzerland
Shenzhen Art Biennale, OCT Contempory Art
   Terminal, Shenzhen, China

2004
New Boundaries, Taikang Top Space, Beijing,
   China
*Dreaming of the Dragon's Nation, Contemporary
   Art from China*, Irish Museum of Modern Art,
   Dublin, Ireland
Shanghai Modern, Museum Villa Stuck, Munich,
   Germany

*Dial 62761232 (Express Delivery Exhibition),
   Contemporary Art Exhibition*, BizArt, Shanghai,
   China
Persona – Ai Weiwei, Ding Yi, Wang Xingwei, China
   Art Archives & Warehouse, Beijing, China

2003
Chinese Maximalism, Millennium Art Museum,
   Beijing; University at Buffalo Art Galleries and
   Museum Studies, State University of New York at
   Buffalo, USA
Subversion and Poetry, Contemporary Chinese Art,
   Culturgest, Lisbon, Portugal

2002
*The First Guangzhou Trienniale – Reinterpretation: A
   Decade of Experimental Chinese Art (1990–2000)*,
   Guangdong Museum of Art, Guangzhou, China
*Quick Look! Shanghai Zhejiang Jiangsu Anhui
   Contemporary Art Exhibition*, Consulate General
   of Switzerland, Shanghai, China

2001
Living in Time, 29 Contemporary Artists from China,
   Hamburger Bahnhof–Museum für Gegenwart,
   Berlin, Germany
*China Art Archives & Warehouse Opening
   Exhibition*, China Art Archives and Warehouse,
   Beijing, China
*Yokohama 2001: International Triennale of
   Contemporary Art*, Yokohama, Japan

2000
Chinese Muren – Chinese Walls, Nederlands
   Gasunie, Groningen, Netherlands
Uncooperative Approach (Fuck Off), Eastlink
   Gallery, Shanghai, China

1999
Concepts, Color and Passions, China Art Archives
   and Warehouse, Beijing, China
Collecting Exhibition, Modern Chinese Art
   Foundation, Caermersklooster, Belgium
BM99, Bienal da Maya, Maya Art Centre,
   Portugal

1998
Every Day, 11th Biennale of Sydney, Museum of
   Contemporary Art etc., Sydney, Australia

Public Collections

Mondrian in China, Art Gallery of Beijing,
International Palace, Beijing; Shanghai Library,
Shanghai; Guangdong Museum of Art,
Guangzhou, China
Jiang Nan, Chinese Contemporary Art, Charles H.
Scott Gallery, Vancouver, Canada

1997
Quotation Marks, Chinese Contemporary Paintings,
National Art Museum, Singapore
*In Between Limits, An Aspect of Chinese
Contemporary Art*, Sonje Museum of
Contemporary Art, Gyeongju, Korea
Handover Exhibition, Hong Kong Convention &
Exhibition Centre, Hong Kong, China

1996
*Shanghai Fax: Let's Talk about Money, International
Fax Art Exhibition*, Shanghai Huashan
Professional School of Art, Shanghai, China
1st Shanghai Biennale, Shanghai Art Museum,
Shanghai, China
China! Touring Exhibition, Kunstmuseum Bonn,
Bonn, Germany

1995
Des Pais del Centre, Avantguardes Artistiques Xineses,
Santa Monica Art Centre, Barcelona, Spain
New Chinese Art: 1990–1994, Vancouver Gallery
of Art, Vancouver, Canada; Chicago Art
Centre, Chicago, USA
Change, China Contemporary Art, Göteborgs
Konsthall, Gothenburg, Sweden

1994
Abstract Works by Six Artists, Hanart TZ Gallery,
Hong Kong, China

1993
*45th International Art Exhibition Venice Biennale:
Cardinal Points of the Arts*, Venice, Italy
The First Asia-Pacific Triennial of Contemporary Art,
Queensland Art Gallery, Brisbane, Australia
Mao Goes Pop, China Post '89, Museum of
Contemporary Art Australia, Sydney; Victoria
National Gallery, Melbourne, Australia

China Avant-garde, Touring exhibition, Haus
der Kulturen der Welt, Berlin; Kunsthall
Rotterdam, Rotterdam, Netherlands; Brandts
Klaederfabrik, Odense, Denmark; Hildesheim
Art Gallery, Hildesheim, Germany; Museum of
Modern Art, Oxford, UK

1992
Documentary Exhibition of Chinese Art of the 90s,
K Gallery, Tokyo, Japan

1991
Shanghai Modern Art, Yokohama Museum of Art,
Yokohama, Japan

1989
China/Avant-Garde Art Exhibition, National Art
Museum of China, Beijing, China

1988
Exhibition of Today's Art, Shanghai Art Museum,
Shanghai, China

1986
1st Shanghai Youth Grand Fine Arts Exhibition,
Shanghai Artists' Gallery, Shanghai, China
First Shanghai Concave–Convex Exhibition, Xuhui
Cultural Centre, Shanghai, China
*Inauguration Exhibition of the Shanghai Art
Museum*, Shanghai Art Museum, Shanghai,
China

1985
Exhibition of Modern Art by Six Artists, Fudan
University, Shanghai, China

CDU Art Collection, Australia
Centre Pompidou, Paris
Chengdu Museum of Contemporary Art, Chengdu
China Art Museum, Shanghai
Chinese Modern Art Foundation, Ghent
City of Hamburg
Daimler Art Collection, Berlin
DSL Collection, Paris
Fosun Foundation, New York
Fukuoka Asian Art Museum, Fukuoka
Guangdong Museum of Art, Guangzhou
Haudenschild Collection, California
He Art Museum, Shunde
Hubei Museum of Art, Wuhan
K11 Art Foundation, Hong Kong
Leeum, Samsung Museum of Art, Seoul
Long Museum, Shanghai
M+ Collection, Hong Kong
Morioka City Library, Morioka
National Art Museum of China, Beijing
Power Station of Art, Shanghai
Sonje Museum of Contemporary Art, Gyeongju
Stichting Van Tuyckom Foundation, Brussels
Taikang Collection, Beijing
UBS Art Collection, Zurich
University of Sydney Art Collection, Sydney
Yuz Foundation, Jakarta

Acknowledgements

Firstly, and above all, we would like to thank Ding Yi for all his patience, good humour, generosity and hospitality in our several meetings. We must also thank his assistant Ariane (Feng Jingfan) for organising many things and events: without her efficiency and intelligence this project would have been far harder. We must thank Lorenz Helbling and ShanghArt Gallery for their support in making this book possible.

Tony would like, firstly, to thank Wang Kaimei for collaborating on this book. It would have been impossible without her input as a Chinese person living in Shanghai; a brilliant translator; and, of course, also a writer. He also needs to thank Jonathan Watkins for an early introduction to the work of Ding Yi, the curatorial team at Xi'an Art Museum for introducing him to the museum and the local cuisine and alcoholic spirits, Deng Yunfei, Ding Yi's assistant, for collecting him at airports and making sure he arrived at the right place, Phil Whittaker and Sotheby's Institute for generously funding and encouraging early trips to China, and Dr Eugene Tan for introducing him to Asia and its contemporary art world. At home he must thank Ate Jose for making sure his desk is not too chaotic; Nenning Espiritu for making sure he always had food or drink; Loki the German Shepherd for his company; and Geraldine Javier, his partner, for companionship and regularly challenging his ideas.

Kaimei wants to thank Tony for taking her with him on this journey exploring the world of Ding Yi. Tony, your trust and respect for me have encouraged me to believe in what I am doing.

Image Credits

Every effort has been made to identify the photographers of images reproduced in this book. Where information was not available, the publisher would be grateful if notified of any corrections or additions to the list below that should be incorporated into future editions or reprints.

Courtesy of the artist: 16, 17, 21, 26, 27, 29, 31, 38, 39, 42, 46, 49, 54, 55, 63, 95, 106
© ADAGP, Paris and DACS 2019, photograph by Alessandro Wang: 19
© DACS 2019, Photo: © Centre Pompidou, MNAN-CCI, Dist. RMN-Grand Palais/ Philippe Migeat: 22
Che Haonan: frontispiece
Justin Jin: 74, 77
Power Station of Art: 100, 104
Alessandro Wang: 1, 2 (both), 3, 5, 7, 8, 9, 10, 11, 12, 14, 20, 56, 76, 78, 90, 92, 93, 94, 96, 97, 98, 99, 101, 102, 103, 105
Huang Yunhe: 51, 52, 53, 57, 58, 59, 60, 61, 64, 66, 67, 68, 69, 70

Index

First published in 2020 by Lund Humphries

Lund Humphries
Office 3, Book House
261A City Road
London
EC1V 1JX
www.lundhumphries.com

ISBN: 978-1-84822-379-0

A Cataloguing-in-Publication record for this book is available
from the British Library.

Copy-edited by Eleanor Rees
Designed by Mark Thomson
Set in Custodia (Fred Smeijers)
Printed in Italy

Frontispiece: Portrait of Ding Yi, 2016,
Photograph by Che Haonan
Cover: *Appearance of Crosses 2019-14*, 2019, Mixed media on
basswood, 120 × 120 cm (47¼ × 47¼ in)